"In other words," Brisbin added, "you have to put the symbol of your hand, or whatever it is—the picture of your hand—in the machine first. And then they compare that when you want access to a secure area, or you want to use it to get money or something..."

Steele asked Brisbin: "Are you saying that the [electronic transfer] card might actually be done away with and there would be some kind of identification on a person's body like the hand, and then—"

"Well, today," Brisbin said, "I don't know of any better system."

—Television interview with Lowell Brisbin, vice president of the U.S. National Bank, and president of the Oregon Automated Clearing House Association.

THE
ECONOMY
TO
COME

*and other signs of Earth's
impending climax*

THE ECONOMY TO COME

and other signs of Earth's impending climax

by
William R. Goetz

HORIZON HOUSE PUBLISHERS
Beaverlodge, Alberta, Canada

© 1983
Horizon House Publishers
All Rights Reserved

ISBN O-88965-063-2

HORIZON BOOKS
are published by Horizon House Publishers
Box 600, Beaverlodge, Alberta TOH OCO
Printed in the United States of America

First Printing, September 1983
Second Printing, February, 1984
Third Printing, (Updated), June 1988

Grateful acknowledgement is made to the following publishers for permission to quote from copyrighted material.

Apocalypse Next, William R. Goetz, copyright 1980, Horizon House Publishers, Beaverlodge, Alberta

The Coming Anti-Christ, Walter K. Price, copyright © 1974, Moody Press, Moody Bible Institute, Chicago, Ill. (Copyright transferred to the author, from whom permission has been obtained.)

Trilateralism, (Ed) Holly Skar, copyright 1980, Boston South End Press, Boston, Mass.

TO
THE FAMILY
God has given
to my wife, Joyce,
and me

—Brenda,
—Brent,
—Bonnie,
—Brad, and
—Bryan

Because of you, God has also given me
much love, joy, happiness, fun,
and many opportunities to grow—
through the difficulties and
disciplines that come with
the heavy, but welcome,
responsibilities of a family

About this edition...

October 19, 1987 was a day that most of us will remember all of our lives. Perhaps we will remember it with a little less trauma than the assassination of President Kennedy, but the word in our office was that the stock market was tumbling by hundreds of points. As you well know, it was an historic decline.

When this book was first written, it was nearly decided to hold it for the "October 19" we knew was coming. But *Economy to Come* was released and we have no regrets. However, the book now takes on new significance -- October 19, 1987 was the day for which it was written. The body of this edition remains intact, except for minimal changes, but the final update chapter is as pertinent as tomorrow's news. This is a message that deserves to be heard and heeded.

K. Neill Foster,
Publisher

Contents

PART THREE
Spiritual Signs

PART FOUR
Other Signs

PART FIVE
The Sign of Safety

Sincere Thanks...

--to the scores of people in many parts of the continent and abroad, but especially to my friend, Danny Spivak, who, since the release of my first book, have graciously shared with me much valuable material--newspaper articles, magazines, books, information;

--to the members of the Sevenoaks Alliance Board of Elders for encouragement and time to write, as well as to the members and friends of the church who urged me on and prayed for me as I worked on this book;

--to Ted and Sunny Cornelson, who once again kindly allowed the use of their secluded Sudden Valley home for a number of writing sessions;

--to Marnie Thomson, typist par excellence, for her exceptionally helpful work in putting my scrawled notes into splendid manuscript form, and to Faith True, my personal secretary, who typed a good part of the early draft;

--to Tammy Kool who typed the 1988 updated material;

--to Linda Jasper, typesetter, for faithfulness far beyond the call of duty;

--to Peter Lalonde, editor of *Omega- Letter*, for permission to quote extensively from several issues;

--and finally, to the friends at Horizon House for their cooperation, encouragement and publishing skills, and my dear friends, ·K. Neill Foster and his wife, Marilynne.

*Everything we know has an end,
as well as a beginning. That the world,
as we know it, should end is
not at all improbable.*

— K. Neill Foster

PROLOGUE

The Climax of Earth's Ages is Upon Us!

The end of the world!

People have been predicting it for centuries.

As far back as A.D. 156, in fact. The year A.D. 1000 was widely feared as a global doomsday. Again in A.D. 1260 a tremendous stir took place in Europe, as apocalyptic predictions became rife.

In the 1500s, Nostradamus, one of the best known seers of the past, made a number of amazing predictions in 1,050 verses, mostly quatrains. He has currently become a very controversial figure, with literally hundreds of books being written about him and his prophecies in recent years. In the summer and fall of 1981, a new translation of his forecasts became a bestseller and *the* major topic of discussion in France — primarily because it was believed he had predicted the rise of socialism to power in that country, as well as the assassination attempt on the Pope. Under Hitler's reign in Germany, Nostradamus's writings were banned because of his predictions (since fulfilled) of a divided Germany. These, and other apparently accurate prophecies, have caused multitudes to ask questions about the future and to examine what this sixteenth century physician and astrologer has said.*

Nostradamus is said to have flatly predicted a climax to earth's affairs before the year 2000 according to *Time* magazine. [1]

Fontbrune's *Nostradamus — Historian and Prophet* has the seer predicting a great war (World War III?) in 1991, after an earlier major conflict (perhaps W.W. II). *La Fin du Monde* (The End of the World), a book published in France in November 1982, details the results obtained by running the predictions of Nostradamus through a computer programmed to take into account

---

*The author is not endorsing or affirming the prophecies of Nostradamus. His amazing predictions and the incredible interest which they have aroused, especially in Europe, are cited merely as an illustration of the fact that such views are widely held and seriously considered.

the positions of the planets. Exact dates and locations for the coming disasters are said to result. The author, Maurice Chatelain, claims this reveals that the immediate future is full of wars, anti-Christs and natural disasters—though he says the 1999 date set by most Nostradamus buffs for the end of the world is wrong, predicting instead the year 3797.

CURRENT DOOMSDAY PREDICTIONS

Widespread terror concerning "Doomsday," as the media dubbed it, on March 10, 1982, was reported around the world. The fear arose as the result of predictions (later withdrawn) by a couple of scientists in their book, *The Jupiter Effect*. The book forecast that the alignment of nine solar system planets on our side of the sun would trigger earthquakes, violent weather and massive upheavals upon earth.

Of course, religious groups have regularly predicted the Apocalypse—setting it variously for 1844, 1914, 1915, 1975. Preachers through the years have frequently made similar prophecies the topic of hair-raising sermons.

Recently several obscure sects have gained a good deal of national publicity by setting specific dates for the "return of Christ" and the onset of the related awesome judgments predicted in Scripture.

A southern U.S. television and radio preacher boldly proclaimed that a day in April 1980 was the date for the "return." A small sect in Arizona set first June 28 and later August 3, 1981, as the time. A tiny Canadian group living in the Alberta bush near Exshaw pinpointed September 16, 1981, as the day, and mailed virulent announcements of the event to many Alberta clergymen.

Unfortunately for the credibility of these self-styled prophets, all of their deadlines have come and gone and, quite obviously, Christ has not returned nor has the Apocalypse or Doomsday burst upon earth. Some of these groups, like the Jehovah's Witnesses, have attempted to save· face by re-interpreting the coming of Christ to be an invisible advent or some other special arrival—a most unsatisfactory explanation.

So when yet another voice is raised to suggest that the return of Christ and the horrendous attendant events that precede His final benign rule on earth really appear to be near at hand, it's not unusual for people to respond with a skeptical, "We've heard all *that* before!"

Fair enough.

And very understandable.

But, in spite of the numerous false prophets with their widely-publicized but inaccurate dating, the fact remains: the Bible *does* clearly predict that Jesus Christ will return to earth.

The Word of God (which lays claims to divine inspiration that can be abundantly verified) makes it clear that a brief but incredibly violent climax to earth's affairs *is* coming.

A PROPHETIC OVERVIEW

In a nutshell, the sequence of events is this. Believers in Christ all over the world will mysteriously disappear in what is called the rapture, or the "snatching away of the church." This will usher in a seven-year period Bible scholars call the great tribulation, with the final three and one-half years being the most awesome span in all of earth's history.*

A global dictator will arise; famine, war,

---

*Not all students of biblical prophecy will agree with the position held by this author, since there are three major views among students of prophecy concerning the end-time sequence of events.

1. One view holds that the return of Jesus Christ to earth will not occur until after a prophesied period of 1,000 years of peace, called the millenium.

2. Another view says that there will be no millennium!

pestilence, earthquake activity, as well as the mind-boggling judgments described in the Book of the Apocalypse (Revelation, the last book of the Bible) will come upon earth, which will literally reel under the impact of these horrendous events.

The climactic battle of Armageddon, in which all nations of the world will participate, will be the final occurrence in this period, precipitated by the revelation of Christ from heaven, and the defeat of the forces of evil. Christ will then consign Satan to the abyss and establish His 1,000-year reign on earth—a reign which will see prevail wonderful, completely ideal conditions, almost beyond human imagination.

---

3. The third view is that the return of Christ precedes, and in fact, precipitates, the millennium. This school of thought holds that the rapture and the tribulation both precede the millennium, with the rapture occurring at one of three times:

  (a) **before** the tribulation (pre-tribulation)
  (b) **during** the tribulation (mid-tribulation)
  (c) **after** the tribulation (post-tribulation)

The author takes the pre-millennium, pre-tribulation position. However, it should be noted that, regardless of the view held on the **exact** chronology of end-time events, all students of prophecy agree that an enormous catastrophic climax to human history is foretold. A **bonafide "CLIMAX OF THE AGES" is unquestionably to be found in mankind's prophetic writings!**

WHAT'S THE EVIDENCE?

Now, what are the evidences for believing that this climax of the ages, which we'll describe in more detail later, is near? Can we be reasonable, rational, intelligent individuals, and still believe that it could happen soon?

Or is all of this merely the wild-eyed ranting of deluded "prophets" — whose fallacies have become clearly evident in the numerous prophetic "bloopers" the world has witnessed in recent times?

These are good questions.

And as the world, early in the decade of the '80s, suffers through the most severe period of economic depression and uncertainty in the living memory of most folks; as the fear of a nuclear holocaust grips us; as endless wars trouble our planet, the arms race heats up and the dire forecasts of economists envision "total collapse" — many are seriously asking such questions. The fear that fuels these queries is well founded.

FEARFUL OUTLOOK

The February 15, 1982, issue of Canada's national news magazine, *Maclean's*, carried what is probably the most solemn cover ever to appear in the country. Its ominous title asked, "Is World War III Inevitable?" The

19

dreadful conclusion of the accompanying article seemed to be that it is — with Murphy's Law ("What *can* go wrong, sooner or later, *will*") being quoted.

A May 1982 U.S. Gallup Poll revealed that half the public "expect a world war by 1992." Red Chinese leader Deng Xiaoping is quoted as saying that "World War III is beyond man's capacity to avoid." Writer Jonathan Schnell of *The New Yorker* declares, "the machinery of destruction is in place, poised on a hairtrigger, waiting for the button to be pushed by some misguided or deranged human, or for some faulty computer chip to send out the instructions to fire." Such a suggestion takes on an added dimension of terror when it is recalled that *The New York Times*, May 26, 1981, detailed 32 nuclear accidents involving weapons, admitted by the Pentagon, over the past 30 years — any one of which "could have been the trigger to a chain reaction which would have turned the world into a massive nuclear crematorium."

It is our purpose to address these fears and questions in the light of the prophetic writings of the Bible.

The aim of this book, then, is to set out as clearly and as simply as possible, an outline of the biblical prophecies which relate to the "end times," and also to examine the current events— particularly in the economic realm—which this author believes are bona fide signs that we *are* approaching earth's awesome climax.

The reader will be asked to examine the prophecies and the evidence, and then to judge for himself just where we stand.

The kind of action which, in the view of the author, is the *only* way to prepare for the eventualities suggested here, will be described in part five.

What a time to be living on planet earth! We may indeed be the generation that will be in on the awesome CLIMAX OF EARTH'S AGES!

PART ONE

The Climax of the Ages

ECONOMIC SIGNS

"...the worst envisioned would be a global monetary collapse, triggered by energy shortages, and characterized by uncontrolled Weimar-style inflation that wipes out paper assets, beggars the middle class, and impoverishes everyone but the speculators."

--*Canadian Business Magazine*
December 1979

"What we are seeing today is not simply an economic upheaval, but something far deeper, something that cannot be understood within the framework of conventional economics. This is why increasingly mystified economists complain that 'the old rules don't work any longer.' What we are seeing is the general crisis of industrialism--a crisis that transcends the differences between capitalism and Soviet-style communism, a crisis that is simultaneously tearing up our energy base, our value systems, our sense of space and time, our epistemology as well as our economy. What is happening, no more, no less, is the breakdown of industrial civilization on the planet and the first fragmentary appearance of a wholly new and drastically different social order: a super-industrial civilization that will be technological, but no longer industrial."

--Alvin Toffler in
The Eco-Spasm Report

CHAPTER ONE

A Basketful of Money for
a Purseful of Groceries

It was August 14, 1923.

Maria's birthday.

The worry lines etched themselves deeply into the face of the pretty German housewife...far too youthful at 28 to be carrying in her features the evidence of such great anxiety.

After their meagre breakfast Maria had kissed her husband, Hans, goodbye, handing him an even more meagre lunch as he set out for his day's work at the railyards.

Alone now, she reflected on how unbelievably things had changed in the past year. There would be no birthday gift for her this year, not even something like the simple token of love Hans had managed last August.

Maria was frightened.

What was happening to Germany? Where was it all going to stop? Since the war had ended, the prices of everything were increasing so fast it made her head swim. She just couldn't comprehend what was going on.

WAGES PAID ON THE HOUR

Yesterday Hans had told her that the workers at the railyard had won the right to be paid on an *hourly* basis—simply because the value of the currency was falling so rapidly that waiting, even to the end of the day, meant they were seriously losing their purchasing power.

Now she would have to come to the railyard fence each morning and afternoon. Hans would rush over and give her the salary, and she would have to go immediately to the shops and stand in line to purchase what food she could. Otherwise inflation would bite so deeply even in the course of an afternoon, that they wouldn't be able to buy the bare necessities of life.

Maria let her mind run along the thought of birthdays. She reflected ruefully on how different it had been when Hans had *his* twenty-eighth birthday, just last January. And the birthday before that, in January of 1922!

Back then, only twenty months ago, she

had been concerned about the cost of the eggs she bought to make Han's birthday cake. In early 1922 an egg, which had sold for a quarter of a mark at the end of the war in 1918, was selling for about 50 marks.

But now, only a year and a half later, eggs cost over 5,000 marks each! *And everything else had gone up comparatively in price!*

Maria fought the rising sense of panic which threatened to engulf her. Even the fact that Hans was now making nearly fifteen million marks a week didn't help. The value of their money was dropping so fast that they just couldn't cope. She had to literally take a basketful of money just to get a few groceries!

What could they do? Nobody seemed to have an answer.

Suddenly Maria gave up the battle against the tide of terror within her. Her stoic self-control crumbled. She put her head down on the table and let loose a flood of despairing tears...a bitter birthday gift to herself. [2]

The kind of despair "Maria" experienced was common in the Germany of 1923, and many people tragically concluded that suicide was the only way out.

Little wonder.

The nation was in the grip of the most extreme case of inflation in history.

After World War I, the victorious Allies, particularly the French, demanded exorbitant redress from a German economy already shaken by the costly and unsuccessful war. Limits were set by the Allies on German industry in 1919, a reparations bill for 132 billion gold marks was submitted in 1921, and half of the Upper Silesian industrial area was given to Poland.

When the inexperienced left-wing German government was unable and unwilling to balance its budget, and the French army moved into the Ruhr in January of 1923 on a "mission of control" designed to squeeze the reparations out of German industry, the seeds of collapse were sown.

Passive resistance to the French and the closure of the factories were supported by the government through the printing of billions of new marks. The German unit of currency was well on its way to destruction.

The mark, which had traded at nine for one U.S. dollar in January 1919, had already declined steadily up to that time. It was 65 to one in January 1920, and 190 to one by January 1922. In July of 1922, it was 495 to one. At the time of the French "squeeze" in January 1923, it seemed to have hit the bottom at an astonishing exchange rate of 18,000 marks to one American dollar.

But with added pressures and the government currency printing program, the slide became an almost vertical plunge. Stupendous denominations of currency were commonplace in Germany in 1923. The bills were printed on one side only because there was no time to let the ink dry, even though the presses were running around the clock. As hyperinflation accelerated, billion- and trillion-mark notes became so common and so worthless, it was cheaper to paper a room with them than to use them to buy wallpaper.[3]

By July 1923, a single U.S. dollar was valued at 350,000 marks. In August it skyrocketed to 4,620,000. September saw an exchange rate of 100 million to one, and in October the rate was an incredible 25 *billion* marks to the dollar.[4]

In November 1923, before the nightmare came to an end, the exchange rate reached a number which only a mathematician could even contemplate: 4,200,000,000,000 (4.2 trillion) marks to a single dollar!

At that point, new "retenmarks" were issued—one for each inflated trillion-mark note. The middle class—those living on fixed incomes from salaries, pensions or investments—was wiped out. Many who had lived comfortably on investment income were literally paid off in full for the cost of a cup of coffee. They had to struggle desperately to stay alive, and some chose rather to end it all.

"Those who survived," says Jerome Smith in *The Coming Currency Collapse*, "were glad to listen to the promises of the National Socialists, who were busy in Berlin as early as 1919. And thus the inflation from one war created the conditions which helped to bring about the next."[5]

This tendency of inflation and economic collapse to create conditions ripe for tyranny will, I believe, be multiplied a thousandfold in the climax of earth's ages—toward which we are unquestionably moving. We'll consider this in chapter four.

MORE LESSONS FROM HISTORY

Though it is undoubtedly the most dramatic, the tragic German experience is not the only lesson from history concerning the effects of unchecked inflation.

The sad experience of an entire people during a series of paper money inflationary periods in medieval *China*, under seven dynasties from the ninth to the seventeenth centuries, is traced in the *Swiss Economic Viewpoint*, October 1, 1976.[6]

The history of *France*, from 1790 to 1796, was one of tragedy when the national currency, the *assignat*, hyperinflated to destruction. The guillotining of the royal family, anarchy and the rebellion of 1795, followed by Napoleon's seizure of power, were bitter fruits of that national financial experiment.[7]

Post-World War II *Italy*, *Poland* and *France* are other sorry examples of massive inflation. In early 1983, Poland's debt was sending shivers through Western bankers who held its massive loans.

Brazil is yet another illustration, along with *Mexico* and *Argentina*, of the enormously disruptive and long lasting effects of inflationary policies in government.[8]

ECONOMIC BLUNDERS CONTINUE

It is the opinion of numerous economists today that these historic inflationary disasters, as well as our current worldwide inflation, are the results of fundamental errors in government fiscal policy.

Most feel that these basic blunders continue to be perpetuated almost universally today.

Douglas Casey, in *Crisis Investing*, says:

...a study of history can result in pessimism and cynicism when one realizes that government never, ever, learns from history; it seems that the only thing we learn from history is the fact that we learn nothing from history.

History is replete with examples of regulation and inflation leading to the worst type of political, social, moral, economic, psychological and military debacles; yet governments continue inflating, regulating, and taxing.

History may be viewed as a record of governments' various depredations upon their subjects. [9]

Casey's pessimistic conclusion, unfortunately, appears to be justified as we look around us today.

Such disastrous global economic mismanagement is unquestionably a major factor in creating the climate for the events we've been calling "the climax of earth's ages" —as we shall shortly see. But first, let's consider the current world economic outlook in more detail in chapter two.

For Further Reading:

Abert, Geoffrey. *After the Crash*. Scarborough: New American Library, 1979.

Casey, Douglas. *Crisis Investing*. New York: Pocket Books, 1980.

Could the sort of inflationary chaos that erupted in Germany and other nations in the past ever occur again? Is such an eventuality inconceivable—or could it happen once more, this time on a global scale?

CHAPTER TWO

The Impending Global Economic Crunch

"Every time history repeats itself— the price goes up."

—Anonymous

An amazingly high percentage of the bestsellers throughout North America in the late 1970s, and the early months of the decade of the 1980s are pessimistic.

They are also books on the economy.

The overlap is not coincidental.

Glance at some of these bestselling titles:

Crisis Investing—Opportunities and Profits in the Coming Great Depression; *The Coming Currency Collapse*; *After the Crash*—How to Survive and Prosper During the Depression of the 1980s; *New Profits from the Monetary Crisis*, and *How to Prosper During the Coming Bad Years*. There are many others of a similar nature, like *The Day the Dollar Dies* and *The Cashless Society*—World Without Money.

Most of these widely read books, as well as the numerous radio or television financial shows and economic newsletters, are written or produced by bona fide economists or analysts—people like Jerome Smith, Harry Browne, Dr. Geoffrey Abert, Howard Ruff, Alvin Toffler and others.

And, as we have indicated, all of them present a very gloomy economic outlook—on a global scale. Even those books whose forewords contain the disclaimer, "This is not a doomsday (or pessimistic) book," do so only on the basis that the authors believe that *they* can offer a way for their readers to prepare for and survive the coming bad times. *None* of the above-mentioned authors disagrees with the prediction that chaotic economic times are ahead.

Abert asks at the outset of his book:

WHAT WILL YOU DO WHEN:

— Money is barely worth the paper it is printed on
— Transportation slows to a virtual halt
— Government services break down
— Cities default
— Banks close their doors
— Crime rises astronomically
— The social fabric is ripped to shreds
— And panic is everywhere

This is not a science fiction nightmare. It is a sober scientific forecast based on unassailable facts. *It is what you have to be prepared for.*[10]

The December 1979 issue of *Canadian Business* carried a major feature on economic prospects in the upcoming decade, entitled "The Unpredictable Decade—the 1980s."

Admitting that no one can say with certainty what will happen, the editors and writers nevertheless concluded that "all... hope the worst [a global monetary collapse] will not happen...and *most fear it will*" (emphasis mine).[11]

Author Douglas Casey predicted a massive depression by 1983-1985. Economist Dr. Abert set the time for the collapse between 1982 and 1985. West German Central banker

Karl Otto Pohl said, "I see the danger of a world recession." [12] *World Market Perspective*, a private Vancouver, B.C., monthly economic newsletter, warned in late 1980:

> Around the corner is what appears to be the final blow-off in the great inflationary cycle of the last 40 years. The result, unfortunately, will be the complete destruction of the dollar. [13]

In an interview in *Gold and Silver Report*, September 1980, Dr. Franz Pick, one of the world's leading authorities on currency matters and precious metals, author of six books and publisher of two yearbooks on currency, says the dollar will be wiped out: "I have lived through the destruction of the Czechoslovak koruna, the German mark and the French franc. Now I'm witnessing the destruction of the U.S. dollar. The destruction process is the same."

Of course, these predictions may be off base. More than a few economists have discovered their crystal ball to be murky in the past! Disagreement among them on what will happen is legendary. And so their forecasts or the specific predicted dates they announce for collapse may not be accurate. [14]

However, whether the economists quoted are right about the exact date is not the issue.

The grim fact is that there is much which would suggest that they definitely *are* on target in their predictions about the general direction of our world economy.

Anthony Sampson, in his book *The Money Lenders*, published in January 1982, raises many ominous questions about our global economic condition. These are listed in the January 18, 1982, issue of *Business Week*:

> ...Is Third World debt spiraling out of control? Can the international financial system withstand the shock of a major default? If Brazil, Mexico, or—to pick a debt-heavy country now on everyone's mind—Poland should repudiate its debt, who will be left holding the bag? [15]

Sampson's answers to these vital questions paint a picture of the international financial system as a sort of global chain letter that, like all chain letters, will collapse if one of the recipients decides not to pay off. [16]

In late 1982, following the Toronto, Ontario, meeting of the International Monetary Fund, "fears that banks could totter under the weight of the world's bad debts [such as Poland's and Mexico's] sent the price of gold soaring from $300 to over $500 per ounce in 10 weeks," according to *The Economist*, September 11, 1982. [17]

And the experts of the International Organization for Economic Cooperation and Development, meeting in Paris in November 1982, voiced pessimism over global economic prospects and fears that protectionist trade measures would trigger food wars and further major worldwide economic problems.[18]

IT SEEMS TO BE HAPPENING

The dire economic predictions of 1980, 1981, 1982 and 1983 appear to be coming to pass. Consider the following news items from late 1982 and early 1983:

A January, 1983 *Province* headline says: "Bankers see 'Doomsday' Drift." Another headline suggests that...

Wheelbarrows may yet replace wallets as Argentines get $20 for a million pesos

Buenos Aires—Argentines have yet to cart their increasingly worthless money around in wheelbarrows, as Germans were said to have done in the 1920s, but government printing presses keep churning out ever-larger bill denominations to keep up.

The latest is the one-million-peso note. On the black market it is worth just $20.

A whole range of slang has developed

to help Argentines keep track of their money. A 10,000-peso note, for example, is called a "palo," which means a stick; a kiosk-owner was charging "three sticks" this week for one chocolate bar. [19]

Typical news stories from January and February of 1983 follow:

World debt crisis forces urgent talks

Paris (AP)—The rich countries of the West start three days of urgent meetings in Paris today in a bid to avert threats of a collapse of the world financial system under the burden of a crushing international debt. [20]

World debt "threat to U.S. recovery"

Washington—Failure to solve the mounting debt problems of developing countries will stall a U.S. economic recovery and threaten 'the cohesion and political relationships of the western world,' Paul Volcker, chairman of the U.S. Federal Reserve Board, told the U.S. Congress on Wednesday. [21]

The cover story of the January 10, 1983, issue of *Time* was entitled "The Debt Bomb Threat." It spelled out the seriousness of the global economic situation in grim terms.

> Never in history have so many nations owed so much money with so little promise of repayment. At stake is a gargantuan debt, a $706 billion lien held by banks, governments and international financial institutions around the world.... It has mushroomed from about $100 billion only twelve years ago, keeping borrowers in bondage and lenders in growing suspense. Much of it may never be paid off, and a major default somewhere, somehow, could trigger far-reaching political and economic reactions everywhere. The global economy is sitting on a debt bomb.
>
> ...Some experts believe that the world needs a new agency to help debtor countries, but to establish one could inflame North-South political tensions that would endanger the present rescue measures.[22]

The crisis appears to be too massive for any one nation, or group of nations, to handle.

Don McGillvary, of Southam News, concluded a five-part analysis of the global economy in September of 1982 with an article headlined, "New World Order Coming." In it McGillvary wrote:

National sovereignty now means little when it comes to economics. Even the U.S., still the strongest economy in the world, can't determine its own destiny...

...As Peter Drucker, the American business guru, said in a recent book, the 'new economics' involve some wider, international unit''

The staggering level of Third World Debt could bring the international banks to their knees. Mexico owes Western banks more than $81 billion; Hungary owes $7.8 billion. Poland alone could topple the financial system by forcing a default on $17 billion owed to the Western banks.

Today, debt pyramids abound. Among the events which might conceivably act as triggers of an overnight tragedy are: a sudden surge of major corporate bankruptcies; a money-market fund panic; a bond-market collapse; a real-estate crash; a Middle East crisis resulting in the Saudis pulling their funds out of the major banks; a grass-roots run on the banks and S. & L.s; or a concerted Third World or East Bloc debt default.[23]

IS THERE A CONSPIRACY TO RULE THE WORLD FINANCIALLY?

Any reference to international financial organizations, agreements or units immediately raises, in the minds of many thoughtful people, at least two major questions.

First, is there indeed (as has been so often suggested) a shadowy global conspiracy by the wealthy elite of earth to totally control the entire world through its economy? And *second*, if there is such a conspiracy, how does the current dismal economic picture fit into their plans? Have our current enormous worldwide economic difficulties come about through the conspirators' *design*? Or has the present situation taken them by *surprise* and, as a result of their manipulation, or ignorance, or inability, is the world economy totally out of the control of anyone?

Let me answer these two vital questions, very directly and briefly, in chapter three and then provide the documentation for my responses.

For Further Reading:

Allen, Gary. "Troubled Bankers," *American Opinion*, October, 1982, pp. 1-6, 97-110. 395 Concord Ave., Belmont, Mass. 02178, U.S.A.

————— "Our Economy Trembles Atop the Banking Pryamid," *American Opinion*, January, 1983, pp. 31-90, 77-82.

Cantelon, Willard. *Money Master of the World*, (Plainfield N.J.: Logos International, 1976).

Clark, Doug. *The Greatest Banking Scandal in History*, (Eugene, Ore.: Harvest House Publishers, 1981).

Novak, Michael. *The Spirit of Democratic Capitalism*, (New York: Simon and Schuster, 1982).

Novak, N.D. "The Changing Scene in World Economics," *Canadian Banker and ICB Review*, August, 1981.

Smith, Jerome. *The Coming Currency Collapse*. Toronto: Bantam Books, 1981.

————— *The Future of Money*, (Vancouver: International Self-Counsel Press Ltd., 1978).

Toffler, Alvin. *The Eco-Spasm Report*. New York: Bantam Books, 1975.

This myth (of a conspiracy to rule the world), like all fables, does in fact have a modicum of truth. There does exist, and has existed for a generation, an international Anglophile network...

Professor Carroll Quigley in
Tragedy and Hope

CHAPTER THREE

Yes, Virginia, There Probably is a Conspiracy

The questions posed at the end of chapter two—whether there is a conspiracy to rule the world financially, and if so, how the current economic morass fits in—are without doubt significant queries.

They deserve thoughtful answers.

First, I have come to believe as a result of my research that there *is* good evidence to support the view that *a conspiracy* to create a one-world financial state *does exist*.

Though I will attempt to support and explain this conviction in a moment, I must say at the outset that I do not believe the *motives* of the "conspirators" to be inherently and necessarily evil—as some have charged.

Second, I frankly confess that I do not know whether the current and projected global economic disaster is engineered or by accident. In my judgment a fairly good case can be made for either position—but, as we will explain later in this chapter, it really doesn't matter. In the final analysis, *the effect is the same*. And that effect, I am convinced, has been clearly foretold in the prophetic writings. More on that later.

WHY DO I BELIEVE THERE IS A CONSPIRACY?

I must preface my response by saying that for years I tended to reject, almost out-of-hand, the material about a mysterious global financial conspiracy that kept coming across my desk. So much of it was extreme, poorly documented and, in some cases, badly written.

I agree with the opinion expressed by Ron

Marr, editor of *The Christian Inquirer*, in this regard, when he wrote in *New World Order—Special Report*, published in June 1980:

> Frankly, the inflammatory rhetoric of many writers claiming to know the secrets of worldwide conspiracy dating back to the Illuminati in 1776, to Machiavelli in the 1300's and to occult traditions in the early days of mankind tends to turn me off.

> So do the findings of those who lay all of our problems at the door of a Communist conspiracy or a Zionist conspiracy or a Masonic conspiracy. [24]

However, as I have read and researched material like Marr's *New World Order*, Hal Lindsay's *The 1980's—Countdown to Armageddon*, *Mystery 666* by Don Stanton, *The Naked Capitalist* by Cleon Skousen, *Tragedy and Hope* by Carroll Quigley, and others, I have become convinced that there is indeed an international, non-governmental group of financiers, intellectuals, industrialists and politicians whose goal is the development of a one-world government, one-world bank and a one-world currency. This "conspiracy," according to Ron Marr, is not to be understood as being a single, unified plot:

It appears much more likely that the dynamic direction which has so evidently emerged in this century is the result of many planners in pursuit of world domination from very different perspectives and purposes, each attempting to use the other—each in the hope that they will emerge as the ultimate controlling force.[25]

Though it is no doubt true as Marr says that there are many independent—even competing—elements at work in any quest for world domination, one particular agency is especially significant and is worth our special attention. That group is the Trilateral Commission.

THE TRILATERAL COMMISSION: HOW DOES IT FIT IN?

Very few people are aware even of the existence, let alone the purposes, of the Trilateral Commission. Hal Lindsey, *The 1980's: Countdown to Armageddon,* says that only one or two percent of his audiences in recent years, have indicated to him even an *awareness* of the existence of the Commission.

Lindsey admits to being baffled by this, in view of the fact that the Commission is an "international non-elected group of the western world's most powerful bankers, media leaders, scholars and government officials bent on radically changing the world." The changes which this group envisions, without obtaining permission to make such changes from any of earth's people through the ballot box, will affect the individual and economic status of every person in the world.

Let me attempt to document that last statement. [26]

TO START AT THE BEGINNING

The obvious need for some kind of system to regulate international trade has always existed.

Prior to World War II, control of world trade was achieved primarily through the posting of tariffs by Britain, France, Holland, Portugal and the United States. These tariffs, under the imperial system, made it difficult for nations outside to trade with those inside—and thus international control was maintained.

However, it became apparent during World War II that the system could not survive in the postwar era. Thus, plans for a replcement system were developed in 1944 by John

Maynard Keynes, an outstanding British economist, and Harry Dexter White, another brilliant economist from the United States.

These plans came to be known as the Bretton Woods system—taking the name from the small New Hampshire town in which they were developed.

The Bretton Woods agreement sought to solve two problems:

1. *The manipulation of national currencies* by their governments so as to protect their own currency and weaken those of other nations, resulting in worldwide financial instability.

2. The problem of *protective tariffs*, raised indiscriminately by nations or groups of nations—resulting in closed markets to the underdeveloped nations and the inhibiting of free international trade.

Fixing currency exchange rates was seen as the solution to the first problem. To achieve this required the establishment of two international institutions—the International Monetary Fund (IMF) and the World Bank. In addition to setting currency exchange rates, these two institutions were given, by agreement, authority to provide credit to the world's "have not" countries and to lend money to nations ravaged by war.

The establishment of the *most favoured*

nation system of trade was the proposed solution to the tariff problem. Under this scheme, under-developed nations which had difficulty competing for international trade were granted this status, and thus were exempt from paying tariffs. Freedom from tariff payments meant that such nations could offer their goods more cheaply, and so international trade was stimulated.

The General Agreement on Tariffs and Trade (GATT) is the international pact which controlled this system.

But any system can be violated, and the success of the Bretton Woods plan depended upon some power capable of enforcing its provisions.

THE "ENFORCER"

The United States was the logical choice to provide that control. In 1944 the U.S. dollar was already the basic world currency: it was stable, backed both by the gold standard and a healthy economy.

In addition, the United States at that time consumed more than half of the world's total exported goods, and thus was in a position to regulate GATT. As the greatest economic power in the world, the U.S. could also effectively deal with violators of the system, using tariff restrictions or credit control to punish infractions.

Bretton Woods greatly encouraged free trade. *It did not tamper with the sovereignty of nations*, working instead on the basis of a *community* of nations. Under it, the world witnessed the greatest growth in international trade in all human history—from virtually nothing at the end of the war, to over $400 billion by the early 1970s.

OH! OH!

But beginning in the decade of the 1960s, the "enforcer"—the United States—began to stumble, and Bretton Woods started to fall.

Here's how it happened.

An increasing deficit in the U.S. balance of payments and the removal of the gold standard robbed the American dollar of its stability and power.

Japan, resurgent after the war, and the increasingly powerful European Common Market became strong competitors to the U.S. in the international marketplace. The result was a weakened U.S. ability to deal with GATT violators.

Third World countries were increasingly forced to limit their trade because of their inability to pay. Many observers feel that it was this lack of Third World purchasing power that finally brought an end to Bretton Woods.

Writing in *The Christian Science Monitor*, February 7, 1977, economist Jeremiah Novak says that the demise of the Bretton Woods system "was (finally) precipitated by...(President) Nixon...in 1971, when the United States devalued the dollar and imposed a tariff surcharge on imports." [27]

Numerous unsuccessful attempts [28] by various groups to revamp the Bretton Woods system made it very clear that a new arrangement was necessary.

Such an arrangement was soon forthcoming.

In July 1973, David Rockefeller recruited some two hundred leading international bankers, businessmen, politicians and labor leaders to join him in research into the complex problems faced in international affairs.

Zbigniew Brzezinski (Special Presidential Advisor for National Security during the Carter administration), who was then Columbia University's specialist on international relations, was handpicked by Rockefeller to be the key intellectual in the formulation of the policies of this new system.

A VISION

What Rockefeller envisioned was the Trilateral Commission.

Newsweek, June 16, 1975, described the commission's inception in these words: "...The Trilateral Commission, a brainchild of David Rockefeller, was transformed into reality by Zbigniew Brzezinski."[29]

He and Rockefeller attracted some of the top intellectuals of Japan, Europe and the United States to join in the task of reshaping world economics.

Senator Barry Goldwater writes: "...Zbigniew Brzezinski and David Rockefeller screened and selected every individual who was invited to participate in shaping and administering the new world order."[30]

The name "trilateral" was adopted because the Rockefeller/Brzezinski task force decided that the basis for a new world economic order would have to be the United States, the European Common Market and Japan, acting in unison. Because these three entities together represented 70 percent of world trade, they therefore had, in the minds of the commission, the "right and duty" to create a new system.

More than this, they had the power (which the U.S. *alone* now lacked) to enforce any replacement for Bretton Woods.

Thus the three spheres of economic influence and power were to be combined into one force—the Trilateral Commission.

Jeremiah Novak, writing in *America*, says:

> The group believes that the policies of the trilateral world must be harmonized, as the U.S. alone can no longer take on responsibility for the international economic system. It also believes that if a new order is created, it must be based on a recognition that *the U.S. is now only the first among equals* in the industrial world....As a result of this conclusion, *U.S. foreign policy must undergo a transformation of gigantic proportions.*[31]

There can be no question that the direction here indicated fits in with the "one-world" concept, which certainly involves the continued lowering of the U.S. leadership profile in the world. Brzezinski himself wrote in the July 1975 issue of the Council on Foreign Relations publication *Foreign Affairs*, "...the world is not likely to unite willingly behind a common ideology or a superpower. The only practical hope is that it will now respond to a common concern for its own survival...the active promotion of such *trilateral cooperation* must now become the central priority of U.S. policy" (emphasis mine).[32]

Novak goes on to show, in his 1977 *America*

article, that the areas which the Trilateral Commission claims the right to regulate are far greater than those dealt with by Bretton Woods.

He writes:

The rules cover such areas as international monetary systems, international trade in raw materials and industrial goods [a new area not covered in Bretton Woods] and use of 'commons,' such as the oceans, space and the (north and south) poles. These rules are seen as universally applicable and subject to sanctions in the event they are violated.[33]

A POLITICAL PLATFORM NEEDED

The Commission recognized that there had to be provisions made for relations with Communist, Third World and OPEC nations in its bid to make the world economically interdependent. It is apparent they did not expect their system to exist in a political vacuum.

Indeed not.

They have handpicked certain of their members to be groomed for the highest political offices in their respective home nations — especially the United States, which is still a major world leader in terms of power and influence.

An article in the *Atlantic Monthly* boldly states this:

Although the Commission's primary concern is economic, the Trilateralists pin-pointed a vital political objective: To gain control of the American presidency. [34]

Georgia's first-term Democratic governor, Jimmy Carter, impressed Rockefeller by establishing a trade agreement with Japan for his state. Already contemplating a run for the presidency, Carter was very responsive to the Commission's interest. He later said "the Commission was a splendid learning opportunity." [35]

Carter's ambition matched the Commission's needs, which were described thus in the *U.S. News & World Report*, February 21, 1977:

The [Commission] founders, anxious to have a liberal Southerner in their ranks, invited Jimmy Carter, then the governor of Georgia, to join them. [36]

And so Carter, after becoming a charter member in 1973, received a thorough indoctrination in Trilateralist views from none other than Brzezinski himself.

The rest is history.

A virtual political unknown, Jimmy Carter came out of nowhere with the unquestionable backing of the enormously powerful Trilateralists in the news media to capture the White House.

He soon rewarded that support.

The *U.S. News & World Report* made this comment on February 21, 1977, shortly after Carter took office:

> The Trilateralists have taken charge of foreign policy-making in the Carter administration, and already the immense power they wield is sparking some controversy. Active or former members of the Trilateral Commission now head every key agency involved in mapping U.S. strategy for dealing with the rest of the world
>
> Altogether, 16 high posts in the administration are held by men and women associated with the organization. Some see this concentration of power as a conspiracy at work.[37]

A similar situation exists elsewhere in Japan and Europe. Economist Novak says:

> Its [the Commission's] membership

roster reads like a Who's Who in business, labor and [Trilateral nation] government.[38]

The 1980 U.S. presidential election saw a conservative, Ronald Reagan, gain the presidency—but in spite of that, a number of Trilateralists, including Vice-President George Bush and Caspar Weinberger, are in the administration. Obviously, one setback will not mean an end to the effort to influence and control.

Hal Lindsey, in *The 1980's: Countdown to Armageddon* writes:

It's been interesting to me to watch various news media heavyweights rush to defend the Commission against charges that it has gained undue power in the world's governments.

In general, they publish articles which minimize the Commission's influence, characterizing its members as a bunch of frustrated and powerless armchair idealists who wish they could institute some of their ideas in world affairs.... (They) call it simply a floating study group with no essential power, and they label the Commission's critics as isolationist conservatives or Marxist-leaning leftists.

I wonder if the fact that so many news media executives are also Commission members has anything to do with these published defenses.

For the media to say that the Trilateral Commission has no essential political power, however, is an insult to the intelligence of the American public. It also assumes that most Americans didn't read or don't remember the many articles which detailed the Commission's growing power and were published in those same newspapers and magazines in the 1977 era.[39]

WHO REALLY RUNS THE WORLD?

Not only is there evidence that the Trilateralists have successfully sought international power—but that the Commission has a close tie with a political entity holding a similar view—one which focuses on U.S. foreign policy.

This group, known as the Council on Foreign Relations (CFR), is a private, non-elected group incorporated in 1921 and chaired by David Rockefeller. Its present headquarters is the Harold Pratt House in New York City.

The extent of the CFR's influence, and its

relationship to the Trilateral Commission, is highlighted by the words of CFR President Winston Lord:

> The Trilateral Commission doesn't secretly run the world. The Council on Foreign Relations does that.[40]

In 1939, the CFR approached the U.S. State Department and offered its services in terms of advice and aid in international affairs. Their efforts were financed by the Rockefeller Foundation.

Senator Barry Goldwater reveals:

> From that day forward the Council on Foreign Relations has placed its members in policy-making positions with the federal government, not limited to the State Department.
>
> Since 1944 every American Secretary of State, with the exception of James F. Byrnes, has been a member of the CFR.
>
> I believe the CFR and its ancillary elitist groups are indifferent to communism. They have no ideological anchors. In their pursuit of a new world order they are prepared to deal without prejudice with a communist state, a socialist state, a democratic state, monarchy, oligarchy—it's all the same to them.

Rear Admiral Chester Ward, of the U.S. Navy (retired), who was a member of the CFR for 16 years, has written, "The most powerful cliques in these elitist groups have one objective in common—they want to bring about the surrender of the sovereignty and the national independence of the United States." [41]

Rear Admiral Ward quotes the president of Yale University, Kingston Brewster, Jr., another CFR member, and author of *Reflections on our National Purpose*, as saying, "Our national purpose should be to abolish our nationality." Ward says, "The lust to surrender the sovereignty and independence of the United States is pervasive throughout most of the (CFR) membership." [42]

VIEW FROM THE INSIDE

Certainly the most revealing disclosure of the origins, aims, and activities of the CFR came from one of their council's own members—Carroll Quigley, professor of history at the Foreign Service School of Georgetown University. His massive 1300-page book, *Tragedy and Hope*, published in 1966 by Macmillan and Co., New York, is an eye-opener! W. Cleon Skousen summarizes the volume in this way:

When Dr. Quigley decided to write his 1,300 page book called *Tragedy and Hope*, he knew he was deliberately exposing one of the best kept secrets in the world. As one of the elite "insiders," he knew the scope of this power complex and he knew that its leaders hope to eventually attain total global control. Furthermore, Dr. Quigley makes it clear throughout his book that by and large he warmly supports the goals and purposes of the "network." But if that is the case, why would he want to expose this world-wide conspiracy and disclose many of its most secret operations?...

He says, in effect, that it is now too late for the little people to turn back the tide. In a spirit of kindness he is therefore urging them not to fight the noose which is already around their necks. He feels certain that those who do will only choke themselves to death. On the other hand, those who go along with the immense pressure which is beginning to be felt by all humanity will eventually find themselves in a man-made millennium of peace and prosperity. All through his book, Dr. Quigley assures us that we can trust these benevolent, well-meaning men who are secretly operating behind the scenes. THEY are the *hope* of the world. All who resist them represent *tragedy*. Hence, the title for his book.[43]

Especially telling is Quigley's own assessment of the "conspiracy" in an oft-quoted passage from his book:

There does exist, and has existed for a generation, an international Anglophile network which operates, to some extent, in the way the radical Right believes the Communists act. In fact, this network, which we may identify as the Round Table Groups, has no aversion to cooperating with the Communists, or any other groups, and frequently does so. I know of the operations of this network because I have studied it for twenty years and was permitted for two years, in the early 1960's, to examine its papers and secret records. I have no aversion to it or to most of its aims and have, for much of my life, been close to it and to many of its instruments. I have objected, both in the past and recently, to a few of its policies...but in general my chief difference of opinion is that it wishes to remain unknown, and I believe its role in history is significant enough to be known.[44]

The October 1982 issue of *American Opinion* further reviews the content of *Tragedy and Hope*:

We learn from Professor Quigley that the conspiracy also has a British branch, among whose instrumentalities is the Royal Institute of International Affairs. In the United States, the Institute "is known as the Council on Foreign Relations." A first purpose of the conspirators was to reunite the British Empire and United States under a single government, which in effect would be a World Government.[45]

Now another book by Quigley, completed in 1944, seventeen years before *Tragedy and Hope* was written, but unpublished because no publisher could then be found who would handle it, has been released in 1982. *The Anglo-American Establishment* (Books in Focus, 160 East 38th Street, New York City) exposes a "Master Conspiracy." Commenting on Quigley's book in an October 1982 *American Opinion* article entitled "Proofs of a

Conspiracy," Alan Stang writes:

So immense, so awesome, is the power of this Conspiracy, that it even scares *Quigley*! He says of the Royal Institute of International Affairs: "...When the influence which the Institute wields is combined with that controlled by the Milner Group in other fields — in education, in administration, in newspapers and periodicals — a really terrifying picture begins to emerge....The picture is terrifying because such power, whatever the goals at which it may be directed is too much to be entrusted safely to any group...."[46]

Alan Stang concludes his article with this summary:

Bear in mind that we have cited but a few examples from Professor Quigley's books. Your intrepid correspondent could just as easily have written this piece with an entirely different set of examples. So we strongly urge you to obtain copies of these books and see for yourself.

When you do, you will see even more undeniably than you do here that there *is* a Conspiracy. You will see, to a great extent, who is running it, including some of their names. Yes, *names*. Real names, composed of familiar letters! You will see how the Conspiracy operates and what it wants. You will see all this couched in a wealth of scholarly footnotes and references that you can and should check for yourself.

When you have finished, you will realize that any conclusion that there is no Conspiracy out to rule the world is simply asinine. Indeed, it is insidious.[47]

Bearing out Quigley's claims, the CFR in one of their own publications has advocated

building a new international order...responsive to world aspirations for peace, for social and economic change...an international order including states labelling themselves as socialist.[48]

Unquestionably, a conspiracy does exist.

SHADES OF ORWELL'S 1984!

The question, however, as suggested before, is whether the current serious global economic conditions (described in chapter two and earlier in this chapter) have been created by the Trilateralists in their efforts to achieve control, or whether the world economy is now totally out of *anyone's* control!

Opinions vary. Some, like Gary Allen, writing in the November 1982 issue of *American Opinion,* feels things are virtually out of control. He says:

In these complex times there are more strings than any single group of men could possibly control. While it is probably true that our Establishment *Insiders* have in the past created wars and depressions for their own benefit, these things happened in the days when such trauma could be somewhat localized. Given today's "interdependent" global economy, it is no longer easy to keep a major crisis localized. Everything affects everything else.

...Which is why we believe the *Insiders* probably do not now wish to try to facilitate a major financial crisis. The probability of backfire is just too great. They want to prevent *any kind* of widespread panic or collapse. Even they must have sweaty palms....

...Nevertheless, there is always the X-Factor: some unforeseen watershed event or panic which can neither be planned for nor controlled.[49]

Others feel the current conditions have been planned. Wally Woods, Jr., author of

Cashless Society: A World Without Money and publisher of two monthly newsletters of news analysis, believes the chaos is by design. In an article entitled "New Money for a New World," published in 1981, he says:

> Space does not allow us to go into much detail at this time. We will say, however, that our present system of economics is on the precipice of total collapse. The depression that is just ahead promises to be more overwhelming than the one in the thirties. *It will not, however, be an 'accidental' depression—it will occur by design*. Its purpose will be to bring the world, especially the United States, to its knees, crying out for something—or, someone—to change things around to alleviate the pain.
>
> That 'something' will be a new world order...that 'someone' will be the new world leader of inestimable charisma and power. And the whole world will be deceived (emphasis mine).[50]

But whether the present chaos is by design or by accident really doesn't matter.

The effect is the same.

When the economic fabric of a society is torn apart, that society begins to disintegrate.

The resulting confusion is the kind of environment in which an elite, or a tyrant, can gain control. John Maynard Keynes has written:

> Lenin was certainly right. There is no subtler, no surer means of overturning the basis of existing society than to debauch the currency. This process engages all the hidden forces of economic law on the side of destruction, *and does it in a manner not one man in a million is able to diagnose* (emphasis mine).[51]

And whether the Trilateralists and their elitist cohorts planned the current economic uncertainty, or if it is simply a matter of circumstances playing into their hands, I agree completely with Hal Lindsey when he says that:

> ...the Trilateralist movement is unwittingly setting the stage for the political-economic one-world system the Bible predicts for the last days. It's happening in concert with all the other pieces of the prophetic scenario falling into place.
>
> What the Trilateralists are trying to establish will soon be controlled by the

coming world leader—the anti-Christ himself.[52]

Unquestionably, there *will* appear on the stage of human affairs a "world class" economist who will offer solutions and controls that will capture the support (both willing and unwilling) of the world.

This economist-to-come, "Mr. 666" (who will have, I believe, a meteoric rise to power through the power of Satan), will become, in the truest sense of the word, a global dictator.

In the next chapter we'll note some of the personal implications in our current scene and then look at the significance—from the prophetic standpoint—of what we've considered to this point.

For Further Reading:

Allen, Gary. *None Dare Call it Conspiracy*, (Rossmoor, Calif.: Concord Press, 1971).
————"Insiders of the Great Conspiracy," *American Opinion*, September 1982, pp. 41-54, 73-78.
Ferguson, M. *The Aquarian Conspiracy*, Personal and Social Transformation in the 80s, (Los Angeles: Tarcher St. Martins, 1980).

Lindsey, Hal. *The 1980s: Countdown to Armageddon*, (New York: Bantam Books, 1981).

Kirban, S. *Satan's Angels Exposed* (Huntingdon Valley, Pa.: Salem Kirban, Inc., 1980).

Quigley, C. *Tragedy and Hope*, (New York: The MacMillan Company, 1966).

Ross, Malcolm. *Web of Deceit*, (Moncton, N.B.: Stronghold Publishing Co. Ltd., 1978).

Sklar, Holly (Ed.). *Trilateralism* (Boston: South End Press, 1980).

Skousen, W.C. *The Naked Capitalist*, (Salt Lake City: Published privately by Skousen, 1970).

—————— *The Naked Communist*, (Salt Lake City: Ensign, 1962).

Stang, Alan. "New Book by Quigley adds more PROOFS OF A CONSPIRACY," *American Opinion*, October, 1982, pp. 19-26, 81-84.

Stanton, Don. *Mystery 666*, (Secunderabad, India, Marantha Revival Crusade, 1978).

Williams, L. *The Energy Non Crisis* (Wheatridge, Co.: Worth Publishing Co., 1980).

*Coming events cast their
shadows before them.*

CHAPTER FOUR

The Universe—
Unfolding as it Should?

Let's review!

We described in chapters two and three two extremely significant conditions existing in our world today.

First, we considered the current economic instability, on a global scale, which leads many observers to fear that Weimar-style international inflation *could* wipe out currency as we know it, and completely shake up our global economy. Even if this does not occur, changing conditions (many of them by design) will force a whole new international, technological approach to economic exchange.

Second, and definitely related, we've looked at evidence for the existence of a serious attempt by a powerful elite to create a new world order, characterized by a "one-world" system of finance and government.

Before we look at the prophetic meaning behind these conditions, let's note in this chapter some of the growing evidences which already have affected, or soon will affect, the average man in the street, and which indicate that we are indeed moving toward "one-world" status, characterized by technological control. In the judgment of the shadowy elite, that undoubtedly means that the universe is indeed "unfolding as it should."

CASHLESS SOCIETY—HERE WE COME!

Back in 1975, Thomas G. Waage, senior vice president of the New York Branch of the Federal Reserve Bank, said in a UPI release that a new electronic system of exchange *had* to be developed or the U.S. banking system would "choke" under an avalanche of checks.[53]

In a nutshell—we *are* headed for a cashless society which will feature computerization, videotex interactive television, "debit card" banking, fiber-optics, the Universal Product

Code, laser scanning and personal (that is, "on-the-person") numbering.

Robert Hendrickson, in his book *The Cashless Society*, summarizes his argument for a cashless society and suggests how it could happen:

> ...large aggregate holdings of cash are...a factor in inflation, international currency imbalances and international monetary crises.
>
> The time to do something effective about all this lawless cash is at hand...
>
> As the first step, all existing credit card systems would be linked, the many duplicating credit ledgers consolidated, the overlaps eliminated and a single credit ledger established for each individual and organization. A single all-purpose credit card and number would be issued to everyone to replace all existing credit cards....
>
> A date would be announced after which the old paper dollar and coin currency would no longer be accepted or honored as valid. All holders would be given a prior period of grace to turn in their paper currency at banks for further credit-card credits recorded in their favor....

Over time, in carefully planned steps, all paper which serves as money...would be eliminated from circulation....

The possibility of limiting, restricting or reducing the credits available to citizens by the elimination of money in the traditional sense, and the use of individual credit controlled through central banks would be the most precise and effective way imaginable of regulating economic activity in a single society.[54]

Hendrickson wrote in 1972. Since then tremendous strides have been made toward what he envisioned.

The marriage of the television to the computer has occurred—with the Canadian-developed Telidon system being "acclaimed internationally as the best of the breed." To be sure, the system has not yet been perfected—but the potential is awesome.

A push-button control box, or keypad, the size of a pocket calculator in the livingroom of the Telidon user is the only *obvious* new wrinkle. But with it the person plugged into the system will be able to do a vast array of different things, such as make catalogue purchases, grocery shop, handle all personal banking transactions, order library books...on and on the list goes. And that's just for starters! [55]

Back in 1966, while I was serving in our denominational headquarters in New York City, I attended a day-long seminar in the old Waldorf-Astoria Hotel sponsored by the U.S. Direct Mail Association. The unquestioned highlight of the event was a very futuristic and dramatic presentation of telephone/TV/computer shopping by Bell Telephone of New York and IBM. The vivid demonstration of the sort of thing which is now in prototype operation (in far more sophisticated form) was mind boggling. It seemed, *then*, it would have to be decades away. Yet only seventeen years later, here it is, and infinitely more advanced than it was then envisioned!

An ad for the First Interstate Bank of California, which appeared in the San Bernadino *News* on August 22, 1981, and was brought to me by a vacationing member of my congregation, is most interesting:

Try Telephone Bill Paying.
It only takes a minute.

All you need is a First Interstate Bank Checking Account and a push button phone. Our telephone Bill Paying service makes paying bills by check old-fashioned.

Use any pushbutton phone. Call any time, day or night. You'll be put in direct contact with our computer, and a "voice" will take you quickly through this sample transaction, step-by-step:

1. The voice will ask for your Customer Number. Push 123456789# (the # symbol always indicates you've finished your response.)

2. The voice will ask for your Security Code. Push 1234#.

3. The voice will ask for the Payee Number of the merchant you're paying. Push 12#.

4. The voice will ask for the amount you want to pay. Use $32.50 as an example. Push 3250#.

5. The voice will ask for pound sign or month and day. Push #.

6. The voice will then repeat the entire transaction back to you for verification. It should all take less than a minute.

7. Push *2# to complete your call.

If you don't have a pushbutton phone, come in to your nearest First Interstate branch, and use our phone to make your call.[56]

What we are seeing is literally a revolution

in banking. Electronic Fund Transfer (EFT) is becoming national in various nations of the world. In 1975, James Smith, then U.S. Comptroller of the Currency, said, "One of the most important competitive considerations today is the utilization of the new electronics technology for funds transfer."[57]

The most obvious indication to the average man in the street of the advent of electronics into financial matters will be the debit card. A *Globe and Mail* article which announced the introduction of debit cards also explains their use and significance:

> Debit cards are expected to come to Canada in August, 1982, when distribution of a special Mastercard by the Saskatchewan and Alberta credit union begins....
>
> Debit cards are not the same as credit cards, although the difference between the combination Mastercard debit-card and the regular Mastercard would not, for example, be evident to a merchant accepting the card for payment of a purchase.
>
> The cardholder, though, would be aware that the amount of the purchase would be debited from his chequing account at his credit union within a short

time after the purchase....If the cardholder has insufficient funds in the account to cover the purchase, a backup line of credit could handle that.

Dale Hillmer, manager of finance for the Credit Union Central of Saskatchewan, said there were a number of reasons behind the Central's decision to opt for a combined debit-credit card.

The Saskatchewan Central has always preferred the debit card to the credit card. It does not view the credit card as financially feasible and also feels that with the advent of electronic fund transfer, debit cards are the best choice. In addition, the Central said a debit card gives the cardholder better control over his finances. [58]

The debit card concept was in fact introduced in these credit unions in 1982, and is presently in use.

Electronic Fund Transfer has already gone international. It began with the introduction of S.W.I.F.T. in 1975. The January 1975 issue of *Burroughs Clearing House* magazine reported:

Burroughs Corp. has been selected by the Society for Worldwide Interbank Financial Telecommunications

(S.W.I.F.T.) to supply data processing and data communications equipment which will be used in a *new international telecommunications network.* S.W.I.F.T., which is based in Brussels, currently has a membership of 246 banks with a private communications system for the transmission of payment and other messages associated with international banking....Most messages transmitted on the S.W.I.F.T. network will be delivered anywhere in the system within a minute of being entered.[59]

Other everyday indications of our direction toward technological change and surveillance may be seen in the Universal Product Code (UPC)—that little black rectangle of thick and thin lines, with a number code which appears now on virtually every product throughout North America. It is designed to go along with the laser scanner and the computer to create computerized checkout systems for retail outlets.

The *laser scanner* is another factor with which the average person is becoming familiar. Many see it used in conjunction with the computerized checkout and the UPC. The products with their UPCs are swept across the scanner, there is a computer "blip" and the transaction is recorded in microseconds.

Progress—it's wonderful!

But not everyone is sold on our astounding technological advances. In an article in *Maclean's* magazine, entitled "Warily into a Wired-up World," Andrew Osler, associate professor of journalism at the University of Western Ontario, says:

I've been looking at the development of videotex interactive television, the marriage of TV and the computer with Canada's Telidon system acclaimed internationally as the best of the breed, and what I see scares the h--- out of me. It's the social equivalent of an atomic bomb with the potential to blow society, as we know it, wide open, and few people seem to be worrying about what to do with the fallout. This new technology could wipe away whatever scraps of individual privacy remain to us, and that's the least of our worries. It also contains the capacity to fine-tune public mind manipulation in a way that makes George Orwell's *1984* scenario look bush league by comparison.

If interactive television is to work, it will have to know an awful lot about us. If it is to monitor Great Uncle Charlie's heart, it will need his medical history. If it is to help with our financial planning, it will need to know everything about our income and spending habits, and if it is to help us find jobs, it will need our full employment and educational records. And there will be nothing to stop the system from acquiring such things as lists of our department-store purchases and library books we borrow, or from logging all the phone numbers we look up in its directory.

And here comes the catch. If someone should ever decide to put all that information—and much, much more—into one computer (which with satellite and fibre-optic transmission systems is no big deal), then that person, or agency or government, or political party, or multinational corporation, could learn more about us than we know about ourselves. The scenario develops. Individual privacy in tomorrow's wired-up world just beyond 1984 could become as archaic as medieval bear-baiting. Sophisticated surveillance of individuals (not just of those with medical problems), and the talented massaging of public opinion become terrifying possibilities. [60]

This increasing power of government on a national scale—let alone on an international "one-world" level—is a concern to many observers. On another level, it already seems that official surveillance of citizens, even in a comparatively free nation like Canada, is increasing.

GOVERNMENT SURVEILLENCE

A 1981 *Toronto Star* editorial, commenting on the expanding usage in Canada of Social Insurance Numbers (SIN) for such things as cheque handling, bond purchasing, opening credit accounts and indexing police records, warned:

No one can argue that the use of one personal identification number is not an efficient, time-saving way to keep track of records—particularly records stored in computer banks. But it is exactly that ease that makes the growing use of social insurance numbers in data banks so dangerous.

As computerization becomes more sophisticated and widespread, so does the use of central data systems, in government and in the business world. It is now possible, through the use of one number, to link separate files containing disparate information, so that one's entire life history, including income and credit information, could be obtained at the push of a button...

Federal Health and Welfare Minister Monique Begin has said Canadians should expect their Social Insurance numbers to be used more widely as identification in the computer banks of government and private industry. She calls it "a policy of common sense." [61]

In the U.S., debate rages over proposals for a compulsory national ID plan. An article in *The Houston Post* describes the issue:

WASHINGTON — Any compulsory, universal identification system implemented to help employers determine if a person is in the United States legally and is eligible for a job would provide a means for a "serious invasion of privacy," the chairman of the U.S. Commission on Civil Rights told a Senate panel Friday.

Arthur S. Flemming told members of the Senate Subcommittee on Immigration and Refugee Policy that compulsory national identity cards, work permits or other standard identifiers would provide the government with an opportunity to undermine individual rights by confiscating, or by threatening to confiscate, the card arbitrarily....

"The existence of a national identity card would multiply by many times the opportunities for bringing together in one file information which would constitute a serious invasion of privacy," Flemming told the subcommittee.[62]

THE DEBATE OVER CONTROL

Disturbing developments have occurred in other areas as well—developments that would seem to undermine individual freedoms and move toward state control.

The four-year McDonald Commission in Canada—a $12-million inquiry into the intelligence gathering activities of the Royal Canadian Mounted Police (RCMP)—concluded:

When a national police force is combined with a security intelligence agency which operates secretly and has been given more potential to damage the liberal democratic fabric of the country, it appears to us that far too powerful an organization has been created.[63]

The commission found that the RCMP had committed a number of illegal acts over the past 40 years and recommended the establishment of a *civilian security agency*.

On the other side of the coin—RCMP supporters dispute the findings of the commission and contend that a civilian agency could more easily come under government control. In either case it would appear official surveillance is growing.

FREEDOM (?) OF THE PRESS

In another area, the Kent Royal Commission on Newspapers—a ten-month inquiry into the Canadian newspaper industry—made its report on July 18, 1981. It created quite a stir, for therein lies the potential for the control of the press.

Professor Lord Oliver Ross McGregor of Durris, England, who was chairman of a similar British royal commission from 1974 to 1977, commented on the Canadian commission in an article written for the Canadian Press. Headlined "Kent proposals would create press 'censors': Independence of the press would be undermined," the article by Lord McGregor expressed reservations about the recommended creation of a....press rights panel which, in association with the Human

Rights Commission, would be an independent agency reporting to Parliament through the minister of justice. The panel of three members, presumably to be appointed by the government, would have the right and duty to supervise the press in a variety of ways....

The British Commission would probably fear that the press rights panel devised by their Canadian colleagues might become the first step toward the establishment of a "ministry of truth".[64]

Serious proposals to control freedom of the press are not limited to Canada. The United Nations Educational Scientific and Cultural Organization (UNESCO) has recently put forward plans for a "New World Information Order." According to Allen Weinstein in *SmithLine Forum*:

> The "New Order" in information would, as a main aim, grant governments and UN agencies insidious new authority: to "regulate" both the gathering and the international transmission of news....
>
> Recognizing that the New World Information Order imperils freedom, 63 leaders of independent news organizations from 21 countries met last May (1981) in Talloires, France.

The Taliores delegates accurately described the goal of their adversaries as, essentially, a New World Propaganda Order.[65]

It does, indeed, begin to appear as though the kind of all-pervasive government intrusion into privacy envisioned in George Orwell's *1984* is becoming a very real possibility.

WHAT DOES IT ALL MEAN?

Do these factors, so briefly reviewed above and apparently pointing to the prospect of a one-world state, with a high degree of control over earth's citizens, have a deeper significance than appears on the surface?

Granted, that apparent significance could be sinister enough in itself.

But, *is* there a deeper meaning?

I believe there most certainly is. A prophetic significance. One clearly detailed in the Scriptures. Spelled out by biblical prophets who have an amazing record of accuracy by which to establish themselves as bona fide foretellers of the future.*

---

*To check out just how accurate, see Appendix A, pages 331-337, for the facts on this vital aspect. After all, if we're going to take the scriptural prophetic writers seriously, we had better consider whether they are worthy of our trust.

We'll look at their predictions in the next chapter.

For Further Reading:

Church, J.R. *New Money, God's 2nd Most Important End-Time Prophecy*, (Oklahoma City: Southwest Radio Church, 1981).

Hendrickson, Robert. *The Cashless Society*, (New York: Dodd, Mead & Company, 1972).

Parker, Donn. *Crime by Computer*, (New York: Charles Scribners Sons, 1976).

Relfe, Mary Stewart. *The New Money System*, (Montgomery, Al.: Ministries, Inc., 1982).

CHAPTER FIVE

Tomorrow's News— From Dusty Writings!

Those ancient Hebrew prophets were "something else"!

Drawn from various walks of life, ranging from a herdsman to a prime minister, they boldly proclaimed that they were speaking for God.*

Their utterances touched on many aspects: their own nation and times, empires through the ages, and the coming, life, death, burial, resurrection and ascension of Jesus Christ, to note but a few.

And what they had to say also relates to events which are appearing in our news media today—as well as *tomorrow's* headlines!

---

*See Appendix A for proofs of their authenticity.

For the prophets predicted that at the end of time a one-world government—headed by earth's final dictator, who is described in Scripture as the Antichrist—would indeed come into existence.

This amazing individual will be energized and controlled by Satan. He will have an incredible rise to power and will quickly assume control over the peoples of earth. The prophetic writings indicate that only those who acknowledge their allegiance to this dictator by taking his mark (either on their foreheads or their right hands) will be permitted to buy or sell. This means he will exercise life or death power over earth's inhabitants.

Only a short while ago such a prospect was considered, by the skeptics, to be a virtual impossibility. Now, however, in the light of developments such as we touched upon in chapter four, that which seemed to be absolutely impossible is now very much an eventuality.

Let's look at the specific predictions to be found in the Word of God.

DANIEL'S DESCRIPTION

The Antichrist first appears in the prophecy of Daniel. Before we look at the specific prophecy about him we need to have some background. In this portion we find that Daniel is enabled by God to interpret a dream which Nebuchudnezzar had, as recorded in Daniel chapter two. The dream is about a great image—head of gold, chest and arms of silver, abdomen and thighs of brass, legs of iron, and feet and toes of iron and clay mixed. A stone then strikes the image on its feet, causing it to collapse, after which the stone begins to grow and fills the earth. The interpretation is given to Daniel by God and is clearly recorded in Daniel 2:36-45.

THE INTERPRETATION

The image represents empires. The golden head is Babylon, the silver chest, Medo Persia; the bronze abdomen, Greece; the iron legs, Rome; and the feet and toes of iron and clay mixed, a ten-nation federation, understood to be the revived Roman Empire.* The stone represents the kingdom of God which is established eternally *in the days of the ten-nation federation.*

---

*Dr. John Wesley White, in **The Coming World Dictator**, quotes **The European Community Magazine**, October 1975, official publication of the European Common Market, as saying, "The EC Rome treaty supports the interpretation of the Books of Ezekiel, Daniel and the Revelation that this 'last days' kingdom is a new Roman Empire" (p. 26). [66]

Further insight is provided in a prophetic vision recorded in Daniel chapter seven, where the same empires are symbolized by four strange beasts. The fourth beast, which like the feet and toes of iron and clay in the first vision represents a revived Roman empire, had in addition to iron teeth ten horns:

> After this I saw in the night visions, and behold a fourth beast, dreadful and terrible, and strong exceedingly; and it had great iron teeth: it devoured and brake in pieces, and stamped the residue with the feet of it: and it was diverse from all the beasts that were before it; and it had ten horns.
>
> —Daniel 7:7

From these ten horns grew an additional "little horn" which uprooted three of the other horns and "made war with the saints." From this we understand that earth's coming final ruler arises out of the revived Roman Empire, probably from one of the lesser nations (a "little horn"). He subdues three of the other ten nations and becomes supreme over the ten. Daniel described this horn in detail:

I considered the horns, and behold, there came up among them another little horn, before whom there were three of the first horns plucked up by the roots: and, behold, in this horn were eyes like the eyes of man, and a mouth speaking great things....

And of the ten horns that were in his head, and of the other which came up, and before whom three fell; even of that horn that had eyes, and a mouth that spake very great things, whose look was more stout than his fellows.

I beheld, and the same horn made war with the saints, and prevailed against them;

Until the Ancient of days came, and judgment was given to the saints of the most High; and the time came that the saints possessed the kingdom.

Thus he said, The fourth beast shall be the fourth kingdom upon earth, which shall be diverse from all kingdoms, and shall devour the whole earth, and shall tread it down, and break it in pieces.

And the ten horns out of this kingdom are ten kings that shall arise after them; and he shall be diverse from the first, and he shall subdue three kings.

And he shall speak great words

against the most High, and shall wear out the saints of the most High, and think to change times and laws: and they shall be given into his hand until a time and times and the dividing of time.

—Daniel 17:8,20-25

Daniel tells us further that this "little horn," Antichrist, will make an agreement with Israel for one "week" of years (seven years) including the reestablishment of the ancient sacrifices—but in the middle of that agreement he will break it:*

And he [the Prince that shall come] shall confirm the covenant with many for one week: and in the midst of the week he shall cause the sacrifice and the oblation to cease, and for the overspreading of abominations he shall make it desolate, even until the consummation, and that determined shall be poured upon the desolate.

—Daniel 9:27

After breaking his agreement with Israel, and the cessation of sacrifices, this diabolical

---

*In Matthew 24:15 and 21, Jesus made reference to this and several other prophecies made by Daniel (Daniel 4:27, 12:11) concerning the future evil ruler. Here Christ spoke of "an abomination that causes desolation" who will cause sorrow unequalled in the history of the people of Israel.

king will exalt himself above every God, claiming that he, himself, *is God and must be worshipped as God.*

And the king shall do according to his will; and he shall exalt himself, and magnify himself above every god, and shall speak marvellous things against the God of gods, and shall prosper till the indignation be accomplished: for that that is determined shall be done.

Neither shall he regard the God of his fathers, nor the desire of women, nor regard any god: for he shall magnify himself above all.

—Daniel 11:36-37

Further, he will be a man who honors force, who will become a blasphemer against God, a persecutor of the saints of God, and one who will adjust laws and times to his advantage.

But in his estate shall he honour the God of forces: and a god whom his fathers knew not shall he honour with gold, and silver, and with precious stones, and pleasant things.

Thus shall he do in the most strong holds with a strange god, whom he shall acknowledge and increase with glory: and he shall cause them to rule over

many, and shall divide the land for gain.
—Daniel 11:38-39

PROPHECY FROM PAUL

A good deal more prophetic information about the Antichrist comes through the Apostle Paul in his second letter to the Thessalonian believers. In Paul's first letter to the believers at Thessalonica, he had written about the Lord's return to earth to take both dead and living saints to Himself (I Thessalonians 4:13-18). However, this wonderful message of hope had confused the Christians there, for in the light of the difficult times they were undergoing, many of them concluded that they had missed that return and were already in the "day of the Lord"—the period of great tribulation.

Paul very quickly and forcefully set that straight by writing, "Let no man deceive you by any means: for that day shall not come except there come a falling away first, and that man of sin be revealed, the son of perdition" (2:3).

Then he went on to describe that "man of sin." This coming ruler will oppose God, seek to exalt himself above God and even declare that he is God. To do so, the man of sin will take his place in the temple and outlaw any worship not directed to him. He will be empowered by Satan to perform all kinds of counterfeit miracles, signs and wonders, deceiving those who are perishing.

The entire personality and mission of the Antichrist will be characterized by rebellion against God. The Greek word translated "falling away" in 2:3 is *apostasia*, which can also mean "rebellion" or "revolt."

Now it is true that since the fall of mankind back in the Garden of Eden, humanity, apart from Jesus Christ, has been in a state of rebellion against God. This spirit of lawlessness, says Paul, is already at work (2:7). In and under the Antichrist, however, that rebellion will blossom into a deliberate, defiant, generalized all-encompassing rejection of God and Christ. In the meantime, it is being restrained, or held back, by what Paul calls the "restrainer" in 2:7.*

The restrainer is the Holy Spirit in the midst of His people, the Church. In that sense, He will be removed when Jesus snatches the Church away. This does not mean that the Holy Spirit will be absent from the earth. No—He will be present as He was

---

*In the language of the King James Version, the restrainer is described as "he who now letteth." "Let" is to be understood as meaning to **hinder**, or **prevent** in this archaic usage.

during the Old Testament period before the birth of the Church. But in His restraining-of-evil work in and through the Church (that body of believers all around the world in whom He dwells) He will be removed at the rapture.

And then the rebellion will spread rapidly, until it is full-blown under the Antichrist, who will be its embodiment.

JOHN WRITES

Finally, John, in one of his letters and in the Revelation, adds several more details on this coming evil one. In I John 2:18-27, John refers to the Antichrist. The Greek prefix translated "anti" in this portion has two meanings. One of these is *against* and the other *instead of*. So we see that the Antichrist is not just against Christ but plans to be instead of Him.

The book of the Revelation describes the apocalypse. The judgments of God upon the earth will be detailed in a scroll with seven seals, each seal containing judgments. When the seventh seal is opened, seven trumpets are blown—each marking a further judgment upon the earth.

In turn, the seventh trumpet will introduce the seven vials or bowls, judgments—the worst part of the tribulation.

In that context, John prophetically describes the Antichrist as well as his *counterfeit* Holy Spirit—the evil false prophet (Revelation 13). The nefarious activity, final struggle and doom of these evil personages is foretold in Revelation 19:11-21.

The Antichrist will be awesome. He will be empowered by Satan. He will blaspheme God. He will apparently rise from the dead, or at least from what would be considered a fatal wound. He will take control of the world through unprecedented political authority and will be worshipped by all except the saints of God. He will appear to be invincible.

While the Antichrist will obviously handle political matters, the false prophet will be in charge of religious affairs. It will evidently be a very religious time, in which the false prophet will perform miracles to win people to the worship of the dictator. One miracle will involve causing the statue of the Antichrist to apparently come to life (Revelation 13:14-15).

Failing persuasion, there will always be economic coercion—with no one permitted to buy or sell unless he or she receives that mark of the Antichrist on either forehead or hand. John declares that the mark is a number—666 (Revelation 13:16-18). Few portions of Scripture have triggered more speculation, since in Hebrew and Greek each letter has a numerical value. Intriguingly enough, the total of those values in the Antichrist's name comes to 666. All kinds of formulas have been unsuccessfully used through the years to "prove" that this person or that is the Antichrist!

John goes on to describe how God's wrath will be poured out on all who do receive the beast's mark. In response, the arrogant, satanic Antichrist will rise against God and seek to destroy God's people, especially 144,000 Jews who (according to Revelation 7:1-8) have been sealed by God—12,000 from each of 12 tribes to bear witness to the true God. Their divine seal will preserve them for this work from both the awesome animosity of the Antichrist and the judgments of God's wrath.

This time period will culminate with the gathering to Jerusalem of armies from all the nations to fight God and the people of God—Israel. This will be the battle of Armageddon (Rev. 14:14-20; 16:13-16).

The sequel to this fearful conflict will be the revelation of the Lord Jesus Christ and His armies from heaven. The Antichrist and his false prophet will be taken and cast into the lake of fire, and all of the rest of godless humanity slain (Rev. 19:11-21).

HOW SOON?

I believe that earth's stage is rapidly being set for the enactment of these awesome events.

And though we know from Scripture that we are not to set any dates, yet we also know that the appearance of the final world dictator must be near.

It is my considered opinion that the developments currently occurring in the world are indeed preparations for the fulfilment of the foregoing biblical prophecies.

Unquestionably what must then follow will be the emergence, on stage, of one of the major personalities of the end time!

Read about why the setting of the stage will demand the appearance of this diabolical dictator—a fearsome wolf in sheep's clothing.

That fact can provide either a wonderful or a fearful prospect, depending on our relationship to Christ—as we'll explain in part five.

For Further Reading:

Anderson, Sir Robert. *The Coming Prince,* (Grand Rapids: Kregel Publications, 1957 Reprint).

Bloomfield, A.E. *How to Recognize the Antichrist.* (Minneapolis: Bethany Fellowship, Inc. 1975).

Goetz, W.R. *Apocalypse Next,* (Beaver lodge: Horizon House, 1981), Chaps. 2, 6, 8.

Marquand, David. *Parliament for Europe,* (London: Jonathan Cape, 1979).

McCall, T. & Levitt, Z. *Satan in the Sanctuary,* (Irvine, Calif.: Harvest House Publishers, 1973).

McDowell, Josh. *Daniel in the Critics' Den,* (San Bernardino, Calif.: Campus Crusade for Christ, 1979).

Price, Walter K. *The Coming Antichrist,* (Chicago: Moody Press, 1974).

Steele, R. *The Mark is Ready, Are You?* (College Place, Wash.: Project Research, 1978).

Stoner, P.W. and Newman, R.C. *Science Speaks* (Chicago: Moody Press, 1976).

And he causes all, both small and great, rich and poor, free and bond, to receive a mark in their right hand, or in their forehead.

Here is wisdom. Let him that has understanding count the number of the beast: for it is the number of a man; and his number is six, six, six.

—Prophet John on Patmos

CHAPTER SIX

Enter Mr. 666!

As a child I had, as most youngsters do, a vivid imagination.

Because I was the youngest by far of three siblings, and therefore like an only child, I had a good deal of opportunity to develop that imagination.

And since prophecy was a topic openly discussed in my home when a particular uncle came to visit, I had a lot of fuel for my imagination.

Uncle Fred was a prophecy buff. One of the areas of his keen interest was the predicted totalitarian control of the Antichrist—Mr. 666. Uncle would wax eloquent in describing what he believed would be the horrors of that reign—I'm sure little realizing the impact such discussions were having on me as I sat and listened intently.

As I look back now I can understand where he was "coming from," for he had known personally what government oppression was, having come to Canada from Russia as a youth.

One of Uncle Fred's contentions was that the Canadian Social Security system, with its individual numbers—then being introduced—was the equivalent of the mark of the Antichrist.

I can recall how at night I used to snuggle down under the bed covers—imagining that I was in a cave hiding from soldiers who were after me because I did not have the mark. For I certainly did *not* intend ever to take the mark. On that point I was firmly settled, though I understood the entire matter only very dimly.

Both my uncle, and my father, have since passed away. Today we are witnessing developments in the area of control, such as the ones discussed in chapters two and three, which would have literally boggled my uncle's mind.

We've seen the "one-world" drive accelerate, even as we've seen global conditions—especially the financial—worsen to the point of virtual crisis.

Technologically, it would appear that total control is now very feasible.

But *could* it really happen?

What about the strong independent spirit—particularly in the U.S. and to a lesser degree in Canada? What about the urge for privacy and individualism? Total control seems almost inconceivable even if it is possible.

I would like to suggest that the will to resist is gone and that under the pressure of financial, political and social breakdown there will be a *ready* acceptance of Mr. 666—who will appear to really have the solutions.

Lester DeKostar, writing in *The Banner*, asks some disturbing questions in his article, "Whither Bound, America?" He outlines the sort of social tensions North America is experiencing—intolerable crime levels, a judicial system that encourages criminal irresponsibility and robs police of their authority, a legislative system manipulated by an elite, the decay of traditional moral standards, a public school system that is inadequate, and the "hawking of cheap grace and heavenly real estate at discount prices in lieu of a vital Christianity."

DeKostar then points out that each of these social tensions has been caused by a minority—whether by criminals, energy moguls, the intelligentsia, or pornographers. He then asks:

What, then, happens when the majority has had enough?

Then the coming storm breaks loose: the so-called silent majority seizes and quickly surrenders its mass power into the hands of a leader. The people give the might they cannot execute into the control of those who can. The minorities who have abused the popular goodwill are summarily destroyed or fall meekly into line. Fascism has come! And its portents today darken the horizons.

So it happened in Italy. So it was in Germany—both of them cultures quite comparable to our own....

There will come a time, here too, when "the masses" whose backs bear "the burden of the world" will cry *enough*! And they will turn eagerly to someone who guarantees a new morality in exchange for but one "little" thing: freedom. [67]

In support of his chilling forecast, DeKostar cites the case of Nazi Germany. In his time, Hitler promised an end to the kind of social ills we are experiencing in our society today. And he carried through on his promises.

As a result "Nazism was hailed as redemptive of a decadent society; and it came almost as a puritanism to a majority sick of perversions and license parading as liberty." Because Hitler was able to provide "work, order and dignity" in Germany, the citizens were prepared to pay whatever price was demanded.

And the people* will buy!

---

*Lester DeKostar says, "In short, Fascism came as an 'angel of light," and the 'German Christians' both Protestant and Catholic welcomed Hitler as a gift of God graciously sent to resolve the tensions which had rumbled on the horizon since World War I. Nazism was hailed as redemptive of a decadent society; and it came almost as a puritanism to a majority sick of perversions and license parading as liberty.

If you doubt this, pick up Milton Mayer's **They Thought They Were Free**, interviews with ten Germans of different strata, done in the 1950s. All longed for the 'good days' when Hitler provided work, order, and dignity—at the expense of a political liberty they really did not miss." [68]

Order and "business as usual" at all costs!

That particular philosophy has been voiced on numerous occasions *since* Hitler and Stalin.

Dr. John C. Bennett, a former President of Union Theological Seminary in New York said in his book, *Foreign Policy in Christian Perspective*:

> Communism needs to be seen as the instrument of modernization, of national unity, of greater social welfare. The brainwashing, the cruel dealing with the opposition, and the political totalitarianism are the cost. At this stage, it is not for us to say whether we would or would not choose the effects at this cost. [69]

A Roman Catholic leader, Msgr. Charles Owen Rice was quoted in the *Pittsburg Catholic*, October 6, 1966, as saying:

> It may sound strange coming from a Catholic priest, but I am convinced we should pray for the survival of the present government of China....The present government, even though Communist, has brought order to its vast nation, order and admirable measures of internal justice and peace. [70]

Former National Security Adviser in the

Carter administration, Zbigniew Brzezinski wrote in his book, *Between Two Ages*:

> Yet though Stalinism may have been a needless tragedy for both the Russian people and communism as an ideal, there is the...possibility that for the world, at large, it was...a blessing in disguise.[71]

The former Canadian Prime Minister Pierre Elliot Trudeau created a storm of protest in Canada over remarks made in a CTV year-end interview, following the imposition of martial law in Poland on December 13, 1981. Trudeau said in the interview that martial law was better than civil war. He later defended his statement and added he hoped that the declaration of martial law would "create stability." [72]

Rule—even oppressive rule—is all right, according to this way of thinking, provided it results in order and stability!

The potential which such a climate creates for the appearance of a dictator is noted by numerous observers.

In late 1980, Dr. Morton Shulman, a leading Canadian economist, warned in a Vancouver, B.C., *Province* article that "Canada is ripe for a Hitler-like economic savior."

Ronald Reaburn, a Vancouver, B. C., community college teacher and free-lance journalist, made some significant observations in an article in *The Vancouver Sun*

Hyperinflation, I fear, can only pave the way to the abandonment of democracy and its replacement by dictatorship. Hitler and Napoleon both rode to power on the back of inflation. [73]

And, according to the prophecies of Daniel, Jesus, Paul and John, as indicated in chapter five, such a man *will* come on the scene.

He will, after his initial "settling-in" period (which will include a treaty with Israel, and the re-establishment of the ancient Jewish sacrifices in a restored temple) reveal his true diabolical and dictatorial nature. He will declare that *he* is god—and will demand that *he* be worshipped in the restored temple.

HIS INFERNAL MAJESTY'S PORTRAIT

The composite picture of the Antichrist, obtained from the prophets, is not an attractive one, though it is most intriguing.

He is obviously a regal character. He is called *"the King of fierce countenance"* in Daniel 8:23; *"the prince that shall come"* in Daniel 9:26; and *"the King who shall do according to his will"* in Daniel 11:36. His self-will is amplified in Daniel 11 where he is characterized as rejecting all the traditional views of diety; he will *blaspheme the God of gods*, verse 36; and will *not regard the desire of women*, verse 37 (which is a reference to the desire of every devout Hebrew woman to be the mother of the Messiah).

Not only will he totally and blasphemously reject the traditional view of God but he will worship the "god of force," verse 38. His confidence will be in military might.

Walter K. Price, in *The Coming AntiChrist*, presents an excellent, well-documented study of earth's final tyrant. In it he clearly demonstrates how the historical tyrant Antiochus IV Epiphanes is a type of the coming Antichrist, and draws a number of parallels between the two.*

From Scripture and the record of Antiochus, Price lists these characteristics of the Antichrist in addition to those we have already noted.

He will be a persecutor of the Jews. (Dan. 9:25; Matt. 24:21, 22 and Dan. 12:1.) He will declare that he is god and *demand worship* (Matt. 24:15). This will mean that he will bring an end to the reinstituted Jewish sacrifices (Dan. 9:27b), place *his* image in the restored temple (Dan. 9:27, 12:11, Matt.

---

*See Appendix F, part one.

113

24:15 and 2 Thess. 2:2-4) and magnify himself as God. (Dan. 8:25, 11:36, 2 Thess. 2:4). He will demand the death penalty for failure to worship and will regulate this by a mark on people (Rev. 13:15-18). More about the future aspects of this worship shortly.

He is called *the man of sin* (2 Thess. 2:2-4); *the song of perdition* (2 Thess. 2:3); *the Antichrist* (1 John 2:18, 22, 4:3 and 2 John 7)*; *the Beast* (Rev. 13:1) and *the lawless one* (2 Thess. 2:7-10).

The details of the predicted coming of a final dictator have certainly caused an enormous amount of speculation—much of it wild and fanciful. However, there are a good many hints in Scripture that give rise to conjecture which may indeed be accurate.

He will obviously be a powerful leader with a good deal of charisma. He will arise out of the ten-nation confederacy, subduing three of the ten in the process and becoming supreme.* Daniel's prophecy explains this in Daniel chapter seven—which is a parallel to Daniel chapter two. In both portions we have a preview of human empires. In chapter two they are seen from *man's* viewpoint as a glorious, overpowering statue, grand and impressive. In chapter seven, they are seen

---

*See Appendix F, parts two to five.

from the divine viewpoint in their bestial nature—a perspective which has been clearly borne out in history.

In Daniel's unusual dream of chapter seven, the first world empire is symbolized by a lion with the wings of an eagle (7:4). The second beast is like a bear that devours "much flesh" (7:5). The third beast, representing a third world empire in Daniel's dream, is like a leopard with four wings and with four heads (7:6).

The fourth beast is "dreadful and terrible," characterized by great strength and great iron teeth. It is different from the preceding beasts, one of its distinguishing features being its ten horns (7:7).

Daniel's attention is particularly focused on the ten horns:

> I considered the horns, and, behold, there came up among them another little horn, before whom there were three of the first horns plucked up by the roots: and, behold, in this horn were eyes like the eyes of man, and a mouth speaking great things....I beheld then because of the voice of the great words which the horn spake: I beheld even till the beast was slain, and his body destroyed and given to the burning flame.
>
> —Daniel 7:8, 11

Understandably, Daniel was baffled by this strange vision of the four beasts and the ten horns, and he wondered what it meant. An interpretation of the dream is given later in the chapter:

These great beasts, which are four, are four kings, which shall arise out of the earth....

Then I [Daniel] would know the truth of the fourth beast, which was diverse from all the others, exceeding dreadful, whose teeth were of iron, and his nails of brass; which devoured, brake in pieces, and stamped the residue with his feet;

And of the ten horns that were in his head, and of the other which came up, and before whom three fell; even of that horn that had eyes, and a mouth that spake very great things, whose look was more stout than his fellows.

I beheld, and the same horn made war with the saints, and prevailed against them;

Until the Ancient of days came, and judgment was given to the saints of the most High; and the time came that the saints possessed the kingdom.

Thus he said, The fourth beast shall be the fourth kingdom upon earth, which shall be diverse from all kingdoms, and shall devour the whole earth, and shall tread it down, and break it in pieces.

And the ten horns out of this kingdom are ten kings that shall arise: and another shall rise after them; and he shall be diverse from the first, and he shall subdue three kings.

And he shall speak great words against the most High, and shall wear out the saints of the most High, and think to change times and laws: and they shall be given into his hand until a time and times and the dividing of time.

But the judgment shall sit, and they shall take away his dominion, to consume and to destroy it unto the end.

And the kingdom and dominion, and the greatness of the kingdom under the whole heaven, shall be given to the people of the saints of the most High, whose kingdom is an everlasting kingdom, and all dominions shall serve and obey him.

—Daniel 7:17, 19-27

The focus in the interpretation of Daniel's dream given above is on the little horn, the Antichrist, who arises from a ten-nation confederacy (the ten horns), subdues three of those nations (the three horns), begins a reign marked by blasphemy and by persecution of the saints, and eventually comes under the judgment of God.

Other Bible prophecies lead us to believe that the Antichrist may be killed (or apparently killed) *and rise again*. Three times in Revelation 13 (vs. 3, 12 and 14) it is said that the Beast suffers a "death wound that is healed."

Whether this is an actual resurrection or an apparent one cannot be positively stated from the scripture available. My personal view is that it is only apparent—since Satan does not have the power of life. But whether real or only apparent, it is obviously an effort to counterfeit the resurrection of Jesus Christ.

THE COUNTERFEIT TRINITY

The counterfeit concept runs through all of this. The Antichrist is indeed part of a counterfeit trinity—with Satan the counterfeit God, Antichrist the counterfeit of the Lord Jesus Christ, and the False Prophet the counterfeit of the Holy Spirit.

In Revelation 13, we see this evil trinity at work, for verse two says that "the dragon [Satan] gave him [Antichrist] his power, and his seat [position], and great authority. Verse four makes it clear that worship of the

Antichrist is really worship of Satan: "And they worshipped the dragon that gave power into the beast: and they worshipped the beast...."

Later in Revelation 13, the activities of the third person of the counterfeit trinity are described. Just as the Holy Spirit represents and magnifies Christ (John 16:13), so the False Prophet will promote the Antichrist:

> And he [the False Prophet] doeth great wonders, so that he maketh fire come down from heaven on the earth in the sight of men,
>
> And deceiveth them that dwell on the earth by the means of those miracles which he had power to do in the sight of the beast; saying to them that dwell on the earth, that they should make an image to the beast, which had the wound by a sword, and did live.
>
> And he had power to give life unto the image of the beast, that the image of the beast should both speak, and cause that as many as would worship the image of the beast should be killed.
>
> —Revelation 13:11-16

Many have speculated that at the time of the death wound, the Antichrist (who most certainly will be a man) will become totally possessed by Satan. He will become Satan incarnate. If so—and there is no good reason for refusing to believe this—it explains why worship of him will be, in fact, worship of Satan.

The tangible indication of that worship according to Revelation 13:16-18 will be the receiving of a mark in either the right hand or the forehead—number 666!

> And he causeth all, both small and great, rich and poor, free and bond, to receive a mark in their right hand, or in their foreheads:
>
> And that no man might buy or sell, save he that had the mark, or the name of the beast, or the number of his name.
>
> Here is wisdom. Let him that hath understanding count the number of the beast: for it is the number of a man; and his number is Six hundred threescore and six.
> —Revelation 13:16-18

Not so very long ago the skeptics had a field day with this one. They delighted in asking how it was going to be possible for anyone to exercise the kind of control which such prophecy envisioned.

They're not scoffing nearly so loudly now. The technology to make possible exactly this sort of surveillance is now available.

We've considered some of that technology already: a cashless society—entailing Electronic Fund Transfer, the UPC, the computer, the laser scanner, fiber optics and videotex interactive television.

And the impetus for using that technology in creating for everyone a national identity number—one that is inseparably related to each individual so that it cannot be stolen—has been given added strength because of growing crime relating both to ID cards and credit cards.

Under the heading "Phony ID's: They're Flooding the Country," the *U.S. News & World Report* declares:

> Authorities say it is anyone's guess how many people, for one reason or another, are using ID's in other than their own names in the U.S. today. There are indications that the number runs will into the millions. In 1971, the Social Security Administration concluded that 4 to 5 million Americans held more than one Social Security number—many of them through error.
>
> A study in the Mid-'70s estimated that the use of phony ID's for check and credit-card fraud and embezzlement cost businesses well over a billion dollars a

year. Fraud against government programs such as welfare, food stamps and medical assistance is believed to cost additional billions, although no one knows the true total. [74]

Add to this the concern over thousands of illegal aliens, living and working in the U.S., and the pressure for a national ID grows. A September 9, 1982, editorial in *The New York Times* comments:

In a well-meaning effort to curb the employment of illegal aliens, and with the hearty good wishes of editorialists who ordinarily pride themselves on guarding against the intrusion of government into the private lives of individual Americans, Congress is about to take this generation's longest step toward totalitarianism. The first step downward on the Simpson staircase to Big Brotherdom is the requirement that within three years the Federal Government come up with a 'secure system to determine employment eligibility in the United States.' Despite denials, that means a national identity card....

Combined with a national identity card...government computers and data banks pose a threat to personal liberty.

Though aimed against 'undocumented workers,' *the computer tattoo will be pressed on you and me.*[75]

Credit card scams are not unusual. Recently *The Province*, Vancouver, reported the news that "Credit Card Scam Hits B.C. Banks" and described "How Forgery Ring Rips Off the Banks." Writing that "a major credit card conspiracy operating between Vancouver and Hong Kong has been uncovered—but not solved," *The Province* crime reporter says that "major banks are extremely worried."

Such occurrences will unquestionably add to the desire to have *everyone* identified by his or her own national identity number—carried *on* or *in* the person.

THE MARK

In recent months the capability and feasibility of *marking people* for identification purposes has become a subject of discussion.

An extremely thorough and careful investigative researcher into this entire area is Ron Steele, author of *The Mark is Ready—are You?* Steele's book is one of the best documented I've ever seen—with photographs and reproductions of newspaper clippings or other data supporting each statement he makes.

Steele's thesis is that the U.S. government is already using sophisticated technology to mark animals—and that the technique is readily transferable to people. He quotes Dr. Keith R. Farrell, developer of Farrell's universal mark (a laser branded mark for livestock) as saying, "It is theoretically possible to include man as another one of these animals" in terms of being marked. Farrell, who is a veterinarian scientist at the Washington State University at Pullman, Washington, has marked himself twice to demonstrate that his laser beam tatooing is harmless. He claims that his technique has the capacity to individually identify every animal upon earth with an unalterable mark.

Steele also warns that technology is being developed by the banking industry to mark human beings for the purpose of electronic fund transfer.[76]

The John Lawrence column in the *Tacoma News Tribune*, Tacoma, Washington, December 14, 1980, adds to the information on the attempt. Describing Steele's research and viewpoint, Lawrence writes:

> [It was on] the TV show, *12 in the Morning* on Channel 12 in Portland, [that] Steele appeared with Lowell

Brisbin, vice president of the U.S. National Bank and president of the Oregon Automated Clearing House Association.

In that interview, the transcript shows that Brisbin has admitted the existence of a palm-scan machine.

"...It has been of great concern to the banking community to develop the best means of identification. There are tests going on—I was describing a little while ago where the hand was being used. If you place your hand on a plate, which measures everything, every mark on the palm of your hand, and that identifies you as being who you are...

"In other words," Brisbin added, "you have to put the symbol of your hand, or whatever it is—the picture of your hand—in the machine first. And then they compare that when you want access to a secure area, or you want to use it to get money or something..."

Steele asked Brisbin: "Are you saying that the [electronic transfer] card might actually be done away with and there would be some kind of identification on a person's body like the hand, and then—"

"Well, today," Brisbin said, "I don't know of any better system."

"In other words," Steele said, "the number you would memorize. You would punch the keyboard, but it [the number] would be with your hand."

"Then you'd put your hand on it, too," Brisbin added.

"Just one other question, real fast," Steele said. "Do you think it could be an alternative...a laser beam number on the hand where you wouldn't have to punch numbers, you could just put it [your hand] down there [on the machine]?"

"I'm sure that there are, Brisbin said. I'm not technically knowledgeable about some of these things..."

"But they are looking for something like this?" Steele persisted.

"Yes," Brisbin said, "there are various research groups looking at better methods." [77]

One of the technological developments which could be used in the sort of personal marking ID Brisbin mentioned is the Palmguard Security System. Produced by Palmguard Inc. of 12810 S.W. Canyon Road, Beaverton, Oregon, the equipment is described in a trade journal ad in this way:

126

PALMGUARD SECURITY SYSTEM

The Palmguard Identification System provides a high degree of access control for areas requiring very positive identification. The palm of the hand is used much like a fingerprint to positively identify the person attempting access. The system serves the need for positive identification of individuals beyond the questionable identity provided by card systems where the card is transferable under duress or through fraudulent intent.

Personnel requiring access must first have had their hand print filed in the system by the security officer for that area. Permission for each access is then determined by the machine, which can limit shift access or days of the week as needed. Each access is logged to provide a permanent record of all transactions or for immediate printout.

When a person approaches the console he finds a green light message, 'ENTER YOUR NUMBER.' He enters a preassigned access number (first level of security) which is not known to any other normal user or intruder. 'PLACE YOUR HAND' directs his hand to the lighted fixture until the message 'REMOVE HAND' appears. If the match is good, a 'THANK YOU' lights and the door is operated. If the first try fails, 'PLACE YOUR HAND' reappears for one more try. Failure on this try will end the attempt.

Should a non-user attempt to enter keyboard numbers, he will normally get a 'WRONG NUMBER' message. If by chance a valid keyboard number is entered, he will then be rejected for not having an image match. Repeated attempts to gain false access will summon a security guard.

The possibility for the misuse of this sort of surveillance is real. As far back as the mid-70s it was revealed

> ...that Federal planners foresee the day when every citizen has a "money card" instead of money—electronically connected to the Federal Reserve Bank. The accounts of tax offenders or political mavericks could be automatically closed—in which case a red light triggered at the point of purchase would prevent the shopkeeper from selling anything to the offender.[78]

and further,

> In an Associated Press release dated August 18, 1975, which appeared in newspapers all over the U.S., Democratic Senator Frank Church, chairman of a committee then investigating U.S. intelligence activities, was quoted as saying that "the government has the technological capacity to impose 'total tyranny' if ever a dictator came to power. There would be no place to hide."[79]

The legislation giving the U.S. Government power to impose economic controls is apparently already in place. On January 10, 1961, in the closing days of the Eisenhower administration, the U.S. Treasury issued a new banking rule called "Emergency Banking Regulation No. 1." Its stated intent is that it will be used if the U.S. is attacked, in order to preserve some sort of banking system in the event of nuclear war.[80]

Given the record of government agencies declassifying information, the potential use of such power for widespread personal control must not be overlooked.

Yes.

The technological capability to exercise control is definitely here. Now!

In the light of all this, it seems significant to me that the computer should have been selected by *Time* magazine as its 1982 "Man of the Year." The machine was singled out as that year's greatest influence for good or evil.

And while the economic, technological and political preparations for potential total control continue, psychological preparations also appear to be underway.

The numerous calls for a "saviour" often issued by responsible leaders, were given a new twist by an interesting publication out of Europe.

A "KING" FOR THE WORLD OUT OF THE UNITED STATES OF EUROPE?

A most intriguing book, containing a

number of startling, controversial and preposterous conclusions was published in England in January 1982.

The Holy Blood and the Holy Grail is the product of ten years of research by the authors, Michael Baigent, Richard Leigh and Henry Lincoln.

In a nutshell, the hypothesis of the book is that:

> Jesus did not die on the Cross.
> He was married and had children.
> His wife and children fled the Holy Land to find refuge in the south of France, and that in a Jewish community there, they preserved their lineage.
> His descendants married into the royal line of the Franks, thus engendering the Merovingian dynasty.
> There are descendants of Jesus living today.
> And, finally, a secret society exists today with the goal of restoring the Merovingian line, which represents those descendants, to power.[81]

The book got started as a result of three BBC films on the mystery of how an obscure 19th century French priest, named Berenger Sauniere, suddenly and inexplicably amassed a fortune, built a stone tower and generally behaved in a most unusual manner. The BBC scriptwriter, Henry Lincoln, became obsessed with the mystery—and *The Holy Blood and the Holy Grail* is the result.

Mark Abley, writing in *Maclean's* magazine, explains the authors' claim:

What Sauniere discovered seems to have been a group of parchments, one dating back to 1244, which were of crucial importance to a clandestine society called the Prieure de Sion (Priory of Sion). To keep the priest silent, the Prieure paid him off extravegantly. Begun in 1090, the society's activities have continued to this day. Baigent, Leigh and Lincoln have held several wary meetings with the order's present grand master, Pierre Plantard, a librarian, French Resistance hero and former associate of Charles de Gaulle. But Plantard may be something more. If the authors and the Prieure are to be believed, he is also a lineal descendant of Jesus Christ. And incredible though it sounds, the Prieure is working to establish one of Christ's descendants on the throne of a united Europe....

The political implications are enormous. The authors report that the present-day Prieure is working to a precise timetable and that Pierre Plantard expects France to have a king on the throne by 1990. Prieure members are said to wield quiet influence in France, Switzerland and the European Parliament. Its members, or close associates, include politicians, financiers, religious leaders and one of the foremost writers of our time, the Mexican novelist (and former ambassador to France) Carlos Fuentes. [82]

WHAT IS THE SIGNIFICANCE?

Now I want to make it *very clear* that I *totally reject* the hypotheses of the book. In spite of the authors' pious protestations, their conclusions are all diametrically opposed to the Scriptures.

A storm of controversy has arisen over the volume. For example, in a scathing review, Marina Warner of *The Sunday Times*, London, called it a "heap of hooey," declaring that the research is "fribbling," the evidence "misused," the hypotheses "ill-considered and poorly argued."

However, the point is not whether the book has any serious intrinsic merit or not. The point is—it claims that a purported descendant of Jesus Christ will become a universal "priest-king" on the throne of a united Europe!

That suggestion fits in extremely well with what the Bible has to say about the coming Antichrist.

I think it is most interesting that such an idea should gain widespread interest *now* at a point in time when the stage is definitely being set for appearance of the prophesied world dictator—Mr. 666, the man of sin!

For Further Reading:

Balizet, C. *The Seven Last Years*, (New York: Bantam Books, 1980).

Kirban, S. *The Rise of Antichrist* (Huntingdon Valley, Pa: Salem Kirban, Inc., 1978).

—————— *Satan's Mark Exposed: 666* (Huntingdon Valley, Pa.: Salem Kirban, Inc., 1981).

White, John Wesley. *The Coming World Dictator*, (Minneapolis: Bethany Fellowship, 1981).

(See also listing at end of Chapter Five.)

And in the days of these kings shall the God of heaven set up a Kingdom which shall never be destroyed.

—Prophet Daniel in Babylon, about 600 B.C.

CHAPTER SEVEN

He'll Be Earth's Last Dictator!

The early morning air was charged with tension that day in Nebuchadnezzar's court back about 600 B.C.

The king had had a dream the night before and now he wanted it to be interpreted for him. Accordingly, he had called in all his court magicians, conjurors, sorcerers and Chaldeans, so that they could tell him the meaning of his vision.

The only problem was that he had forgotten the dream—though it had made a tremendous impression upon him.

Nevertheless he was insisting that his prognosticators tell him not only its meaning—but the forgotten dream as well!

Their frightened protests that this was unfair and unheard of produced a royal rage—and the decree that, since they could not reveal *both* dream and interpretation, they should *all* be destroyed.

Before the mass execution could be carried out, however, Daniel—a captive Jew who had become prominent in Nebuchadnezzar's court as a wise man—made a promise to the captain of the guard that *he* would tell the king both the dream and its interpretation—if he were but given a little time.

A temporary reprieve was granted. Daniel and his three Hebrew friends gave themselves to prayer that God would reveal these secrets to him.

And God did reveal both to Daniel in a night vision.

He was hurried before Nebuchadnezzar and, after giving the credit for his knowledge to God, proceeded to tell the king what he had dreamed *and* what the dream meant.

The revelation, which we've already briefly considered in chapter five, is one of the most significant prophecies ever uttered, and explains why we say that the coming Antichrist will be earth's last dictator.

Before we look at the prophecy—a brief comment about Daniel.

The authenticity of Daniel's prophecy has been viciously attacked over the years by many critics. In spite of the fact that both Jews and Christians accept the book as part of the bona fide Old Testament Scriptures, the critics who do not accept the inspiration of Scripture claim that Daniel could not have written it. One of their main reasons is that the prophecies of the book, especially in chapter eleven, give such an accurate picture of the future that it has to be history—not prophecy. So they assert that Daniel was not written by Daniel and is dated about 165 B.C., instead of prior to 500 B.C.

There is ample evidence to defend both Daniel's authorship and the book's authenticity. Such defense is beyond the scope of this volume, and besides, it has been admirably presented by others far better qualified than this author. A recent and notable apologetic is Josh McDowell's book, *Daniel in the Critics' Den*. It is most scholarly and convincing.

You can safely count on it. Daniel's prophecy is bona fide. Jesus obviously believed Daniel to be genuine. He called him a prophet and quoted him several times (Matt. 24:15).

So study Daniel's writings in complete

confidence.

A PARADE OF EMPIRES

Nebuchadnezzar's dream, as recorded in Daniel, was of a great image—dazzling in its brightness and overpowering in its size and form. It had a head of gold, chest and arms of silver, abdomen and thighs of brass, legs of iron and feet of iron and clay mixed.

Then, in the dream, a stone was cut out without hands. It came and struck the image on its feet of iron and clay. The entire great statue collapsed and disintegrated into dust which was blown away by the wind.

The stone began, then, to expand—until it became a great mountain and filled all the earth.

We're not left to ponder what all of this means. The interpretation, as given by Daniel, has already been briefly considered in chapter five. However, since it is so significant, we should look carefully at exactly what Daniel said:

> This is the dream; and we will tell the interpretation thereof before the king.
> Thou, O king, art a king of kings; for the God of heaven hath given thee a kingdom, power, and strength, and glory.

And wheresoever the children of men dwell, the beasts of the field and the fowls of the heaven hath he given into thine hand, and hath made thee ruler over them all. Thou art this head of gold.

And after thee shall arise another kingdom inferior to thee, and another third kingdom of brass, which shall bear rule over all the earth.

And the fourth kingdom shall be strong as iron: forasmuch as iron breaketh in pieces and subdueth all things: and as iron that breaketh all these, shall it break in pieces and bruise.

And whereas thou sawest the feet and toes, part of potters' clay, and part of iron, the kingdom shall be divided; but there shall be in it of the strength of the iron, forasmuch as thou sawest the iron mixed with miry clay.

And as the toes of the feet were part of iron, and part of clay, so the kingdom shall be partly strong, and partly broken.

And whereas thou sawest iron mixed with miry clay, they shall mingle themselves with the seed of men: but they shall not cleave one to another, even as iron is not mixed with clay.

And in the days of these kings shall the God of heaven set up a kingdom, which shall never be destroyed: and the kingdom shall not be left to other people, but it shall break in pieces and consume all these kingdoms, and it shall stand forever.

Forasmuch as thou sawest that the stone was cut out of the mountain without hands, and that it brake in pieces the iron, the brass, the clay, the silver, and the gold; the great God hath made known to the king what shall come to pass hereafter: and the dream is certain, and the interpretation thereof sure.

—Daniel 2:36-45

As Daniel told Nebuchadnezzar, the Babylonian empire of which he was king, was the head of gold. The silver chest represents Medo-Persia; the bronze abdomen, Greece; the iron legs, Rome; and the feet and toes of iron and clay, a ten-nation confederacy. During the rule of this ten-nation entity, which arises out of the old Roman Empire, the God of heaven will establish *His* kingdom, which will have no end.

The coming of *that* kingdom will mark the culmination of all human rule—symbolized by the destruction, disintegration and sweeping away of everything that remains of the "grand" statue of human empires.

Thus, the coming Antichrist, who will reign over that final ten-nation empire—and through it over the world—will be the *last* dictator which this poor old earth will see.

The world has witnessed a dreary parade of tyrants and dictators—some of the Pharoahs, the Assyrians, Roman emperors, Hitler, Stalin, Mao tse Tung, Amin and a host of lesser-known but nonetheless diabolical rulers.

Nothing which any of them has done, however, will equal the incredible, devilish tyranny of Antichrist—but he will be the *last* dictator.

No more after him.

His defeat by God will usher in the reign of Christ, first in the millennium and then eternally in the new heaven and earth.

In both chapter two and seven of Daniel's prophecy (parallel passages on the same subject, which we also considered briefly in chapter six) we saw how this future timetable is clearly presented.

Let's look a bit more closely at Daniel 7:19-25:

> Then I would know the truth of the fourth beast, which was diverse from all the others, exceeding dreadful, whose teeth were of iron, and his nails of brass;

which devoured, brake in pieces, and stamped the residue with his feet;

And of the ten horns that were in his head, and of the other which came up, and before whom three fell; even of that horn that had eyes, and a mouth that spake very great things, whose look was more stout than his fellows.

I beheld, and the same horn made war with the saints, and prevailed against them;

Until the Ancient of days came, and judgment was given to the saints of the most High; and the time came that the saints possessed the kingdom.

Thus he said, The fourth beast shall be the fourth kingdom upon earth, which shall be diverse from all kingdoms, and shall devour the whole earth, and shall tread it down, and break it in pieces.

And the ten horns out of this kingdom are ten kings that shall arise: and another shall rise after them; and he shall be diverse from the first, and he shall subdue three kings.

And he shall speak great words against the most High, and shall wear out the saints of the most High, and think to change times and laws: and they shall be given into his hand until a time and times and the dividing of time.

—Daniel 7:19-25

The message is clear.

In the days of a ten-nation political entity (the ten horns) which arises out of the old Roman Empire (the fourth beast) a diabolical world ruler will arise (the one predominant horn). He will be the final one—for in his reign the climax of earth's ages will occur and Christ's kingdom will be established.

How close are we to that time?

I believe very close.

In the preceding chapters we have attempted to document the powerful and accelerating drive for a one-world government. We've considered the economic crises which (if history teaches us anything at all) could precipitate the rise to power of any global strong man who can provide solutions. And we've looked at the technological advances which make possible the kind of totalitarian control the prophets envisioned.

While we referred to a united Europe in chapter six, we have not yet looked in any detail at what could well be that final ten-nation bloc (or at the very least, its forerunner)—the European Economic Community.

We need to.

That the EEC may be Daniel's "ten-toed" or "ten-horned" kingdom is not at all far-fetched, as we will see.

The EEC began in 1957 with the Treaty of Rome. Back then it was a six-member economic partnership. But even then it was envisioned as much more than that. Dr. Walter Hallstein, the president of the EEC (or European Common Market, as it is also known) described the vision:

> Three phases of the European unification are to be noted. First, the customs union, second, the economic union, third, the political union....What we have created on the way to uniting Europe is a mighty economic-political union of which nothing may be sacrificed for any reason. Its value exists not only in what it is, but more in what it promises to become....At about 1980 we may fully expect the great fusion of all economic, military, and political communities together into the United States of Europe.[83]

Hallstein was inaccurate on the timing, but the direction and goal he described are right on target.

The six-nation partnership has become a ten-member entity which held its first elections to a European parliament in June

144

1979. Though the EEC member nations do not get along too well (just as iron and clay don't mix well) they *are*, nevertheless, a unity. A European Monetary System (EMS) was founded on March 13, 1979 and, in 1980, a common currency—the ecu—was put into circulation in the Common Market. It is backed by 20 percent of the EEC nations' gold reserves—3,150 tons of gold valued at $34 billion. On October 6, 1981, the EMS realigned exchange rates of four European currencies to improve the stability of the continent's money markets.

The importance of this power bloc is suggested in a January 10, 1982, article in *The Vancouver Sun*:

> Do not be misled by appearances. The recent presidential election for the European Parliament lacked the hoopla normally associated with elections, but that in no way reflects the importance of either the position or the institution....
>
> The new president [Pieter Dankert of the Netherlands] will have the honor of overseeing the 25th anniversary celebrations of the European Economic Community, for which preparations are already under way. Since its small beginnings in 1958 the community has,

among its many other achievements, grown from six to 10 members, become the world's largest trading bloc, and garnered the largest concentration of wealth and technical expertise in the world.

Only 6½ years ago the community held the first direct elections in the European Parliament, a body which, under [former president Simone] Veil, has strengthened, and will probably grow stronger in relation to the executive bodies of the community.[84]

A common passport for member nations is in the final stages of planning and approval, as reported in a late 1980 *Vancouver Sun* release:

Giuseppe Zamberletti, Italy's secretary of state for foreign affairs, announced in the European Parliament recently that some of the details have been settled and that member governments may be asked to approve the plans this year.

"Such a passport would be a practical and obvious symbol in bringing Europeans closer," Zamberletti said before the Parliament approved a resolution advocating quick adoption of the passport.[85]

The current member nations of the EEC are Britain, France, Germany, Holland, Denmark, Luxembourg, Ireland, Belgium, Italy, Greece, Spain and Portugal. Austria has made application to join. Exactly how these fit into the prophetic picture is not known.

Certainly the current EEC membership is not necessarily the final one envisioned by the prophets.

That a united Europe is well into the process of development cannot be denied. Hal Piper, of *The Baltimore Sun*, writing from Bonn, West Germany, says:

> Seated comfortably in his spacious office above the Rhine, an immaculate, grey-suited West German government official recently talked about the "United States of Europe."
>
> "At the end of the road, we envision a federal state like the United States," he said. "A United States of Europe. Of course, that would be a long way off."
>
> The idea, as outlined by West German Foreign Minister Hans-Dietrich Genscher and members of his tiny coalition party, is to draft a "European constitution" that would formalize existing political links between the 10

member countries of the European community.[86]

Piper goes on to explain that up to that time the Common Market had been primarily an economic group. But more recently, the ten member nations have begun an attempt to come to some agreement on foreign policy. As a result, the ten nations "worked out a common approach to the Middle East problem" and "a joint proposal on Afghanistan." Piper also points out that the 1980 combined gross national product of the Common Market countries was greater than that of the United States for the first time. He comments that "a common European political institution could secure for Europe a comparable political mass that might enhance its influence on U.S. foreign policy."[87]

So if indeed the ten-nation power bloc—which will be in place when God sets up His Kingdom—is now forming, certainly the climax of the ages cannot be too far distant.

How essential to make preparation for such an event—as we will suggest in part five.

For Further Reading:

Lindsey, H. *The Late, Great Planet Earth* (Grand Rapids: Zondervan Publishing House, 1970).

PART TWO

The Climax of the Ages

POLITICAL SIGNS

One of the clear indications that the world is moving into its predicted climax is to be seen in the current alignment and activities of the nations.

Jesus indicated in His discourse on future events, given on the Mount of Olives, that the nation of Israel and the other nations of earth are likened to the fig tree and "all the trees," respectively.

Jesus said further that, just as the person who sees leaves beginning to appear on the trees can know that summer is near, so the person who sees certain political signs appear can know that the climax of all human affairs is near at hand.

In part two, we'll look at what I believe are current political events which definitely qualify as "the bursting forth of the leaves."

"Summer" is unquestionably near!

And Jesus spoke unto them a parable: Behold the fig tree [Israel], and all the trees [the nations];

When they now shoot forth leaves, you see and know that summer is now near at hand.

So likewise, when you see these things come to pass, know that the kingdom of heaven is near at hand.

—Luke 21:29, 30
(author's paraphrase)

And in that day will I [the Lord] make Jerusalem a burdensome stone for all people.

—The Prophet Zechariah,
writing about 487 B.C.

CHAPTER EIGHT

Israel—A Problem to the Nations

It was an invitation which I certainly did not intend to pass up!

The opportunity, in late 1982, was to attend a large private dinner in Vancouver at which Colonel Yehuda Levy, the Israeli Defense Forces spokesman during the 1982 Lebanese war, was to be guest speaker, with a question and answer period promised.

The invitation arrived about the time that the intense wave of worldwide indignation against Israel over the "Refugee Camp Massacre" in Lebanon was just beginning to

151

subside. At that point, also, I was at work on this volume, and so I really wanted to hear the colonel.

The Israeli invasion of Lebanon was, of course, one of the major events of 1982. It was another in the continuing series of confrontations, developments and struggles which have kept Israel in the media spotlight of our global village for decades now.

One of the purposes of the colonel's address was to "set the record straight" concerning the alleged atrocities perpetrated by Israel in the war. His claim was that, by and large, the world media (and especially the North American segment) was biased and even dishonest. He claimed that many of the frequently televised photos of damaged buildings were actually pictures of damage effected *before* the war, during the previous eight-year Lebanese civil war. In that intense struggle, over 120,000 casualties occurred, a state of terror developed, and the Palestinian Liberation Organization (PLO) grew into a powerful "government-within-a-government," a "state-within-a-state," and an "army-within-an-army." They became entrenched within the state of Lebanon to the extent that, according to the colonel, the PLO were in scores of non-military buildings and areas, "hiding behind innocent civilians who did not want them in their country."

Certainly there can be no simplistic, black-and-white conclusion on the tragic 1982 Lebanese war. Nor is this in any sense an attempt to endorse all Israeli actions or to condone everything that happened.

Nevertheless, having said that, it does appear that a definite negative bias, in relationship to Israel, can be documented.

A "Dry Bones" cartoon in *The Jerusalem Post* summarizes it somewhat humorously. Shuldig, the hero, soliloquizes:

> "So we're [Israel's commission] investigating the extent, if any, of our connection with the [Palestinian] mass-acres.
>
> "But what about the Phalange unit that slaughtered the civilians?
>
> "How come nobody is demanding *their* arrest?
>
> "Nobody!!
>
> "Not the Americans; not the Palestinians; not the Egyptians; not the Lebanese...
>
> "And not *us*, either!?"

It's a valid question. Why is there no outcry against, or questions about, the people who actually did the slaughtering?

Certainly the *difference* in world reaction to the Israeli responsibility (whatever that may be) for the unquestionably tragic Lebanese massacre, and to the brutality of the Soviet invasion of Afghanistan, with its many-times-greater destruction of life, is an astonishing commentary on the slant in world opinion.

It serves to underscore that there is, indeed, a widespread and often inexplicable anti-Israel attitude abroad in the world. Israel *has* been "a burden to the nations," and though the prophecy of Zechariah has certainly not yet seen its complete fulfilment, the attitude it describes is unquestionably a factor today.

I submit that the very existence of Israel as a nation in our modern family of nations is a major indicator of the times in which we live. She is, in fact, *the foremost political sign* of the impending climax of the ages.

Let's consider why this is so.

PROPHECIES ABOUT ISRAEL

The textbook on the history of Israel and on her future is the Bible. The Bible describes how, in the beginning, God chose Abraham and promised to make of him a great nation, with whom He would sustain a special relationship. The record is found in Genesis, chapters 12-18. It contains, as well, promises of a permanent homeland, which is clearly described, for Israel.

The fulfilment of God's word to Abraham began with the growth of his family. Later, in Egypt, where the Abrahamic descendants had gone to escape famine, the children of Israel grew and became a nation. Under Moses, they subsequently escaped the cruel Egyptian bondage which had arisen, and finally were led in the conquest of Canaan, the promised land, by General Joshua.

Enroute to Canaan, they were given the divine moral code and the first portions of God's Word—in the Ten Commandments and the Pentateuch.

And in a dramatic incident which took place at the Mounts Ebal and Gerizim, God made it very clear to them, through Moses, that His blessing would be theirs as a *nation*, if they obeyed His word, but that His judgments would be visited upon them, *nationally*, if they disobeyed.

In a formal way, the nation agreed to this contract between themselves and God. The document is recorded in the Old Testament book of Deuteronomy. The date of its enactment was approximately 1400 B.C.

Here, in part, is that amazing contract:

BLESSINGS PROMISED
FOR OBEDIENCE

And it shall come to pass, if thou shalt hearken diligently unto the voice of the LORD thy God, to observe and to do all his commandments which I command thee this day, that the LORD thy God will set thee on high above all nations of the earth:

And all these blessings shall come on thee, and overtake thee, if thou shalt hearken unto the voice of the LORD thy God....

The LORD shall cause thine enemies that rise up against thee to be smitten before thy face: they shall come out against thee one way, and flee before thee seven ways.

The LORD shall command the blessing upon thee in thy storehouses, and in all that thou settest thine hand unto; and he shall bless thee in the land which the LORD thy God giveth thee....

And the LORD shall make thee plenteous in goods, in the fruit of thy body, and in the fruit of thy cattle, and in the fruit of thy ground, in the land which the LORD sware unto thy fathers to give thee.

The LORD shall open unto thee his good treasure, the heaven to give the rain unto thy land in his season, and to bless all the work of thine hand: and thou shalt lend unto many nations, and thou shalt not borrow.

And the LORD shall make thee the head, and not the tail; and thou shalt be above only, and thou shalt not be beneath; if that thou hearken unto the commandments of the LORD thy God, which I command thee this day, to observe and to do them.

And thou shalt not go aside from any of the words which I command thee this day, to the right hand or to the left, to go after other gods to serve them.

CONSEQUENCES OF DISOBEDIENCE

But it shall come to pass, if thou wilt not hearken unto the voice of the LORD thy God, to observe to do all his commandments and his statutes which I command thee this day; that all these curses shall come upon thee, and overtake thee....

The LORD shall cause thee to be smitten before thine enemies: thou shalt go out one way against them, and flee seven ways before them: and shalt be removed into all the kingdoms of the earth....

Thy sons and thy daughters shall be given unto another people, and thine eyes shall look, and fail with longing for them all the day long, and there shall be no might in thine hand....

The LORD shall bring a nation against thee from far, from the end of the earth, as swift as the eagle flieth; a nation whose tongue thou shalt not understand;

A nation of fierce countenance, which shall not regard the person of the old, nor shew favour to the young....

And he shall besiege thee in all thy gates, until thy high and fenced walls come down, wherein thou trustedst, throughout all thy land; and he shall besiege thee in all thy gates throughout all thy land, which the LORD thy God hath given thee.

And thou shalt eat the fruit of thine own body, the flesh of thy sons and of thy daughters, which the LORD thy God hath given thee, in the siege, and in the straitness, wherewith thine enemies shall distress thee....

If thou wilt not observe to do all the

words of this law that are written in this book, that thou mayest fear this glorious and fearful name, THE LORD THY GOD....

And the LORD shall scatter thee among all people, from the one end of the earth even unto the other; and there thou shalt serve other gods, which neither thou nor thy fathers have known, even wood and stone.

—Deuteronomy 28:1,2,7,8,11-15,25,32, 49-50,52-53,58,64.

PROPHET EZEKIEL ADDS A WORD

There are numerous other prophetic utterances concerning Israel in the Old Testament writings, but the prophetic visions of Ezekiel are of particular significance in the context of our consideration.

Ezekiel wrote at a point (approximately 586 B.C.) after which some of the national consequences for disobedience, outlined in Deuteronomy, had already occurred. Chapter 36 of Ezekiel charges Israel with defiling their own land by their disobedience (v. 17). As a result, God poured judgment upon them, and the Israelites were "scattered...among the heathen, and they were dispersed through the countries..." (v. 19).

But that was not the end of God's plan for Israel. A part of Ezekiel's divinely inspired forecast for the nation follows:

And I will sanctify my great name, which was profaned among the heathen, which ye have profaned in the midst of them; and the heathen shall know that I am the LORD, saith the Lord GOD, when I shall be sanctified in you before their eyes.

For I will take you from among the heathen, and gather you out of all countries, and will bring you into your own land.

Then will I sprinkle clean water upon you, and ye shall be clean: from all your filthiness, and from all your idols, will I cleanse you.

A new heart also will I give you, and a new spirit will I put within you: and I will take away the stony heart out of your flesh, and I will give you an heart of flesh.

And I will put my spirit within you, and cause you to walk in my statutes, and ye shall keep my judgments, and do them.

And ye shall dwell in the land that I gave to your fathers; and ye shall be my people, and I will be your God.

—Ezekiel 36:23-28

The famous prophecy of Ezekiel 37, which inspired the Negro spiritual "Dry Bones," reiterates that exciting outlook for Israel's future in a strikingly graphic way. Ezekiel was set down in the midst of a valley full of dry, lifeless bones. Then the Lord said to Ezekiel:

Prophesy upon these bones, and say unto them, O ye dry bones, hear the word of the LORD.

Thus saith the Lord GOD unto these bones; Behold, I will cause breath to enter into you, and ye shall live:

And I will lay sinews upon you, and will bring up flesh upon you, and cover you with skin, and put breath in you, and ye shall live; and ye shall know that I am the LORD.

So I [Ezekiel] prophesied as I was commanded: and as I prophesied, there was a noise, and behold a shaking, and the bones came together, bone to his bone.

And when I beheld, lo, the sinews and the flesh came upon them, and the skin covered them above: but there was no breath in them.

—Ezekiel 37:4-8

Then the Lord commanded Ezekiel to speak to the four winds, causing them to "breathe upon these slain, that they may live" (vs.19). Ezekiel did as he was commanded, "and the breath came into them, and they lived, and stood up upon their feet, an exceeding great army" (v. 10). Then the Lord interpreted the vision for Ezekiel:

> Then he said unto me, Son of man, these bones are the whole house of Israel: behold, they say, Our bones are dried, and our hope is lost; we are cut off for our parts.
>
> Therefore prophesy and say unto them, Thus saith the Lord GOD; Behold, O my people, I will open your graves, and cause you to come up out of your graves, and bring you into the land of Israel.
>
> And ye shall know that I am the LORD, when I have opened your graves, O my people, and brought you up out of your graves,
>
> And shall put my spirit in you and ye shall live, and I shall place you in your own land: then shall ye know that I the LORD have spoken it, and performed it, saith the LORD.

—Ezekiel 37:11-14

Later in the same chapter, the Lord reveals through Ezekiel that the divided kingdom will be reunited as a political unity:

> And I will make them one nation in the land upon the mountains of Israel; and one king shall be king to them all: and they shall be no more two nations, neither shall they be divided into two kingdoms any more at all...
>
> —Ezekiel 37:21

A FURTHER WORD

The Lord Jesus Christ, who during His earthly ministry lived and was crucified under Roman dominion, added to the prophetic forecast on Israel. He said:

> And when ye shall see Jerusalem compassed with armies, then know that the desolation thereof is nigh.
>
> Then let them which are in Judaea flee to the mountains; and let them which are in the midst of it depart out; and let not them that are in the countries enter thereinto.
>
> For these be the days of vengeance, that all things which are written may be fulfilled.
>
> But woe unto them that are with child, and to them that give suck, in those

days! for there shall be great distress in the land, and wrath upon this people.

And they shall fall by the edge of the sword, and shall be led away captive into all nations: and Jerusalem shall be trodden down of the Gentiles, until the times of the Gentiles be fulfilled.

—Luke 21:20-24

WHAT ARE THE FACTS OF HISTORY?

Now, having noted some of the many prophecies relating to Israel, let's look very briefly into the historical record, and at the current scene, to get a perspective on where we stand.

History records the tragic story. National disobedience to God's laws, followed by His judgment, followed by repentance and God's promised aid, followed by disobedience, became a continuous cycle. The nation went steadily downhill spiritually—*and* in every other way!

Finally, the chosen people were divided into two nations—the ten tribes of Israel to the north, and the two tribes of Judah in the south.

These two nations lived side by side for 200 years, often engaging in war between themselves, as well as with the nations around them.

Meanwhile, their national disregard for God, worse in Israel, continued and became so great that finally divine judgment permitted Israel's complete destruction as a nation—with her people carried away into captivity from which they would not return for centuries.

Judah, the southern nation, also experienced the judgment of God for her sin and was later conquered by a succession of enemies, though permitted to remain in the land.

Later, under the Macabees, a Jewish state did exist for a brief time about 140 B.C. until the armies of Rome conquered all of the then-known world, including Judah.

The prophecy of Jesus in Luke 21:20-24 was literally fulfilled when in A.D. 70—as a "final solution to the Jewish problem"—the Roman general Titus brutally put down a rebellion, crucified hundreds upon thousands of Jews, sold thousands more into slavery in other lands and totally destroyed Jerusalem, even razing the Temple by fire.

A band of about 1,000 Jewish soldiers,

women and children did hold out against the might of Rome for months in the desert stronghold of Masada, but when that heroic community finally fell in A.D. 100, the nation of Israel literally ceased to exist. [88]

Her people were dispersed among the nations. Her national homeland, in ruins and desolate, was under the control of others. Just as God said. You can read it in the history books.

So—at that point, there simply was no longer, within the family of earth's nations, a nation of Israel.

They were finished.

They had NO homeland.

They had NO government, NO army.

They were DEAD and BURIED, in terms of being a national entity.

Now, it is a fact that when a people are deprived of a homeland, of self-government and are dispersed among various nations for any length of time, they usually lose their national identity quite quickly.

This has happened to peoples in South America and Southeast Asia in a period of as little as 300 or 400 years. In America, "the melting pot of the world," it has occurred in 200 years.

But it has *not* happened to the Jews.

The fact is that, though existing for over 2,500 years without self-government, and for more than 1,900 years without a homeland, the Jews have maintained their distinctive nationality.*

OUT OF THEIR GRAVES

But the Jews have not merely retained their national identity, as remarkable and unlikely as that is. Against unbelievable odds, they have regained and are actually *in* their original homeland—as a nation among nations. Unquestionably, this phenomenon among nations, unique in the history of the world, must be the *beginnings* of the fulfilment of the "dry bones" prophecy from Ezekiel, quoted earlier.

It is not the *complete* fulfilment, in terms of the spirit of the Lord being placed within the nation, but certainly it is the beginning. The "bones" are coming together, as the people of Israel have come up out of their "graves," nationally, to exist again as a nation.

The actual rebirth of Israel developed over many years of struggle, including World War

---

*This becomes all the more amazing when one compares them to larger, stronger contemporary nationalities, who have either vanished from the earth, as such, or have been assimilated into other cultures.

I, during which Palestine came under British control. The culmination came on May 14, 1948, when the Jewish National Council proclaimed from Tel Aviv the establishment of the Sovereign State of Israel.

Both the United States and Russia recognized the fledgling nation, which, after much debate, was accepted as a member nation into the United Nations.

The "bones" had come together!

SURVIVAL IN WAR

But Israel has been born to a turbulent national life.

In the 35 years since Israel became a nation, she has been through five major wars.

In 1948, immediately upon declaration of statehood, the tiny, newly-formed nation was plunged into a life-and-death struggle for its very survival. It should have been no contest, with the neighbouring Arab states vastly outnumbering Israel, as well as holding an incredible military advantage in terms of men and materials.

Nevertheless, when the "war of independence" ended on January 7, 1949, Israel had not only survived, but had gained possession of key areas of Palestine.

Tensions remained, however. They inevitably built up until, on October 29, 1956, Israel invaded the Sinai, shortly after Egypt nationalized the Suez Canal and denied Israel's ships passage through it.

The invasion, which was supported by Britain and France, was a complete success from the Jewish point of view. In just seven days, before the U.N. established the first international police force to supervise a truce, Israel routed 40,000 Egyptian troops, overran the Sinai and closed the Canal.

Again a shaky peace prevailed, but the inevitable build-up in the cycle of tension soon developed. The eruption came on June 6, 1967, in the famous Six-Day War. As a result of that phenomenal Jewish blitz—once again against tremendous odds in terms of manpower and military equipment—the entire Sinai, the Golan Heights in Syria, the territory to the Jordan River, and the Old City of Jerusalem fell into Jewish hands.

Israel's fourth war *could* have been her last. It is generally agreed that the Yom Kippur War of September 1973 took Israel by surprise, and, as the late Golda Meir, then Prime Minister, said: "For the first time in our 25-year history, we thought we might have lost."

The Arab armies, powerfully equipped with the latest in sophisticated weapons provided by the Russians, attacked on two fronts simultaneously. The surprise assault, which came on the Jewish high holy day, was massive. History's greatest tank battle was fought in the Sinai during this war. It was also the world's first truly technological war.

The accounts of the Yom Kippur War are intriguing, telling the story of Israel's "miraculous" survival and victory (of sorts), as well as suggesting that the United States and Russia actually went to the brink of nuclear war over the conflict.[89]

But—"peace" settled down, and in 1979 the dramatic Israeli-Egyptian peace treaty was signed. (We'll have more to say about the prophetic significance of this in chapter nine.) The treaty resulted in the "normalization of relationships" between Israel and Egypt, which continued after the assassination of Egyptian President Sadat, one of its three architects, in 1981. A major result of the treaty was the unprecedented return, in April 1982, of the Sinai peninsula to Egypt by Israel, marking the first time in history that a territory taken in battle had been voluntarily returned.

In June of 1982, Israel initiated war once again. The Israel Defense Forces (IDF) invaded Lebanon in an effort to destroy, once and for all, the Palestinian Liberation Organization (PLO) army—that international terrorist force dedicated to the destruction of the State of Israel—which had become deeply entrenched in the nation neighbouring to Israel. Lebanon had, in fact, become a base from which PLO terrorist attacks on Israel's Galilee were regularly launched.

The effort was dubbed "Schlomal Galilee"—Operation Peace for Galilee.

Israel's military objective, the defeat and dislodgement of the PLO from Lebanon, was achieved. In late September of 1982, the remnant of the PLO army left Beirut, to be dispersed to the various Arab nations who would allow them entry.

However, in the aftermath of the war, Israel suffered a severe propaganda defeat, being made to appear "inhumane" by much of the world media, largely as a result of questions over her role in the brutal massacre of hundreds of refugees in a Palestinian camp, in October.

Nevertheless, the fact remains that Israel is very much a modern-day nation. And, according to the International Institute For Strategic Studies, the definitive authority on armaments, the Israelis are the world's fourth most powerful military force—an incredible achievement for so small a nation.

And, in spite of the continuing external pressures, and the enormous burden of maintaining such a huge military, the nation has grown in strength and stability through its brief, turbulent history.

Religiously, Israel has been more given to an agnostic approach. Though there are various strong orthodox groups active in Israeli life, the prevailing mood is one of secularism.

One major religious event in recent years, however, has been the construction and dedication, in 1982, of the Great Synagogue, near the site of the ancient temple (now occupied by the Muslim Dome of the Rock). Some observers feel this synagogue could be the predicted "Tribulation Temple." Another significant factor has been the establishment, in December 1970, of a special school for the training of young Levites in the ancient rites of sacrifice. [90]

WHAT DOES ALL THIS MEAN?

The point of all this is that, in a very special way, a regathered, somewhat secure nation of Israel is *the* most significant sign of prophecy's impending fulfilment.

In our introduction to part two, we referred to the parable which Jesus told about the fig tree putting forth its leaves, thus indicating that summer was near. Jesus told that parable as a part of His answer to the disciples' questions: "What will be the sign of your coming?" and "What will be the sign of the end of the age?" (Matthew 24).

In the first part of His answer to those questions, Jesus described many general world conditions, like wars, famines and earthquakes, which He said would increase in frequency and intensity like labor pangs prior to the birth of a child.

We'll look at some of these indicators in Part Four.

Then, as a *major* part of His response, Jesus spoke of Israel being back in the land of Palestine (Matthew 24:16) with the Temple rebuilt (Matthew 24:15) and with even their ancient worship restored (Matthew 24:20)—following, of course, a lengthy worldwide dispersion.

Jesus added (in Matthew 24:34) that the generation which saw "the fig tree putting forth its leaves"—Israel, whose national tree is the fig tree, reborn and in the land—would not pass away "until all these things come to pass."

Many prophetic students have concluded that we are that generation. Hal Lindsey, the dean of prophetic writers, boldly states on the back cover of his book, *The 1980's: Countdown to Armageddon*, "*we* are the terminal generation" (emphasis mine).

Unquestionably, regardless of one's viewpoint, the existence and survival of the nation of Israel—an existence and survival which defies incredible odds—*is a most significant political signal* that ancient prophecies are beginning to be fulfilled.

The climax of the ages nears!

For Further Reading:

Collins, L. and Lapierre, D. *O Jerusalem!* (New York: Pocket Books, 1973).

Goetz, W.R. *Apocalypse Next*, (Beaverlodge: Horizon House, 1981), Chapter Five.

Latham, L. *Israel: A Secret Documentary*, (Wheaton, Ill: Tyndale House, 1975).

Lewis, David A. *Magog 1982 Cancelled*, (Harrison, Ark.: New Leaf Press, 1982).

Lindsey, H. *The 1980s: Countdown to Armageddon*, (New York: Bantam Books, 1981).

McDowell, J. *Evidence That Demands A Verdict* (Arrowhead Springs, Calif.: Campus Crusade for Christ, 1972).

Phillips, M. *The Spirit World* - An abridgement of "The Bible, The Supernatural, and the Jews," (Wheaton, Ill.: Victor Books, 1972).

Shottish, Anis A. *Jesus, Prophecy and the Middle East*, (Nashville: Thomas Nelson Publisher, 1981)

Van Impe, J. *Israel's Final Holocaust*, (Nashville: Thomas Nelson Publisher, 1979).

Weldon, J. and Levitt, Z. *Encounters With UFO's*, (Irvine, Calif.: Harvest House Publishers, 1975).

Weldon, J. and Wilson, C. *1980's Decade of Shock*, (San Diego: Master Books, 1978).

Our aim is the complete liberation of Palestine, and the liquidation of the Zionist entity, economically, politically, militarily, culturally and ideologically.

> —Yassar Arafat, PLO leader, May 1977

We call for closer ties between Moscow and all elements of the PLO–

> —joint statement by Soviets and PLO, following an August 1977 conference.

CHAPTER NINE

The Russian Connection

There *will* be a Russian invasion of Israel.

That *fact* is not in question. Only the timing is.

And the prediction of this invasion, uttered some 2,700 years ago by the prophet Ezekiel, could quite conceivably have its fulfillment soon.

Even some Israeli military personnel are of this opinion.

I mentioned my hearing Colonel Yehuda Levy (Israeli Defense Forces spokesman) speak at a November 1982 dinner in Vancouver, B.C. On that trip to Canada, the colonel was interviewed by Dr. Kenn Opperman on the television program "Eleven W10." Dr. Opperman referred to the prophecy of Ezekiel concerning a Russian invasion of Israel, and asked Colonel Levy for his response.

The colonel acknowledged that he was aware of the prophecy and of the very real probability of its fulfillment. More on that shortly.

Let's look, first, at exactly what Ezekiel predicted, and then relate current events to his prophecy.

AMAZING PREDICTIONS

In chapters 37, 38 and 39 of the prophecy of Ezekiel, there are several very specific predictions.

In Ezekiel 37:11-25 we have the prophecy that Israel, which would be scattered and cease to exist as a nation, would be regathered and dwell in the land given by God to Jacob. This was considered in our last chapter.

In chapter 38 of Ezekiel, there is the prediction that a northern power, leading a confederacy of nations (which are named) will come against Israel in an invasion.

The amazing outcome of that invasion is predicted in the first part of chapter 39.

The outcome truly *is* amazing.

Instead of the expected annihilation or enslavement of tiny Israel by the mammoth Russian war machine, it is the *Russian* confederacy which is dealt a crushing defeat. That trouncing is not a military victory for Israel, but rather a supernatural destruction of the Red army.

We need to explore these prophecies in greater detail.

ISRAEL REBORN

The documentation for the already partially fulfilled prophecy of Israel's rebirth was provided in our previous chapter. Israel's miraculous preservation for centuries while without a homeland, her rebirth and regathering as a nation, her miraculous survival through five wars since then, and her continued prominence in world affairs (out of all proportion to her size) are major indicators of the lateness of earth's hour.

THE INVADERS IDENTIFIED

Concerning the coming invasion, the prophet wrote:

And the word of the Lord came unto me, saying,

Son of man, set thy face against Gog, the land of Magog, the chief prince of Meshech and Tubal, and prophesy against him....

Persia, Ethiopia, and Libya with them; all of them with shield and helmet:

Gomer, and all his bands; the house of Togarmah of the north quarters, and all his bands: and many people with thee.

Be thou prepared, and prepare for thyself, thou, and all thy company that are assembled unto thee, and be thou a guard unto them....

Therefore, son of man, prophesy and say unto Gog, Thus saith the Lord God; In that day when my people Israel dwelleth safely, shalt thou not know it?

And thou shalt come from thy place out of the north parts, thou, and many people with thee, all of them riding upon horses, a great company, and a mighty army:

And thou shalt come up against my people of Israel, as a cloud to cover the land; it shall be in the latter days, and I will bring thee against my land, that the heathen may know me, when I shall be sanctified in thee, O Gog, before their eyes.

—Ezekiel 38:1-9; 16

That's not the entire prophecy, so I do urge you to obtain a Bible and read all of Ezekiel 37-39. However, the portion we've quoted tells us that a northern power, named "Gog, of the land of Magog," will lead the invasion.

THE LEADER IS RUSSIA

For centuries scholars have believed that this northern power is Russia. *The Destiny of the Nations*, written by Dr. John Cummings back in 1864—long before Russia was a major power—put forth this view.

There are three reasons for believing this. *The meaning of the names* used is one. Josephus, the most famed of ancient Jewish historians, held this view. It is based on the fact that Genesis 10:2 lists "Magog" as the second grandson of Noah. History records that he and his descendants moved to and settled north of the Black Sea. "Tubal" and

"Meshech," the fifth and sixth grandsons of Noah, moved to the south of the Black Sea. Intermarriage over the centuries followed. The descendants of Meshech and Tubal are identified, thus, as the Mushki and Tubali of the Volga River basin, and present day Moscow and Tobolsh.[91]

The famous nineteenth century lexicographer, Dr. William Gesenius, emphatically states that the word Gog could properly be translated "the prince of Rosh" and says that Rosh is definitely to be equated with Russia.

Scofield's *Bible Notes*, the *Watson Bible Dictionary*, the *Schaft-Hertzog Commentary*, and others, support this view.

The homeland location of the leader of the invaders is another reason for believing it to be Russia. Ezekiel 38:15 says that he will come "from thy place out of the north parts"—or, as it is rendered in some translations, "out of the *northernmost* parts."

Now, remembering that compass directions in the Bible are always given in reference to the Holy Land, we can identify the invader. There is only one nation which fits the description of being to the uttermost north of Israel—Russia. To check this out for yourself, get a globe. Run a line from Israel to the North Pole. You'll discover that it passes almost through Moscow. Without question,

Russia, and *only* Russia, is to the *uttermost* north of Israel.

A final reason for saying Russia is the leader is *her character*. God says to Russia, through Ezekiel (as recorded in Chapter 38:3): "Behold, I am against you, O Gog." Such a statment seems contrary to God's very character, for He is revealed in Scripture as being a God of love, mercy, and patience. Obviously, if God is against Russia, it must be because of the extreme way in which Russia is against God.

And she is anti-God, officially.

Article Twelve of the 1918 Soviet Constitution decrees that no church or religious organization "shall enjoy the rights of judicial person." Instruction of children under age 18 in religious matters, whether in public *or* private, is against the law. Article 135 allows religious bodies to practice, but not propagate their religion.

The founder of communism, Karl Marx, rejected the idea of God, saying religion is merely an opiate of the people. The Manifesto clearly states that "Communism abolishes 'eternal' truths; it abolishes all religion." Lenin wrote, "Atheism is a natural and inseparable part of Marxism." Zinoviev said in 1924, "We shall vanquish the Lord God in His highest heaven." The official program of the Soviet Party, published in 1932, states that "the real emancipation of the working masses from religious prejudices" is one of the Party's objectives.

And the actions of the Communists support their words. Communist U.S.S.R. has done more to destroy faith in God than any other power or ideology in the history of the world!

In the four years after the 1917 Bolshevik takeover, 28 bishops and 1,219 priests were killed. Churches were closed. By 1935, according to *Soviet* statistics, 42,800 clergymen had been put to death.

The murderous disregard and disdain for human life saw the slaughter in the 1917-35 era (in addition to the clergymen) of 6,000 professors, 9,000 doctors, 12,900 landlords, 50,000 officers, 70,000 policemen, 193,290 shopworkers, 355,150 intellectuals and 815,000 soldiers, with 3 million more being sent to Siberian concentration camps. A grisly total of 11,700,000 persons were either killed or enslaved during that time.[92]

Such action is against all that God demands of the leaders of a nation.

But most serious of all is Russia's *official* treatment of the Jews and Israel. God has said that Israel is His chosen people, and that "I am against them that are against thee." So the Communists' cruel persecution of the

Jews and fierce opposition to Israel are strong reasons why God says. "I am against thee, O Gog."

For these reasons we may unequivocally state that the leader of the predicted invaders of Israel is none other than Russia.

THE ALLIES LINE UP

Nearly 2,700 years ago God told Ezekiel to list the allies of Russia when she invades Israel. He did so in Chapter 38:5-6, as follows:

Persia, Ethiopia, and Libya with them;
all of them with shield and helmet:

Gomer, and all his bands; the house of
Togarmah of the north quarters, and all
his bands: and many people with thee.

PERSIA

Ancient Persia, of course, covered present-day Iran and Iraq.

Iraq has been in the Soviet orbit for some time now, though apparently the Soviets have decided to cool their relationship, according to reports such as the one carried in the March 11, 1982, issue of the *Baltimore Evening Sun*. This decision came, it is believed, in favor of an effort to make Iran a major Soviet ally.

Such a move would have immense benefits for the U.S.S.R. It would give Moscow a warm-water port facility on the Persian Gulf, and access to oil as well as to Afghanistan's "back door."[93]

Russia and *Iran* have had a Mutual Defense Alliance, dating back to 1921, with an updating in 1935. The pact calls for intervention by either signatory in the event of invasion, instability or other incident affecting the security of either nation. Everyone knows, of course, about the chaotic conditions in Iran, under the Khomeini and with the Iran/Iraq war.

Recently the Red Bear has been tightening his embrace on the Iranian section of ancient Persia. A quick review of several news-clips shows how rapidly it's happening:

November 30, 1981: The Soviet Union appears to be gaining a toehold in Iran, thanks mainly to an economic policy that allows Ayatollah Ruhollah Khomeini's regime to barter oil for technology....The clergy-led government appears to have swallowed its traditional distaste for communism and moderated its attacks on their Soviet neighbors to the north.[94]

January 18, 1982: For months the Soviet Union has been gaining a long-coveted foothold in Iran. In mid-October the ruling Islamic Republic Party accepted Moscow's offer to send agents to Iran to strengthen Tehran's intelligence and security forces.... Another Soviet team was dispatched to assist in rebuilding the country's devastated economy. Now the Soviets, in their boldest ploy to date, are pressing Iran to sign a mutual cooperation pact that would effectively draw Khomeini's revolutionary government into Moscow's sphere of influence....(Soviet Ambassador Vinogradov's) deal: increased Soviet protection, presumably in the form of arms and technical advisers, in exchange for a formal five- to ten-year 'friendship and mutual assistance treaty' between the U.S.S.R. and Iran...the Kremlin wants a signed deal....The talks about the friendship treaty...are...continuing.[95]

February, 1982: Moscow has, during the last 2½ years, successfully infiltrated more than 4,000 KGB agents into the country [Iran] ruled by the religious, fundamentalist Khomeini.[96]

Mar. 1, 1982: Last week Iran and the Soviet Union concluded an agreement

187

for 'accelerated' economic and political cooperation. Under the new arrangement, the Soviets will finish constructing a hydroelectric dam and two power plants in Iran that they had begun building under the Shah. Iranian Energy Minister Ghafurifard declared in Moscow that the Soviet Union is a 'friendly country.'[97]

March 16, 1982: With Iran's approval, the Soviet Union is building a military base and seaport on Iran's southern coast, Scripps-Howard News Service has learned. The base will be just outside the strategic Strait of Hormuz. (One of the world's vital "choke points"—particularly in terms of mid-east oil movement.)[98]

March 22, 1982: Iran, the most populous country in the Near East after Egypt, with a historically powerful role, may slip into a Soviet embrace. Iranian exiles believe that KGB agents, masquerading as Islamic fundamentalists, now number at least 5,000 in Tehran. The Tudeh (Masses) Party, the Soviets' traditional vehicle in Iran, has expanded its activities—even though its leadership was underground in January.

Iran has sold the Russians a half-billion dollars' worth of oil in the past year, apparently in exchange for arms.[99]

Yes, Iran is virtually in the Soviet camp. The tilt is a very rapid one at this point, early in 1983. It could have gone all the way even by the time this is in print, or it could be that, for the U.S.S.R.'s purposes, the situation as it now stands is adequate.

ETHIOPIA

Ethiopia is a translation of the ancient Hebrew word *Cush*, according to Dr. Gesenius. Based on his scholarly conclusions, it is correct to say that the present-day Ethiopians make up a part of the Cushites, though not all of them. Thus, a reasonable view is that Ezekiel's Cush represents a number of present-day north African nations.

Such a conclusion also fits in with the prophecy of Daniel 11, which speaks of the "king of the south"—believed by some scholars to be a description of Cush, or the African-Arab power bloc.

Ethiopia had a pro-Communist coup in 1976, and since then has moved from her previous pro-western stance under the late Emperior Haile Selassie to a strong communist state, solidly entrenched in the Russian orbit.

LIBYA

Libya is the ancient *Put*. Gesenius' *Hebrew Lexicon* indicates that the descendants of Put became the forefathers of the north African Arab nations such as Libya, Algeria, Morocco and Tunisia. Therefore, the Libya of Ezekiel's prophecy most certainly includes the present-day Libya at least, and probably more.

Libya went communist in a 1969 coup. The nation today is firmly in the Russian camp, primarily because of an almost maniacal hatred of Israel by the "madman" ruler Colonel Maummer Kaddafi. He is a known "broker" of terrorism on an international scale, as well as being known for his surprising ties to Moscow; surprising in view of his Islamic messianic obsession.

There is little question but that Libya, under Kaddafi, would gladly join in any serious invasion of Israel.

GOMER

Gomer was the first grandson of Noah, as

recorded in Genesis 10:2, and, according to tradition and history, migrated north up the Danube. He became the father of Ashkenaz, Riphath and the head of many families. In the Jewish Talmud, Gomer is spoken of as Germani—that is, Germany. The present divided land of Germany was originally called "the land of Gomer" or Gomerland.

Ashkenaz, Gomer's son, was the name given to German Jews. Josephus called this people, described as "all Gomer's bands," the Rheginians. They are the adjacent Germanic peoples, believed to be found in the areas of modern Poland, Czechoslovakia and East Germany. Thus, Gomer and "all his bands" is *that part of eastern Europe found behind the Iron Curtain today.*[100]

This set of allies to Russia were arbitrarily, and generally unwillingly, taken into her camp at the close of World War II in 1945.

TOGARMAH

Many Bible scholars consider *Togarmah* to be *Turkey*, or the Turkoman tribes of northern Turkey and southern Russia.

Turkey is the only nation mentioned in Ezekiel's prophecy which is not either in, or tilting to, the Russian lineup. And though Turkey has been a member of NATO—the western defense alliance—since 1950, she is now under intense pressure from her ambitious northern neighbor.

Since 1978, when for the first time in 45 years a Soviet senior military official visited Turkey, there has been a subtle but strong drive on by the Communists to influence Turkey. The Communist party was recently legalized and a transmitter for it constructed on Turkish soil. A great deal of Soviet aid has been channelled into Turkey and Soviet "advisors" have entered in large numbers to assist in several joint projects. [101]

Severe economic and labor problems, which produced a lot of turmoil and headlines like "Turkey and its PM sliding toward ruin" in August 1979 and "Now It's Turkey on Brink of Collapse" in April 1980 have given way to slightly more stable times. However, as Georgie Anne Geyer reported to the Vancouver *Province* from Washington, D.C., on November 10, 1981: "the evidence points to Soviet-backed terror in Turkey."

So, preparations for the entry of the last mentioned confederate for the invasion appear to be well under way.

A SURPRISING ABSENTEE

But as intriguing as is the list of Russia's

confederates, particularly in view of current affairs, an even more intriguing aspect is an absentee from the list, whom you would think, in the light of history, *should* be heading the group.

That "unlisted" nation is *Egypt*!

Ezekiel did not include Egypt in the line-up of nations he predicted would join Russia in her invasion of Israel—unless, of course, she is unnamed and included in the phrase "and many people with thee" at the end of verses 6 and 9 of Ezekiel 38. That's what commentators have thought, for years, in an effort to explain Egypt's surprising absence. But the explanation has never been too satisfying.

For historically, Egypt has been too important and over the years too much an enemy of Israel to be relegated to inclusion as a mere unnamed part in an "umbrella" phrase.

A historic event which occurred on March 26, 1979, may be the explanation for Egypt's omission from the list of invaders.

On that date Egypt and Israel signed a peace treaty.[102]

In New York City that day for a meeting, I picked up a suburban newspaper (the major New York dailies were on strike) the front page of which was dominated by the headline "Let There Be No More Bloodshed," and a huge full-color photo of the late Egyptian President Anwar Sadat, Israeli Prime Minister Menachem Begin, and then U.S. President Jimmy Carter, on the lawn of the White House, signing the historic document. The improbable signing created a tremendous stir, a lot of Arab and Russian opposition, and many dire predictions that it could never be practically worked out.

However, it *does* seem to be working, with the unprecedented April 1982 withdrawal of Israel from the Sinai (won in War) and its return to Egypt, being a major milestone on the road to full ratification of this most improbable truce between centuries-long implacable enemies.

I fully realize that the treaty may yet fail to hold, and that Egypt could yet turn against Israel and become one of those unnamed "people with thee," in Russia's invasion. But I don't think it will happen. I believe the previously unexplained omission of Egypt from Ezekiel's prophecy has its explanation in the 1979 peace treaty, that it is a strong proof of the inspiration of Scripture, and an indicator of the lateness of the hour!

A GROUP OF PROTESTORS

The prophet foretells, in verse 13 of chapter 38, that there will be a feeble protest, uttered by *Sheba, Dedan, the merchants of Tarshish, with all the young lions thereof.*

Who are they?

According to Dr. W.F. Albright in the *Bulletin of the American Schools of Oriental Research* published in 1941, Sheba and Dedan were land-bound traders located east of Palestine, while Tarshish was the leader of sea traders and marine merchants west of Palestine.

The term "Tarshish" came to be used, in time, as a synonym for any maritime power or area where mining, smelting and trading in metal ore was carried on. Great shipping interests got the nickname "Tarshish," for Ezekiel's "Tarshish" is evidently also a nation of merchants.

Because of this, Ezekiel's reference is believed to be an expression broad enough to take in *all* the younger nations of the Old and New Worlds—especially Britain and her former colonies.

This is reinforced by the fact that the protestors would have to be kindly disposed toward Israel, strong enough to at least protest, and symbolized by a lion, or by a young lion (a colony).

Britain, primarily, and her colonies (like the U.S.) are held to be in view here, as will be readily apparent. However, it is my view that this is at best a rather tenuous indentification and one which I offer only as a possibility. I do feel, though, that it is the *only* possible reference, of which I am aware, in *Scripture* to the U.S. or Britain.

It should be noted that they apparently do no more than protest. No action is taken by them.

Such a scenario, unfortunately, fits in with our times. Many observers feel that since Viet Nam, the will in the United States to resist aggression is gone. The Afghanistan invasion appears to support this view.

And now, though it is still debated, it appears that the shift to Soviet military superiority has occurred. *Aviation Week and Space Technology* reported in its February 22, 1982, issue that:

Massive investments by the Soviet Union in strategic nuclear forces have shifted the strategic balance vis-a-vis the U.S., placing in jeopardy this country's intercontinental ballistic missile force.... "As a result of their [USSR] massive investment in strategic nuclear systems, the Soviets have wrought a dramatic shift in the strategic balance," Air Force Chief of Staff Gen. Lew Allen, Jr., told Congress....The trend of continuing Soviet strategic weapons modernization..."has resulted in...increased uncertainty in U.S. capabilities to deter both nuclear and non-nuclear conflict," according to the joint chiefs.[103]

This may explain why there is nothing more than a *protest*, when the invasion comes!

REASONS FOR RUSSIA'S INVASION

The question may well be asked, "Why would Russia invade Israel?" Israel is really quite insignificant in size, with a population of only about three and one half million. Why invade?

The reason, according to Ezekiel, is that the invaders will think an evil thought—of "taking a spoil."

The words of the prophecy are:

Thus saith the Lord GOD; It shall also come to pass, that at the same time shall things come into thy mind, and thou shalt think an evil thought:

And thou shalt say, I will go up to the land of unwalled villages; I will go to them that are at rest, that dwell safely, all of them dwelling without walls, and having neither bars nor gates,

To take a spoil and to take a prey; to turn thine hand upon the desolate places that are now inhabited, and upon the people that are gathered out of the nations, which have gotten cattle and goods, that dwell in the midst of the land.

— Ezekiel 38:10-12

The idea of a spoil, which means "booty or plunder taken or stripped in war," from Israel was until recently a foolish one. Palestine was a desolate, barren place, called "the forbidding land."

But things have changed.

Since 1948, the desert has begun to "blossom like the rose." Lush fields, through irrigation, have replaced barren landscapes all over the country. Agriculture has become a great industry, with Israel now the No. 1 supplier of citrus fruits to Europe. Four crops a year of many vegetables are produced.

There is an abundance of copper in Israel. And the Dead Sea, with its incredibly rich mineral deposits valued by some sources as high as US $13-15 trillion, contains strategic deposits of potash (used for fertilizer), bromide (useful in oil production), magnesium (a possible replacement for aluminum), and lithium (a uranium replacement in nuclear processes)—to name but a few of the most important, readily available minerals.

Israel also has oil capacity. Not only is there, in early 1983, exploration for oil under way with high hopes, but the world's largest oil refinery is located at Haifa. Though the oil flow was turned off after 1973, the capacity is there, including two pipelines to the large seaports of Eilat and Ashdod. Those major world-class ports are in themselves highly desirable factors from Russia's viewpoint. Israel's major airfield at Haifa, located at the head of the Valley of Megiddo, is one of the world's largest, most sophisticated airfields, and as such would be an important prize for Russia.[104]

More than this, Palestine is the "navel of the earth"—the land bridge between the three continents of Africa, Europe and Asia. Russia's goal of world domination would be made much easier by control of Israel, both through its location and its wealth.

Certainly, Russia would consider "taking a spoil" through an invasion of Israel.

HORSES...

Ezekiel 38:4 and 15 says that the invader

will come with "horses and horsemen," "riding upon horses."

A good deal of speculation has arisen over whether this is to be taken literally, or simply understood as being Ezekiel's way of saying that the invading army would be exceptionally well equipped, inasmuch as, in his day, cavalry was the "ultimate" weapon.

It is most interesting to note that in recent years, Russia has come into possession of 70 percent of the world's horses. From a drop of 38 million horses in 1914 to 14 million during World War II (when the Russian cavalry, the Cossacks, were still a big factor in the defeat of the Nazis) the horse in Russia is making a comeback. On June 15, 1981, a U.S.S.R. decree was issued offering a 50 ruble bonus for each horse raised to maturity on collective and state farms.

For years Russia has been buying horses on the world market in huge quantities, at the same time as they have been breeding a special strain called the Kirghiz. This new type of horse is said to be untiring, with great endurance, able to resist sub-zero temperatures as well as heat, and to survive on dry and scanty food while still doing a maximum day's work.[105]

Certainly a major cavalry force with this sort of animal would not be affected by the

energy crunch, nor subject to radar detection!
It would appear made to order for at least
some aspects of a campaign in Israel, for
(though the Russians have the nuclear
capacity to utterly destroy Palestine) the
U.S.S.R. would obviously not wish to destroy
the wealth, but rather take it as a spoil.

...AND LIGNOSTONE

Another interesting aspect of Ezekiel's
prophecy which has created a good deal of
speculation is this section in Chapter 39,
verses 9 and 10:

> And they that dwell in the cities of
> Israel shall go forth, and shall set on fire
> and burn the weapons, both the shields
> and the bucklers, the bows and the
> arrows, and the handstaves, and the
> spears, and they shall burn them with
> fire seven years:

> So that they shall take no wood out of
> the field, neither cut down any out of the
> forests; for they shall burn the weapons
> with fire: and they shall spoil those that
> spoiled them, and rob those that robbed
> them, saith the Lord GOD.

In my first book, *Apocalypse Next*, I said
this (p. 151):

A good deal of discussion has arisen over the description here of the kind of weaponry described, particularly over the burning of the discarded weapons of the invaders as fuel. Skeptics have had a field day with this, pointing out that steel doesn't burn. Others have suggested it describes a yet-to-be-developed nuclear fission potential.

In recent years, there have been numerous reports circulated of a substance called "lignostone"—said to have been developed in Ter Apel, Holland, in the mid-1960s. According to such reports, lignostone is a chemically treated wood which is very lightweight but which, like steel, can be used for armor plating. It reportedly burns more readily and intensely than coal. Moreover, the Russians are said to be the principal producers and users of it.

All of this fits the prophetic picture extremely well—except that I have been completely unable to confirm the existence of such a substance. Extensive research at several university libraries failed to turn up even so much as the mention of the name in *anything*—dictionaries, technical journals or scientific bulletins. This does not prove its non-existence, of course, but it does appear that the story is unfounded.

Since the release of *Apocalypse*, I have been inundated with letters and phone calls from people who assure me that such a substance *does* exist. Many skiers have told me that skis used to have their edges lined with it. More than this, a personal friend, Dr. Emil Gaverluk of Oklahoma City, sent me a piece of lignostone, which is being marketed in the U.S. under the trade name, "Lignilite." It must be tooled with carbide-tipped tools because of its hardness. It is obviously a composition of compressed wood, chemically impregnated.

Another *Apocalypse* reader, a doctor from West Virginia, sent me a copy of a syndicated column by Jack Anderson in which the national columnist reports that a secret CIA document indicates that the Russians are "away ahead of the U.S. in the development of 'composites' for military purposes."

The pieces of the puzzle seem to be coming together.

HOW SOON?

Certainly, there can be little question that the preparations *are* being made for an invasion of Israel.

A November 14, 1982, *New York Times* report strongly suggests that, contrary to the stated purpose in 1979 of the Soviet invasion of Afghanistan being just to stabilize the government, a program of airfield construction there seems to be a vital part of their mission.

Six Soviet airfields in southern Afghanistan, which would put the Persian Gulf and the Middle East within range of Russian jet fighters, were nearing completion in late 1982. Quite apparently the Red Bear has designs on this area of the world.[106]

The statement of Soviet Ambassador Anatoly Dobrymin to Henry Kissinger, as related in *The White House Years*, is significant. He said: "...if the Israelis threaten us, we will wipe them out in two days. I can assure you *our plans are made for this eventuality*" (emphasis mine).[107]

Perhaps he had in view the deployment, now complete, of Russia's SS-20 mobile ballistic missiles (with over 250 now operational) which can easily cover a distance of 3,107 miles and could destroy all Israel.

If there is any doubt, the fact that Russia fully supports the position of the Palestinian Liberation Organization should be the clincher. Now, it is true that the U.S.S.R. failed to come to the aid of the PLO in Lebanon in 1982. Just why is not clear—at least to this author.

But, in spite of the military defeat of the PLO army in Lebanon and its dispersal into at least eight Arab nations, the aims of the terrorist organization remain the same. And Russia still supports them.

News releases by Arafat and other PLO leaders, even as they left Beirut, in September 1982, made that clear. Under an August 31, 1982, Vancouver *Province* headline "Arafat: Fight to Go On," it was reported that the Manama, Bahrain newspaper *Al-Khaleej* quoted Arafat as saying, at the time he left Beirut to join some of his scattered forces, that the Palestinians will "take account tomorrow and take vengeance [on Israel] the day after tomorrow." He said his troops have "sworn to fight until victory." [108]

According to an Associated Press account in *The Vancouver Sun*, September 11, 1982, Nayef Hawatmeh, a pro-Soviet PLO leader, said "The Palestinian guerrillas are regrouping...to continue their war against Israel." A late August *New York Times* headline said "PLO pressure will continue." [109]

The goal of the PLO has been clearly

spelled out. On May 5, 1977, Yassar Arafat, the acknowledged head and spokesman for the terrorists, said, in Oslo, Norway:

> Our aim is the complete liberation of Palestine and the liquidation of the Zionist entity economically, politically, militarily, culturally and ideologically.

The charter of the PLO calls for "dismantling the Jewish state and replacing it with a non-sectarian Palestinian nation." [110]

Even in the face of its 1982 defeat, the PLO has not officially departed from its stated purpose, written shortly before it came into existence in 1964. At its congress in 1980, Fatah, which represents 70 percent of the PLO membership, renewed its vow to "liquidate the Zionist entity."

This goal, apparently, is still held.

And it is one in which the Russian leadership has freely shared. Over the years Arafat has frequently held what have been termed "successful" talks with the highest ranking Soviet leaders (including the late Brezhnev). As recently as the late '70s, the Soviets and PLO issued a *joint* statement calling for "closer ties between Moscow and *all* elements of the PLO." [111]

And in her book *The Terror Network*,

published in 1981, Claire Sterling offers well-documented proof that the PLO terrorist training camps in South Yemen, established to develop a multi-national terrorist network, have definite links to Moscow. Apparently the ties continue.[112]

There can be little doubt that the U.S.S.R. was arming the PLO.

The Israeli Defense Forces, on their drive into Lebanon, uncovered vast stores of arms, particularly in Tyre and Sidon.

In June 1982, *The Economist*, of London, carried the eye-witness report of its Israel correspondent concerning the I.D.F. claims that it had "discovered quantities of arms underground—often under office buildings, schools, clinics and mosques—far larger than even they expected; it was the infrastructure of an *army*, they say, not of an irregular force."[113]

The correspondent reported that his own examination of one area beneath the playground of a Tyre school, run by UN agencies, revealed telescopic photos of Galilee and a huge armory of weapons crated in boxes lettered in Russian and Chinese.

Evidence in Sidon confirmed links between the PLO and numerous terrorist groups from outside the Middle East.

THE COLONEL RESPONDS

I had heard radio reports in June of the discovery of these massive arms stores—and the uncovering of some one million Russian-made army uniforms in Tyre and Sidon. I was unable to personally confirm these, and so it was with tremendous interest that I participated in the question and answer time following the November dinner, referred to earlier, at which I.D.F. Colonel Levy spoke.

The first of two questions I asked was a request for confirmation, if available, of the reports I had heard concerning the discovery of uniforms and weapons.

The Colonel's response was that he could not confirm the *number* of one million uniforms, but he did say that he personally had seen "stores of weapons and military materials many, many times the quantity which would have been needed to supply an army the size of the PLO."

In a July 11, 1982, article in the *Jerusalem Post*, the question of the size of the captured arsenal was raised:

> One of the mysteries of this war is why the PLO had so many weapons stockpiled in Lebanon. There is simply no correlation between the size of the organization, or even its most optimistic

growth potential, and the quantities of arms, ammunition and explosives found.

These weapons were sophisticated— some of them the best the Soviets have produced....

Prime Minister Menachem Begin has speculated that the *Soviets* were stockpiling arms in Lebanon. In other words, the PLO was establishing a storehouse of weapons for future Soviet use in the region. [114]

All of this is extremely interesting when viewed in terms of Ezekiel's prophecy.

The second question I asked Colonel Levy had to do with Israel's national sense of security, following the ousting of the PLO from Lebanon. Could the Colonel say how much greater was Israel's confidence now, compared to what it had been prior to the "Operation Peace for Galilee"?

Yehuda Levy replied that from the first four days of the war, when the I.D.F. drove to the gates of Beirut, and destroyed the Syrian SAM's in the Bekka Valley, there was a tremendous increase in the sense of national security and confidence in Israel.

Shortly thereafter the *Jerusalem Post* reported that "Begin tells United Jewish Appeal: 'Borders will be peaceful now.' "

Addressing an enthusiastic crowd of over 1,000 American UJA leaders in Jerusalem, Begin maintained that as a result of Israel's military showing in Lebanon, "Syria won't dare attack us! Egypt has signed a peace treaty; Jordan is unable to attack; and Saudi Arabia will not attack," the Premier said.[115]

But why ask about Israel's national sense of confidence and security?

Simply because one of Ezekiel's prophetic utterances relates to Israel's confidence at the time of Russia's invasion.

Here's that passage:

Therefore, son of man, prophesy and say unto Gog, Thus saith the Lord GOD; In that day when my people of Israel dwelleth safely [or, as some translations render it—*confidently*], shalt thou not know it?

And thou shalt come up against my people of Israel, as a cloud to cover the land; it shall be in the latter days, and I will bring thee against my land, that the heathen may know me, when I shall be sanctified in thee, O Gog, before their eyes.

And thou Gog shalt say, I will go up to the land of unwalled villages; I will go to

them that are at rest, that dwell safely
[*confidently*], all of them dwelling
without walls, and having neither bars
nor gates.

—Ezekiel 38:14,15;11

The fact that Israel now enjoys a degree of
confidence that is unprecedented in her
modern history, and that she dwells in
unwalled villages—something unheard of in
the prophet's time—certainly adds substance
to the view that the impending invasion must
be nearing. A regathered nation *is* dwelling
comparatively confidently in "unwalled
villages."

THE RESULT

As has already been briefly stated, the
invasion results in the crushing defeat of the
Russian army, as Ezekiel's prophecy
indicates:

And I will turn thee back, and leave
but the sixth part of thee, and will cause
thee to come up from the north parts,
and will bring thee upon the mountains
of Israel:

And I will smite thy bow out of thy left
hand, and will cause thine arrows to fall
out of thy right hand.

Thou shalt fall upon the mountains of Israel, thou, and all thy bands, and the people that is with thee: I will give thee unto the ravenous birds of every sort, and to the beasts of the field to be devoured.

Thou shalt fall upon the open fields: for I have spoken it, saith the Lord GOD.

And I will send a fire on Magog, and among them that dwell carelessly in the isles: and they shall know that I am the LORD.

So will I make my holy name known in the midst of my people Israel; and I will not let them pollute my holy name any more: and the heathen shall know that I am the LORD, the Holy One in Israel.

—Ezekiel 39:2-7

Apparently *unusual natural disasters* like earthquake and upheaval, pestilence, torrential rain and hailstones combined with *supernatural* fire, brimstone and the outbreak of vicious *fighting among the invaders themselves* will result in the destruction of five-sixths of the entire Soviet military force.

In addition, God says He will rain fire upon Magog (Russia itself) and on those who dwell in the coastlands. Some have speculated that this refers to nuclear destruction. It could indeed, but whether this is so or not, one fact is very clear: all the world will realize that the destruction of the Russian confederacy was the work of God—not man.

EXACTLY WHEN WILL IT HAPPEN?

Again, it is not possible to be dogmatic about every move or the exact sequence of events, inasmuch as differing views are held by competent scholars. However, this could be the scenario—taking into account both Ezekiel's prophecy and that of Daniel in chapter 11: Sometime after the Antichrist, head of the ten-nation confederacy, signs a seven-year treaty with Israel, the king of the south—the Arab bloc—will invade Israel (Daniel 11:40).* At this point, the entire Russian confederacy will come down upon the Jews like a whirlwind—with chariots, horsemen and many ships.* Apparently the

*Daniel 11:36-40 refers to the Antichrist. However, verse 40 introduces the "king of the north" (Russia) who, grammatically, **must** remain the subject for the rest of the chapter.

*Whether this reference to chariots and horses is to be taken literally or is merely a description of military might is the subject of some debate among prophetic students. I tend to feel that it is the latter, but would not rule out the possibility of the use of horses, with which Russia is extremely well supplied, as described earlier in this chapter.

Russians will doublecross the Arabs, for Daniel 11:40-43 indicates that their hordes will enter not only Israel, but many countries—with Egypt, Libya and Ethiopia specifically singled out as being taken. This fits the apparent desire of the Soviets to control the entire Middle East because of its oil.

It is at this juncture that the nations (which we have already indicated could be the NATO powers) utter their feeble protest, to which Russia, the superpower, pays no attention whatever (Ezekiel 38:18).

At this point, the tidings from the north (the north of Africa) where the king of the north is at this moment in the prophetic preview, and from the east (the European Common Market and the Oriental armies) cause the principal invader to set up headquarters in Israel. Here, upon the mountains of Israel, Russia's war machine is destroyed.

IN SUMMARY

Unquestionably, one of the major political indicators that the time of the rapture and the attendant events in earth's climax of the ages is nearing has to be the way things appear to be shaping up for the long-foretold invasion of Israel from the north.

*[China] is a sleeping dragon. Let her sleep.
When she awakes, the nations will be sorry.*

—Napoleon Bonaparte

CHAPTER TEN

The Nations Are Stirring

Ours is a rapidly changing world—one in
which relationships between nations, in
particular, are very fluid. National alignments
and friendships seem to lack the permanency
of past eras when the world was less a "global
village" than it is today, and the pace of
international affairs was much slower.

Such conditions, I feel, have prophetic
meaning.

It will be recalled that Jesus, in a message
given on the Mount of Olives shortly before
His crucifixion, likened Israel to "the fig

tree" and other nations to "all the trees." He implied that just as the appearance of leaves on trees indicates the nearness of summer, so certain events in Israel and among "the nations" would signal the nearness of His return.

I believe that current volatile national alignments and developments are, at the very least, the beginnings of the "trees shooting forth their leaves" — indicating that "summer is near."

We've looked already in part two at the significance of Israel, and of Russia's apparent preparations for an invasion of that nation.

Let's now consider some of the other nations and their activities to see whether or not these qualify as indicators of the impending climax.

The nations, or alignments of nations, which are described in the prophetic scriptures in addition to Israel, Russia and confederates in her impending invasion of Israel, are these:

—The "revived" Roman Empire,
—The "kings of the east," and
—The "princes of Ishmael," or the "king of the south."

Let's examine these groupings of nations in the light of prophecy and current affairs.

The prophecy of Daniel, of which I am convinced we are seeing—in the European Economic Community—at least the foreshadowings of the fulfilment, has been considered in part one.

Briefly, in summary, that prophecy is given twice in Daniel, in chapter two and in chapter seven. The first was in a dream of a great statue and the second in a vision of strange beasts. These companion revelations, as we considered in chapters five and seven of this book, depict empires—with the final empire (which is in existence at the time when the God of heaven establishes *His* never-ending reign) being clearly identified as a 10-nation confederacy which emerges out of the fourth empire—the old Roman Empire.

As described earlier, the European Economic Community began as a six-member economic partnership in 1957 in an agreement known as the Treaty of Rome. By 1988 it had become a 12-member power block which now has held elections several times to a European parliament.[116]

The ultimate goal is a complete unification of Europe—in trade, in economics and in the political realm. Though it has experienced many internal problems (well symbolized in the prophecy as feet and toes of iron and clay, which do not mix) it is nevertheless steadily gaining in stability and power.

The European Economic Community is a *major* power bloc. Its population is almost equal to that of the U.S. and Russia combined. The combined Gross National Product of the EEC is the greatest in the world. It has tremendous potential. The major shift of gold and silver deposits to EEC member-country banks could, as described earlier, be a most significant factor during the anticipated global economic chaos, giving the Community tremendous power.

It is also interesting to superimpose a map of the Old Roman Empire over a map of the 12 EEC nations. There is a remarkable similarity! And while the current membership may not be the final form of the revived Roman Empire, the EEC must certainly be at least a forerunner of the final fulfilment of Daniel's vision.

Unquestionably, these nations are like trees putting out leaves as "summer" approaches!

THE ORIENT FACTOR

China—the world's largest nation with a population of some one billion—is considered by many to be another of the nations which are astir, in accordance with biblical prophecy.

In the context of the three end-time wars predicted in the Bible (see chart p 265) there are references to a massive eastern power. Revelation 16:12 refers to the "kings of the east" who come over the Euphrates to do battle in Israel at the time of Armageddon. In what many feel is a companion reference, Revelation 9:14-16 states that the number of the army is 200 million, demonically energized. Daniel 11:44 contains another reference to this eastern power which figures in end-time events.

To me, it is quite significant that Mao Tse Tung boasted on several occasions before his death that China could "field a people's army of 200 million militia." This is particularly interesting if it is remembered that, at the time when the Apostle John penned his prophecy in the Revelation, some 1,900 years ago, such an army was absolutely unthinkable. Two hundred million was virtually *earth's entire population* at that time! For anyone to say, then, that just one nation could have such an army was utterly fantastic! Yet today it is a very real possibility.

China has nuclear capacity, and in 1979

completed the Karakoram Highway from Singkiang province down through Pakistan to the Indian Ocean. A spur of this highway goes through Afghanistan and Iran to Iraq, where the Euphrates River runs from Turkey to the Persian Gulf.[117]

Certainly it requires no great imagination to see that this great eastern power is no longer asleep, but appears ready, or gearing up, to play the role envisioned for her by the ancient prophets.

THOSE INTRIGUING ARABS

God unquestionably has a plan for the Arab peoples. Abraham's son, Ishmael, the forerunner of the Arab nations, received certain predictions and promises from God, recorded in Genesis 16:10-12 and 17:20.

God said that Ishmael would be a wild man whose hand would be against every man, with every man's hand against him. God said he would become fruitful and multiply exceedingly; he would beget twelve princes and he would become great, nationally, dwelling in the presence of his brethren.

Certainly these promises have seen at least a partial fulfilment. The Arab nations have been "wild"—that is, free and roving and fiercely independent. They have also been

220

against every man, in that they have
traditionally been warlike and have experienced much military opposition throughout
history.

Salem Kirban, a Christian Arab author and
publisher, suggests in his *Reference Bible*
that the twelve "princes" of Ishmael may
well be the present-day peoples of Lebanon,
Lyria, Yemen, Jordan, Egypt, Saudi Arabia,
Sudan, Libya, Algeria, Tunisia, Morocco and
Iraq.[118]

There are also several references in the Old
Testament, particularly Daniel 11, to the
"king of the south" (believed by many
scholars to be a reference to Egypt and/or the
north African nations) who figures promi-
nently in end-time affairs.

Unquestionably, the Arab bloc has become
a factor in our era. Far from being the
unimportant, backward desert countries
which world opinion once held them to be, the
Arabs have become a major consideration in
global affairs. Oil has done it.

The twelve nations considered to be the
"princes of Ishmael" today control three
million square miles of territory in which are
to be found two-thirds of the world's proven
oil reserves.[119] They comprise almost all of
the OPEC nations, and whether they are
raising the price of oil, as they did after the

1973 war with Israel, or forcing a glut and threatening to dump oil on the market, as they did in the early 1980s, or fighting among themselves—they are a significant factor in world affairs.

They are, without doubt, part of the end-time stir among the nations.

IN SUMMARY

The "fig tree"—Israel—and "the other trees"—all of the nations or groups of nations mentioned in end-time prophecy—certainly are on the scene and in the news today.

It is not unreasonable to conclude that their existence and activities may well be called the "putting forth of leaves."

Such a conclusion must mean that "summer"—the climax of earth's ages—is near, according to the political signs.

For Further Reading:

Campbell, D. *Daniel, Decoder of Dreams*, (Wheaton, Ill.: Victor Books, 1972).

Lindsell, H. *The Gathering Storm*, (Wheaton, Ill.: Tyndale House Publisher, Inc., 1980).

PART THREE

The Climax of the Ages

SPIRITUAL SIGNS

Satan *always* boldly attempts to counterfeit whatever God does. This drive will become surpassingly blatant at the time of the end.

Are there evidences in our day that counterfeit spiritual entities are developing, or are already in place?

Let's look, in part three at *spiritual signs* of the impending climax of human affairs.

CHAPTER ELEVEN

A Counterfeit
Church Takes Shape

One of the most unusual and graphic prophecies in all the Bible is the one found in Revelation, chapters 17 and 18.

This portion contains the description of what has come to be called the "harlot church." Most people, I am convinced, either do not understand the prophecy, or use it to condemn some church or other.

As a child I frequently heard my Uncle Fred wax eloquent in "proving" that a particular church, which I will not name, was the harlot of Revelation. It caused me, then, to give that church and its members a wide berth.

I have since come to believe very strongly that my uncle, and the school of interpretation to which he subscribed, was only *partially* right.

IT IS A CHURCH

I am convinced that the harlot of Revelation is *indeed* a church—in fact, a powerful global religious system. But I am also quite certain it is *not* the particular church my uncle believed it to be...with all due respect to his memory. I believe the harlot church definitely will contain elements of that church and many others—but that it will not be just any *one* church.

Now—if all of this talk of a church being a harlot, and of a powerful global religion is confusing to you, please "hang tough" as we attempt to explain.

LET'S DEFINE THE TERMS

Let's start with some definitions.

A harlot is a woman who has prostituted her God-given sexuality in order to sell her body's sexual functions to any number of "lovers"—in direct contrast to a wife who becomes one with her husband in a faithful, pure union.

The man/woman relationship is frequently found in Scripture as a symbol of spiritual relationships. For example, the symbol used in Scripture to describe the Church (the body of born-again believers from around the world through the ages) is that of a Bride. In Ephesians 5, and in Revelation 19, the Lord Jesus Christ is depicted as the Bridegroom— the One to whom the true Church will be married. We who are believers are the Bride of Christ whose union has not yet been consummated. In the Old Testament, Israel was said by God to have been married to Him, with sin and straying being described as "adultery."

Spiritual departure from God is frequently symbolized in Scripture by the use of terms like "adultery," "whoredom," "harlotry." A woman used symbolically in Scripture signifies religion. A good woman, like a "bride" or "wife," means good religion—the true Church. A bad woman, like a "harlot," or "whore," means an evil religious system that deceives the souls of humanity.

So when the prophet John used the term "whore" in describing the vision he had received, he was writing about a religious system which had prostituted its very existence to that which is totally contradictory to the true purpose of the Church.

A MOST UNUSUAL VISION

Look now at what John was inspired by God

to write in Revelation 17. Remember as you do that the harlot, or whore, represents a false church, and the strange beast upon which she rides represents a confederacy of nations. Read the prophecy carefully and then consider its explanation:

And there came one of the seven angels which had the seven vials, and talked with me, saying unto me, Come hither; I will shew unto thee the judgment of the great whore that sitteth upon many waters.

With whom the kings of the earth have committed fornication, and the inhabitants of the earth have been made drunk with the wine of her fornication.

So he carried me away in the spirit into the wilderness: and I saw a woman sit upon a scarlet coloured beast, full of names of blasphemy, having seven heads and ten horns.

And the woman was arrayed in purple and scarlet colour, and decked with gold and precious stones and pearls, having a golden cup in her hand full of abominations and filthiness of her fornication:

And upon her forehead was a name written, MYSTERY BABYLON THE

GREAT, THE MOTHER OF HARLOTS AND ABOMINATIONS OF THE EARTH.

And I saw the woman drunken with the blood of the saints, and with the blood of the martyrs of Jesus: and when I saw her, I wondered with great wonderment.

And the angel said unto me, Wherefore didst thou marvel? I will tell thee the mystery of the woman, and of the beast that carrieth her, which hath the seven heads and ten horns.

The beast that thou sawest was, and is not; and shall ascend out of the bottomless pit, and go into perdition: and they that dwell on the earth shall wonder, whose names were not written in the book of life from the foundation of the world, when they behold the beast that was, and is not, and yet is.

And here is the mind which hath wisdom. The seven heads are seven mountains, on which the woman sitteth.

And there are seven kings: five are fallen, and one is, and the other is not yet come; and when he cometh, he must continue a short space.

And the beast that was, and is not, even he is the eighth, and is of the seven, and goeth into perdition.

And the ten horns which thou sawest are ten kings, which have received no kingdom as yet; but receive power as kings one hour with the beast.

These have one mind, and shall give their power and strength unto the beast.

These shall make war with the Lamb, and the Lamb shall overcome them: for he is Lord of lords, and King of kings: and they that are with him are called, and chosen, and faithful.

And he saith unto me, The waters which thou sawest, where the whore sitteth, are peoples, and multitudes, and nations, and tongues.

And the ten horns which thou sawest upon the beast, these shall hate the whore, and shall make her desolate and naked, and shall eat her flesh, and burn her with fire.

For God hath put in their hearts to fulfil his will, and to agree, and give their kingdom unto the beast, until the word of God shall be fulfilled.

And the woman which thou sawest is that great city, which reigneth over the kings of the earth.

—Revelation 17:1-18

The two main figures in this prophecy are as fascinating as they are repulsive and weird.

The harlot is described as lavishly decked in jewels and gorgeous garments, holding a rich gold cup—attractive on the outside, but full of putrefaction inside. Written across her forehead is the name, "Babylon the Great, Mother of Harlots and [the] Abomination of the Earth." Most disgusting of all is the fact that she is drunk—but not with wine. She is drunk with the blood of saints and martyrs.

This brazen woman sits upon a seven-headed beast—standing near a great body of water—with the seventh head having ten horns. The Beast turns upon the harlot, strips her and devours her, finally burning her remains with fire.

Now, as I have suggested, this harlot is the substitute for the Bride of Christ, the true Church. She will spiritually seduce not only kings (that is, she will not only wield control over the leaders of nations) but also mankind in common. This is clearly indicated by the explanation that the waters by which the harlot sits are peoples, nations, races (17:15). All mankind, apart from the saints, is included.

In biblical terms, a "mystery" is something that was previously hidden but, at a definite point in time, is revealed. We perceive, then, that Mystery Babylon is a spiritual system.

SUCH A PERVERSE SYSTEM

But what kind of religion could possibly hold such sway and gain such control over Moslems, Hindus, Christians (the *nominal* kind only, since the Church will have been raptured by this time), Buddhists, atheists and so on?

Quite apparently, no *one* religion like Protestantism, or Islam, or Catholicism could get all the other religions to join it, though many such attempts have been and are being made. Unquestionably, whatever religion it is, it will have to have a strong appeal—far stronger than the pull of watered-down liberal Christianity today.

What sort of religion could this be?

The solution to the mystery is found in the name on the harlot's forehead: "Babylon the Great." The "harlot" religious system is thus associated with Babylon—a city which was more than just a city. It was an entity which, as far as the world of its day was concerned, embodied in itself *a world church*, *a world empire*, and *a world ruler* whom all nations were compelled to worship as supreme. Thus, depraved religion, enforced by government decree, and a sinful, lustful lifestyle, come to mind when Babylon is mentioned.

Proper biblical interpretation, which demands that the first use of a term in Scripture be followed in every successive use, soon confirms that we are close to solving the mystery of what religion the harlot could possibly represent.

Babylon was born when the first "world ruler," Nimrod (whose name meant "we will revolt"), built Babylon on the Plains of Shinar in the process of constructing his kingdom (Genesis 10:8-10). The first united religious act undertaken by mankind was the construction of a tower whose top would reach into the heavens (Genesis 11:4). This was the famed Tower of Babel.

There has been much misunderstanding about this tower. Those first Babylonians were *not* attempting to build a tower which could actually reach the heavens. They weren't that stupid. Rather, they were building an astrological tower—a ziggurat—which could be used to study the stars, chart their courses, cast horoscopes and make predictions. *Halley's Bible Handbook* declares that idolatrous worship was the whole purpose for the construction of the ziggurats.[120]

The prophet Isaiah, in chapter 47:12, 13, indicates that Babylon "labored with sorceries and astrology from her youth" — from the very beginnings of her history. Isaiah also prophesied that Babylon could not be delivered by her prognosticators — indicating that these practices were deeply engrained in Babylon's life.

It is a fact that astrology, sorcery, clairvoyance, conjuring and magic had their origins in the writings of the Chaldeans, who divided the heavens into the twelve sections of the zodiac and claimed that the stars control the destiny of mankind.

This religion, which obviously had its roots in the effort to build the tower of Babel, reached its pinnacle in the Babylonian Empire. History reveals that each of the Babylonian rulers built giant ziggurats for the use of their astrologers and Chaldeans.

DANIEL ADDS SOME DETAILS

The book of Daniel, which we considered in chapter six, lists the magicians, astrologers (conjurers), sorcerers and Chaldeans whom Nebuchadnezzar summoned to reveal his dream and its interpretation. These religious practitioners dealt in black magic, contact with demon spirits, materialization, witchcraft and astrology. According to Hal Lindsey in *There's a New World Coming*, the Chaldeans were a special priestly caste who could trace their family history back to the very originators of the art of astrology.[121]

The harlot represents this religion. Her dazzling external appearance suggests the appeal the system has to the sensual nature. The gold cup full of putridness symbolizes the corruption of her teachings, while her intoxication with the blood of believers indicates her method of dealing with those who oppose her.

And, for the first part of John's prophecy, the harlot rides or controls the Beast. In other words, the religious system rules the nations. John is saying that an occultic amalgamation of the world's religions—the revived Babylonian religion—will control the final world power.

A look at Revelation 17:9 and 10 confirms this. Here's what the prophet says:

And here is the mind which hath wisdom. The seven heads are seven mountains, on which the woman sitteth.

And there are seven kings: five are fallen, and one is, and the other is not yet come; and when he cometh, he must continue a short space.

This tells us that the seven heads of the beast represents *two* things: seven mountains and seven kingdoms. The seven mountains undoubtedly represent Rome—a city known around the world to be built upon seven hills.

The city of Rome in John's time was indeed controlled by the Babylonian religious system. It was the center of pagan worship and was even called "Babylon" in Scripture.

But the seven heads are also seven kingdoms—and there's more information given about these. Note Revelation 17:10 and 12:

> And there are seven kings: five are fallen, and one is, and the other is not yet come; and when he cometh, he must continue a short space.
>
> And the ten horns which thou sawest are ten kings, which have received no kingdom as yet; but receive power as kings one hour with the beast.

Five of the seven kingdoms had fallen, one was in existence at the time John wrote and one was yet to come—the seventh. The seventh is to be different from the rest—having ten horns.

THE SEVEN KINGDOMS

Now what does history reveal? Have there

been seven kingdoms controlled by the religion of Babylon? Indeed, there have been six so far.

THE FIVE THAT "ARE FALLEN." The first of these was *Assyria*, with its capital of Nineveh given over to the occult, as Nahum 3:4 clearly shows.

Next was *Egypt*, which has left us evidence of her preoccupation with the occult in those fabulously costly pyramids—all built according to astrological specification. The sphinx is supposedly the key to the twelve sections of the Zodiac.

Then there was the *Babylonian* empire, in which Daniel lived and served God. The Babylonian religious system obviously reached its zenith during this empire.

Medo-Persia conquered Babylon but was in turn "enslaved by the Babylonian religion."

The fifth of the five which had fallen by John's time was *Greece*—in which occultic religion also held sway, as history abundantly reveals.

These empires all had in common an underlying belief in astrology, which bound together witchcraft, sorcery and magic. The practitioners of these arts usually enjoyed great stature and power—with kings seldom making any move without first consulting advisors steeped in Babylon's occultic art.

THE ONE THAT IS." John referred to a kingdom that "is"—which also came under the sway of the occultic beliefs that have their origin on the plains of Shinar at the Tower of Babel. There can be no doubt that this was the mighty empire of *Rome*, whose dependence upon her augurs, sorcerers and astrologers has been immortalized in Shakespeare's Roman plays such as *Julius Caesar*.

THE ONE THAT IS "YET TO COME." This leaves only the seventh kingdom, the one described as "the other is not yet come; and when it comes it must continue a short while."

Recalling our discussion of Daniel's prophecy about the ten-nation confederacy arising out of the old Roman Empire, and comparing it with the ten horns of John's symbolic beast, it seems that this kingdom "yet to come," to be influenced by the ancient religion of Babylon, is the revived Roman Empire—the *European Common Market*.

Now, having provided this panorama of world powers seduced by the harlot, the prophet narrows his focus to the final world power—" the beast that was, and is not and will be"—and says that this king will be destroyed (17:11).

John says "even he is the eighth." His destruction fits the picture we have had sketched elsewhere, when we recall (as was discussed in chapter eight) that the Antichrist, who takes charge of the revived Roman Empire, later sets *himself* up as God.

This satanic culmination of the adulterous religious activity of sinful, rebellious mankind is in effect the eighth and final form of this diabolical, counterfeit system. But in deifying himself, the Antichrist will destroy the harlot. Though the revived Roman Empire is initially controlled by the religious system (and the Antichrist apparently goes along with it), the two are strange bedfellows. Each is trying to use the other.

Thus, at the midpoint of the seven-year treaty the Antichrist decides he no longer needs the false church. He and the false prophet have become wonder workers themselves—energized by Satan. Thus, he proclaims himself to be god—and the harlot is destroyed by him. How ironic!

COULD IT HAPPEN SOON?

Is there anything on the world religious scene today that would cause us to believe that these events could occur in the near future? I believe there is.

There are at least three trends in the world today which appear to be foreshadowings of the harlot's appearance.

The *first* is the continuing drive for a one-world church—regardless of doctrine or even religion. If you're not ''into'' this sort of thing you may not be aware of the fact that a World Council of Churches exists and has as its goal the unification of all religions—Protestant, Catholic, Buddhist, Jewish—and so on.

The World Council of Churches traces its roots back to the Universal Christian Council on Life and Work, held in Stockholm, Sweden, in 1925. Joint conferences between this council and the older International Missionary Council resulted in the formation, in Amsterdam, of the World Council of Churches in 1948.

The WCC meets every seven years in a General Assembly of delegates appointed by member churches or religious organizations. It convened in Vancouver, B.C., Canada, July 24 to August 10, 1983, for its Sixth Assembly. A 150-member Central Committee meets every six months, but the real power resides in the Secretariat in Geneva.

As Dr. J. De Forest Murch says in *The*

is composed of a wide assortment of churches which have great differences in theological doctrine, church organization and worship. They represent many nationalities, political viewpoints and sociological backgrounds. They are unitarians and trinitarians....There are dozens of different rites and liturgies of communion and worship. There are Soviet Russian Communists, other Communists, Socialists, Democrats and Republicans.[122]

On June 11, 1970, *Christian Beacon* reported "Theologians Take Steps in Dialogue With Men of Other Faiths" as the heading to a story from Zurich, Switzerland, by Ecumenical Press Service, June 2, 1970. The World Council of Churches is the main organization working for dialogue with pagan faiths.

The EPS story said: Christians must place their faith in Christ in a positive relationship to the faiths of other men if conversations between each other should *neither* betray the commitment of the Christian *nor* exploit the confidence of men of other faiths, 23 Christian theologians said here recently. They were attending a consultation on "Christians in dialogue with men of other faiths" which was a follow-up to the recent World Council-sponsored conference between Hindus, Buddhists, Christians and Muslims in Ajaltoun, Lebanon.[123]

The WCC has been the center of a great deal of controversy recently over its policy of granting funds to militant rebel groups—a total of 3.4 million since 1969, according to a March 1981 report on page seven of *The Inquirer*. One of the WCC funded groups—the Patriotic Front of Zimbabwe—was accused of the 1978 murder of 40 Rhodesian missionaries. Such a policy by a church body is quite apparently a prostitution of the biblical function of the Church. Nevertheless, the grants continue.[124]

In the March 1983 issue of the *Readers' Digest*, a major article described the involvement of the World Council of Churches (through grants) to Communist-related terrorist groups in various parts of the world.

Also early in 1983, the CBS-TV documentary program *Sixty Minutes* focused on the same topic, with devastating detail.

The World Council of Churches has been

understandably disturbed by these revelations. The April-May 1983 issue of *Canadian Ecumenical News* called them "attacks" and said that the *Digest* and *Sixty Minutes* had "deliberately chosen to slander the ecumenical movement." However, they did not deny the grants to leftist terrorist groups, but only said that this program "represents less than half of one percent of the Council's budget." [125]

The drive for a world church was reemphasized at the WCC-related European Conference of Churches, October 1979, when Dr. Lukas Vischu, a Swiss Reform clergyman, and the Eastern Orthodox Ecumenical patriarch Dimitrios I, united in urging the Roman Catholic church to join forces with the World Council of Churches.

The Signs of the Times, (January 1981 issue) under the headline "Churches Building Bridges," said that "the movement to bridge gaps among the churches, to unite them all into one great super church, may not get headlines these days, but it is advancing with increasing momentum." [126]

The 1979 visit of Pope John Paul II to the Orthodox Ecumenical Patriarch Demetrios in Istanbul; the January 1982 Lima "convergence document," agreed upon by representatives of the Roman Catholic, Eastern Orthodox, Oriental Orthodox, Lutheran, Reformed, Anglican, United, Baptist, Methodist, Disciples and Adventist traditions; the 1982 moves toward Protestant union in the U.S.; the visit of the Pope to Canterbury Cathedral and a joint worship service there in May 1982 — all are indications of an accelerating push for church union within the *Christian* realm.

In addition to the WCC's one-church drive within the Christian world, consultations between the WCC and various other religions continue. In 1982, two such meetings were held. The first was in Sri Lanka, March 30-April 1, and was jointly sponsored by the WCC and by the World Muslim Congress of Karachi, Pakistan. It brought together representatives from 30 different Christian churches to confer with 33 Muslims. The consultation ended with a call for "the establishment of a joint Standing Committee between the World Muslim Congress and the World Council of Churches." A report of the meeting concluded with

...It is very much hoped that the joint Standing Committee could seek representation soon from other international Islamic organizations and from the

Roman Catholic Church. This meeting certainly represented a historic first in the reconciliation process between Muslims and Christians. [127]

A second 1982 meeting was called by the WCC Unit on Dialogue with People of Living Faiths and Ideologies. It met June 28 to July 6 in Hawaii to "grapple with the complex question of traditional cultures," including how to *reaffirm* these faiths and cultures.

If the concept of bringing together faiths with such widely divergent views as the ones mentioned in the foregoing news stories seems strange, the words of the WCC's First General Secretary, Willem Visser't Hooft, must be recalled. He said, "In the World Council, there is a new creation—churches agreeing to disagree *on aspects of faith* but committed to seeking its fullness together" (emphasis mine).[128]

While the goal of a single global church has undoubtedly been in the minds of churchmen for many years, the concrete efforts to achieve it are only of recent vintage. Now the amazing spread of the philosophy of secular humanism, defined in the *Humanist Manifestos I and II*, published in 1933 and 1973, has given this drive a powerful global push, especially in the West.

Certainly an ecumenized, doctrinely liberal church of externals, without real spiritual life, could easily accept all religions into one super-church in the climate which now exists. I may offend some of my readers, but I am certain that the global drive for a one-world church is a forerunner, at least, of the counterfeit church.

THAT OLD BLACK MAGIC

A *second* trend is the turn to the *supernatural*—including the occult—on the part of North Americans, accompanied by a great revival of spiritism all over the world. At a conference in Arrowhead Springs, California, in late 1979, I heard Dr. Charles Malik, former president of the United Nations, cite the revival of paganism and spiritism as one of the most disturbing trends of our day.

Even in "sophisticated" America interest in witchcraft, the occult, the horoscope and numerous related supernatural topics has mushroomed.

Many magazines, like *McCalls*, *Esquire* and *Time*, ran feature articles at the beginning of the 1970s on what then was termed "the occult explosion." Movies, books, magazines and encyclopedias of the supernatural abound. Entire bookstores devoted to the occult are not uncommon. Universities regularly offer courses on witchcraft and magic—usually the so-called "white" variety. Myriads of mystical Eastern religions, bizarre and often demonic, have invaded North America—discovering in most cases an amazing responsiveness.

Some time ago, I visited a neighbor who was hospitalized in a nearby city. As we sat and chatted I was amazed to see, out on the lawn of the hospital, a young woman engaged in a series of physical gyrations that suggested to my mind a form of bizarre worship. I later discovered that her antics were, indeed, acts of worship to an Eastern deity! And this in public—in a "Bible-belt" section of conservative Canada!

THE "TURNED ON" CROWD

Then there's the *drug epidemic*, which scarcely needs to be documented. The reason for its being related to the emergence of a one-world counterfeit church does need to be spelled out, however.

In Revelation 9:21, a group of people whom the prophet foresees as experiencing the judgments of God are described as, in spite of that judgment, "repenting not of their murders, nor of their sorceries, nor of their fornication, nor of their thefts." The nationally-known Canadian evangelist, Barry Moore, in a message on the source of the drug problem, points out that the word translated "sorceries" in the above portion is significant. It comes from the Greek word *pharmakeia* which is the word from which we get our English word "pharmacy"—or drugstore. It means a drug-related kind of occult worship or black magic. [129]

And Revelation 18—referring to the harlot's false religious system—charges that "all the nations were deceived by your *sorcery*"—using the same word, *pharmakeia*.

There can be little question that Satan uses hallucinatory drugs to take people to a deeper level of satanic influence and control. An individual whom I, along with others, had the awesome privilege of helping to deliverance from deep entanglement in witchcraft and demonic control confirms that this is so—from personal experience and observation.

So when these three trends are observed to be having a strong impact on the world, it is apparent that the prophecies concerning "mystery Babylon" must be in the early stages of their fulfilment.

An additional comment must be made here concerning the belief (held by some observers of the religious scene) that *certain* aspects of the charismatic movement could be a unifying factor in terms of the final phony super-church.

It *is* a fact that a wide variety of groups, ranging all the way from bona fide Pentecostals, through cults like "The Way," to pagan, eastern and Satanic religions, practice speaking in unknown tongues.

It is also a fact that the charismatic experience in *some* Christian circles tends to make people ready and willing to accept fellow charismatics *regardless* of their stand on biblical or doctrinal matters.

While I do recognize that there is a true and valid charisma, such attitudes as described above provide a basis for the view that a strong *counterfeit* charismatic movement *could* be a powerful added force in creating the harlot church. If indeed a counterfeit charismatic element does play a future role, certainly what is occurring in the world today has to be viewed as creating the climate for the pressure for religious union.

IN CONCLUSION

Brooks Alexander, of Spiritual Counterfeits Project, Inc., sums it up well in his article, "The Coming World Religion."

He points out that one of the startling features of early stages of the awful period during which the Antichrist is on the scene will be an unprecedented religious *unity*!

Alexander says that the apocalyptic vision of John is one of "ultimate totalitarianism, in which political power, economic control, *religious worship*, *occult gnosis*, *psychic power*, and personal charisma will be combined in a unified system of oppression and delusion called 'Mystery Babylon'!" (Emphasis mine).[130]

The realization of such a prediction is certainly well within the realm of the foreseeable—at this point!

For Further Reading:

Cumbey, C. *The Hidden Dangers of the Rainbow*, (Shreveport, La.: Huntingdon House, Inc., 1982).

Goetz, W.R. *Apocalypse Next*, (Beaverlodge: Horizon House, 1981), chapter nine.

Lindsey, H. *There's a New World Coming* (Santa Ana, Ca: Vision House Publishers, 1973).

As non-theists, we begin with humans, not God—nature, not deity.

Humanist Manifesto II

CHAPTER TWELVE

The Battle
For The Mind

In an article entitled "Humanism...the Grand Delusion," Dr. Bill Bright, founder of Campus Crusade, suggests that if you were asked, "What do you think is the most dangerous religion in America?", you might name Scientology, the Unification Church, or some other cult or eastern religion.

Dr. Bright goes on to say that "...it may surprise you to learn that I believe the most dangerous religion is *humanism*." [131]

I agree fully with his view. Not only has humanism, in his words, "become the greatest threat to our Judeo-Christian heritage and is doing more to destroy the moral and spiritual fiber of our society than any other peril," but it is, I am convinced, *setting the stage, spiritually, for the Antichrist and Armageddon.*

What, precisely, do we mean by the term "humanism," and why is it called a religion?

A CLEAR DEFINITION

Note: This may take a while, but it is extremely important. And if you're tempted to ask, "What has this to do with the end times?"—hang tough. I hope to show you how it relates very definitely to earth's awesome climax.

Webster's *New World Dictionary* defines humanism as being "any system of thought or action based on the nature, dignity, interests, and ideals of man....A modern, non-theistic, rationalist movement which holds that man is capable of self-fulfilment, ethical conduct, etc., without recourse to supernaturalism."

In other words, Man can make it, just fine, on his own—*without God!*

Humanism actually can be traced back to the Garden of Eden and "The Lie" of Satan by which he deceived Eve. There, he said that if Eve ate of the fruit of the tree—forbidden to her by God—she and Adam would "be as gods, *knowing* [that is, *deciding for themselves*] good and evil" (Genesis 3:5). The Hebrew word translated "knowing" is *yada*—meaning "to ascertain." So Satan's appeal was: Eat the forbidden fruit. Then *you'll* be able to decide, without any recourse to God, what is good or evil, right or wrong!

In more "modern" times, philosophers like Protagoras ("Man is the measure of things"), Socrates and Aristotle expounded humanistic themes.

In the renaissance in Italy and in the 18th century French Enlightenment, there was a revival of humanistic philosophy, with people like Voltaire and Rousseau as leaders. The European universities became secular and this bias was later transferred to America.

Then, in 1933, 34 humanists in America drafted and signed what was called a "Humanist Manifesto." In 1973, *Humanist Manifesto II* was written and endorsed by thousands of humanists in America and abroad.

Secular humanists completely deny the existence of God. "We find insufficient evidence for belief in the existence of a supernatural; it is either meaningless or, irrelevant to the question of survival and fulfilment of the human race," says *Humanist Manifesto II*. "As non-theists, we begin with humans, not God—nature, not deity."

The 1973 *Manifesto* goes on to state, "Promises of immortal salvation or fear of eternal damnation are both illusionary and harmful."

Humanists insist that man is the product of evolution—which, of course, rules God out. Humanist Corliss Lamont in his book, *The Philosophy of Humanism*, writes:

> Biology has conclusively shown that man and all other forms of life were the result, not of a supernatural act of creation by God, but of an infinitely long process of evolution probably stretching over at least two billion years. [132]

Humanists also maintain that man is basically good and any sinful tendencies are the product of environment, not man's nature.

So of course, if you believe (as the humanists do) that man is the product of evolution, and is basically good, then what's wrong with adultery, premarital sex, lying, abortion, homosexuality—provided no one is hurt? "We affirm that moral values derive their source from human experience," states the *Humanist Manifesto II*. "There are *no* absolutes."

Thus, euthanasia, even suicide, are okay too. Why not?—since there is no God or divine law.

Quite logically, the *Humanist Manifesto* advocates the creation of a global community "based upon *transnational* federal government" and ordered by humanistic principles: Man is supreme. There is no God.

Now, before we underscore how this fits into the end-time prophecies, let's note why humanism is properly considered a religion.

LET US WORSHIP

Humanism is recognized as a religion, even by many humanists, because it advocates *"worshipping"* man instead of God as a philosophy of life.

And the Supreme Court of the United States, in the Torcaso v. Watkins case, in 1961, stated, "Among *religions* in this country which do not teach what would generally be considered a belief in the existence of God are Buddhism, Taoism, Ethical Culture, *Secular Humanism* and others" (emphasis mine).[133]

Dr. Tim La Haye, in his *Battle For the Mind*, contrasts the two religions of

Christianity and Humanism in the following way (read from the bottom up): [134]

	Compassion-ate World View	Socialist One-World Order
WORLD VIEW	Compassion-ate World View	Socialist One-World Order
WHY ARE WE HERE?	Servant Attitude	Autonomous Man
HOW SHOULD WE BEHAVE?	Morality	Amorality
HOW DID WE GET HERE?	Creation	Evolution
SOURCE	God	Atheism
BASIS	The Bible	The Writings of the Philosophers
	CHRISTIANITY	**HUMANISM**

This religion has gripped the thinking of modern man. Dr. Francis Schaeffer, considered by many to be the foremost evangelical philosopher of the day and author of more than a dozen books and originator of three epic film series, has written, "...The consensus of our society no longer rests on a Judeo-Christian base—but rather on a humanistic one. *In our time* humanism has replaced Christianity as the consensus of the West." (emphasis mine).[135]

256

Renowned Russian author, Aleksandr Solzhenitsyn, in a memorable commencement address to the 1978 graduating class of Harvard, said that

> ...destructive and irresponsible individual freedom has been granted boundless space [in the western culture].
>
> Such a tilt of freedom in the direction of evil has come about gradually, but it was evidently born primarily out of a humanistic and benevolent concept according to which there is no evil inherent to human nature; the world belongs to mankind and all the defects of life are caused by wrong social systems which must be corrected.... [136]

Humanist Paul Kurtz, editor of *Humanist Manifesto II*, wrote in 1975: "Humanist attitudes are becoming more firmly established in our society."

HOW HAS IT HAPPENED?

The public educational systems and the media throughout North America (and the world, for that matter) have played key roles in "humanizing" our culture.

Humanist Paul Blanschard wrote, "I think that the most important factor moving us toward a secular society has been the educational factor. [It]...tends to lead toward the elimination of religious superstition.''[137]

The effect of the media, especially television, on manners and morals scarcely needs documentation. Pay television and earth dishes make available rank pornography and violence. And the continual chipping away at morals and values in the entire media suggests that morality really is ''an individual choice.''

IT'S PREPARATION FOR ARMAGEDDON

Because of these conditions, I feel that as never before in human history the climate is right, the soil is fertile, and the times are receptive for the rapid, widespread acceptance of ''The Lie.''

The degree to which the climate has been dramatically changed is well documented by McCandlish Philipps (a Pulitzer award-winning journalist, formerly of the *N.Y. Times*) in his massive book, *The Bible, The Supernatural and The Jew*. Philipps points out that when a deliberate attempt was made, early in the century, by proponents of eastern religions to ''invade'' North America, they were rebuffed by the spiritual life of this continent. However, even by the 1970s when

Philipps wrote, the tide had turned. Acceptance of eastern and occult religions was widespread. Such acceptance is even greater today.

In this, a similarity to ancient Rome at the time of its fall may be seen. Then (as now) any and all religions were acceptable—except true Christianity! Such a bias is frequently to be found today on university, college and high school campuses—whereby non-Christian religions are allowed freedom to function on campus, and in many cases are actually taught in courses, but Christian groups and activities are banned! [138]

This continued acceptance of "The Lie," while biblical truth is ruled out, will lead logically to Armageddon—the second of three prophesied end-time wars yet to come (see chart on page 265)—in which a godless mankind is united to do armed conflict with God.

IT'S ANTI-GOD

Armageddon *will not be just a conflict between men and nations*, though there will be an attack upon the chosen people, Israel. Rather, Armageddon is *a battle between a Satan-inspired and controlled world and Christ!*

The confrontation at Armageddon is incited by the unholy trinity of Satan, the Antichrist and the False Prophet. They will send dispatches to all nations ordering them to come to Palestine for this battle against the One whom they consider to be their heavenly oppressor.

They will come to shake their fists in the face of God in a massive demonstration and protest against His devastating judgments. They will rattle their sabres of war in battle against God. While such insanity appears now to be inconceivable, remember the strong delusion under which they will labor, the absence of the Church, and the increased depravity of mankind. Three years or more of steady brainwashing by the Antichrist and the false prophet while experiencing the continuous wrath of God will thoroughly condition mankind to do Satan's bidding and rise up against God. In their deluded state, they will think that, with advanced missile technology and nuclear weapons, they can blow God out of His heaven.*

Psalm Two describes their condition:

Why do the heathen rage, and the people imagine a vain thing?

The kings of the earth set themselves, and the rulers take counsel together, against the Lord, and against his anointed, saying,

Let us break their bands asunder, and cast away their cords from us.

He that sitteth in the heavens shall laugh: the Lord shall have them in derision.

Then shall he speak unto them in his wrath, and vex them in his sore displeasure.

The outcome will be swift and deadly. By a word from His mouth Christ will destroy the armies of the ungodly. Antichrist and the false prophet will be cast into the lake of fire. Satan will be bound in the abyss for a thousand years—all by Christ's mighty power.

PAUL AND JOHN FORESEE THE BATTLE

The outcome of Armageddon is described by both the Apostle Paul and John. These portions of Scripture very definitely indicate that a Christ-rejecting, anti-God mankind will obviously be so completely deceived by "The Lie" of Satan, his counterfeit Christ, the Anti-Christ, and the false prophet, that it will be thought possible for godless humanity to actually fight against God!

In his letter to the Thessalonians, Paul reassures his readers that the day of judgment has not yet come, since there must first be a "falling away" and the coming to power of Antichrist (2 Thess. 2:3). Paul goes on to describe this "man of sin" as one "who opposeth and exalteth himself above all that is called God, or that is worshipped; so that he as God sitteth in the temple of God, shewing himself that he is God" (verse 4).

Only the presence of the Church—"who now hindereth" (verse 7)—now prevents the full revelation of the Antichrist. When the Church is "taken out of the way" in the rapture, the result will be devastating. The acceptance of "The Lie" will be tremendously accelerated when the salt and light of the world have been snatched away. Then virtually nothing will hold back its global acceptance.

And then shall that Wicked [Antichrist] be revealed, whom the Lord shall consume with the spirit of his mouth, and shall destroy with the brightness of his coming:

Even him, whose coming is after the working of Satan with all power and signs and lying wonders.

And with all deceivableness of

unrighteousness in them that perish; because they received not the love of the truth, that they might be saved.

And for this cause God shall send them strong delusion, that they should believe a lie: [Many translate this as *"the* lie."]

That they all might be damned who believed not the truth, but had pleasure in unrighteousness.

—2 Thessalonians 2:8-12

As Paul states in the passage from 2 Thessalonians above, Antichrist and his forces will be destroyed by the Lord—a reference to the battle Armageddon. John gives us a vivid picture of Christ and His victorious army in Revelation:

And I saw heaven opened, and behold a white horse; and he that sat upon him was called Faithful and True, and in righteousness he doth judge and make war.

His eyes were as a flame of fire, and on his head were many crowns; and he had a name written, that no man knew, but he himself.

And he was clothed with a vesture dipped in blood: and his name is called The Word of God.

And the armies which were in heaven followed him upon white horses, clothed in fine linen, white and clean.

And out of his mouth goeth a sharp sword, that with it he should smite the nations: and he shall rule them with a rod of iron: and he treadeth the winepress of the fierceness and wrath of Almighty God.

And he hath on his vesture and on his thigh a name written, KING OF KINGS, AND LORD OF LORDS.

—Revelation 19:11-16

The incredibly rapid rise and spread of the secular humanistic philosophy in the world today is, I believe, an all-important part of the preparation for, as well as an indicator of, the nearness of Armageddon.

Indeed, the hour must be late.

For Further Reading:

Gothard, W. *Be Alert to Spiritual Danger* (Wheaton, Ill.: IBYC, 1979).

La Haye, T. *The Battle for the Mind*, (Old Tappen, N.J.: Flemming H. Revell, 1980).

The Humanist Manifestos, I and II, 1933, 1973. (Buffalo: Prometheus Books, 1973).

EVENT	PARTICIPANTS	TIME	REASON	OUTCOME
First War Invasion of Israel Ezek. 38, 39	Russia and allies vs. Israel	Just before the Tribulation or possibly during the very first part of the first 3½ years.	Russia desires Israel's vast mineral wealth, oil and strategic location.	God will intervene and through an earthquake in Israel plus supernatural rain and hail, five-sixths of the Russian army will be wiped out. It will take the Israelites 7 months to bury the dead and 7 years to collect and burn the debris.
Second War Armageddon Joel 3:9, 12 Zech. 14:1-4 2 Thess. 2:8 Rev. 16:13-16 Rev. 19:11-21	Armies from all nations vs. God and Israel	At the end of 7-year Tribulation period.	Flushed with power, and furious over God's judgments in the Tribulation, the Anti-Christ will defy God, seek to destroy the nation of Israel, and Jerusalem.	The Lord Jesus Christ comes down from heaven and destroys, by His very appearance, the combined armies of more than 200 million men. The bloodbath covers 185-200 miles of Israel and blood is splashed "even unto the horse bridles" (Rev. 14:20). Antichrist and the false prophet are cast alive into the Lake of Fire (Rev. 19:20). Satan is bound in the bottomless pit for 1000 years (Rev. 20:1-3).
Third War Final Rebellion Rev. 20:7-10	Satan and those deceived by him vs. God	At end of 1000-year Millennium period.	God allows Satan one more opportunity on Earth to preach his deceiving message in order to give those born in the Millennium a 'Garden of Eden' choice.	Satan will be successful in deceiving millions of those born during the millennial period to turn away from Christ. This horde of people will completely circle the believers and encompass Jerusalem in a state of siege. When this occurs God brings fire down from heaven killing the multi-millions in Satan's army. Satan is then cast into the Lake of Fire where the false prophet and Antichrist are, and they will be "tormented day and night forever."

Three End-Time Wars

PART FOUR

The Climax of the Ages

OTHER SIGNS

Birth pangs.

They begin at a given point in time, and then—usually gradually—begin to increase in both *frequency* and *intensity* until the actual moment of birth occurs.

Nearly 2,000 years ago, Jesus Christ foretold that certain events would occur in the future. He called these events "birth pangs" which would precede His revelation from heaven and the establishment of His Kingdom in earth's climactic age.

Let's look at the evidence for believing that this generation is witnessing the onset of those prophesied "birth pangs."

"What will be the sign of Your coming?"
— question of the disciples to Jesus

CHAPTER THIRTEEN

The Prophecies Of Jesus And Daniel

The time was just two days before Jesus Christ was crucified.

The location was outside the Temple in Jerusalem.

In the crowd which thronged that special place were Jesus and His disciples. The disciples, undoubtedly with a sense of pride, were commenting on the beauty of the stately building with its fine stonework and elaborate ornamentations. And properly so. For, though it could never compare for magnificence with the original Solomon's Temple, still Herod's Temple was a splendid structure.

Suddenly, and totally unexpectedly, Jesus said, "Do you see all these things? Truly I say to you, there shall not be left one stone upon another that shall not be thrown down."

The disciples were astonished and dismayed. Later they came to Jesus privately and asked Him three questions. They inquired:

1. "When shall these things be?"
2. "What shall be the sign of Your coming?" and
3. "[What shall be the sign] of the end of the world?"

Jesus' reply is recorded in Matthew 24 and Luke 21. It is called "the Olivet discourse" because it was uttered on the Mount of Olives.

Here is the Luke account of that answer:

And he said, Take heed that ye be not deceived; for many shall come in my name, saying, I am Christ; and the time draweth near; go ye not therefore after them.

But when ye shall hear of wars and commotions, be not terrified; for these things must first come to pass; but the end is not by and by.

Then he said unto them, Nation shall rise against nation, and kingdom against kingdom:

And great earthquakes shall be in divers places, and famines, and pestilences; and fearful sights and great signs shall there be from heaven.

But before all these, they shall lay their hands on you, and persecute you, delivering you up to the synagogues, and into prisons, being brought before kings and rulers for my name's sake.

And it shall turn to you for a testimony.

Settle it therefore in your hearts, not to meditate before what ye shall answer:

For I will give you a mouth and wisdom, which all your adversaries shall not be able to gainsay nor resist.

And ye shall be betrayed both by parents, and brethren, and kinsfolks, and friends; and some of you shall they cause to be put to death.

And ye shall be hated of all men for my name's sake.

But there shall not an hair of your head perish.

In your patience possess ye your souls.

And when ye shall see Jerusalem compassed with armies, then know that the desolation thereof is nigh.

Then let them which are in Judaea flee

to the mountains; and let them which are in the midst of it depart out; and let not them that are in the countries enter thereinto.

For these be the days of vengeance, that all things which are written may be fulfilled.

But woe unto them that are with child, and to them that give suck, in those days! for there shall be great distress in the land, and wrath upon this people.

And they shall fall by the edge of the sword, and shall be led away captive into all nations: and Jerusalem shall be trodden down of the Gentiles, until the times of the Gentiles be fulfilled.

And there shall be signs in the sun, and in the moon, and in the stars; and upon the earth distress of nations, with perplexity; the sea and the waves roaring;

Men's hearts failing them for fear, and for looking after those things which are coming on the earth: for the powers of heaven shall be shaken.

And then shall they see the Son of man coming in a cloud with power and great glory.

And when these things begin to come to pass, then look up, and lift up your heads; for your redemption draweth nigh.

—Luke 21:8-28

These events, then, are to be seen as *preliminary* to the coming of the Son of Man in a cloud with power and great glory—even as birth pangs precede a birth.

LET'S SET SOME GROUND RULES

Now before we proceed any further in categorizing the signs, or in looking at current events in their light, we need to lay a few basic ground rules.

To do so, it is necessary that we become a bit ''technical'' in theological terms. However, it is essential for us to do so; otherwise it would be very easy to jump to the wrong conclusions. So bear with us for this brief review.

There are several ways of interpreting this prophecy of Jesus:

One view says it was all fulfilled in the past and applies only to what has already occurred. The problem with such a view is to explain how Jesus could have already returned—at the time of the destruction of Jerusalem!

A second view holds that the prophecy applies to this entire ''church age'' in which we now live, and especially the closing days of it. Proponents of the view hold that the Church thus experiences the Tribulation.

A third view, and the one held by this author, is that *the prophecy has exclusive reference to the Jewish nation and Jewish believers.* It also has a double reference—part of it having had its fulfillment when the Romans under Titus destroyed the Temple and Jerusalem, with the remainder yet to be fulfilled in the final period of God's dealing with the entire earth in relation to, and through, the Jewish nation.*

Obviously, the actual signs of His appearing which Jesus prophesied had in many instances a prior fulfillment at Jerusalem's fall. But while they will be finally literally fulfilled in the last seven years prior to the establishment of Christ's kingdom upon earth, *they will not burst suddenly upon the world. They will rather be preceded by a building toward their appearance.* Just as a

---

*Reasons for holding that this has exclusive reference to the Jews are that the term "synagogue" is frequently used; specific geographical locations such as Jerusalem and Judaea are mentioned; and the hearers are urged to pray that their flight would not be on the sabbath--all indicators pointing to the fact that Israel, not the Church, is in view here.

birth is preceded by birth pangs which increase in intensity and frequency, so these actual signs—the literal ones to occur right before the appearing of Christ—will be immediately preceded by similar signs or the *beginning* of the *same* signs throughout the earth.

And, if the soon return of Christ with His saints is indicated by the appearance of these indicators, how much nearer must be the snatching away of the Church which, I believe, precedes the return by seven years?

So, to summarize these preliminary components, the *actual* events prophesied by Jesus in Matthew 24 and Luke 21 will occur *between* the rapture and the return, during the tribulation. The *indicators* we will consider now are *similar* events obviously building up to those actual fulfillments.

TEN IMPORTANT INDICATORS

A synopsis of the two accounts of Jesus' prophecy provides us with the following ten great indicators of His return:

1. *Wars*, and as a part of that sign, rumors of wars, commotions, nation rising against nation and kingdom against kingdom.

2. *Great earthquakes* in various places.

3. *Famines*.

4. *Pestilences.*

5. Unusual, frightening *signs in the heavens*, including fearful sights, great signs from the heavens, signs in the sun, moon and stars, with the powers of heaven being shaken.

6. *Jerusalem restored to Jewish control* AFTER a worldwide dispersion and return to Israel by the Jews.

7. *Distress* of nations, *with perplexity.*

8. Men's hearts failing them for *fear* of what is coming on the earth.

9. *False Christs.*

10. *A worldwide proclamation of the Gospel.*

That's the list Jesus gave His disciples.

LOOK AT WHAT'S HAPPENING TODAY

When I wrote *Apocalypse Next* just over two years ago, I included a chapter on the prophecies of Jesus which we are considering now. After listing the ten signs of the beginnings of birth pangs, or sorrows, I prefaced a look at the then current scene with these words:

As we set out to see what's happening in our world today in relationship to these indicators, I frankly confess a major problem. There is so much

276

material about each of these that a whole chapter, or even an entire book, could be written on each one. My problem is to somehow adequately condense these mountains of data into the space available and still do justice to it all.

In the few months since I wrote that, the indicators have become, in my judgment, *far* more numerous and *far* more obvious. The problem of selecting for this chapter those which are most illustrative is much more difficult now than it was when I wrote *Apocalypse*. And that fact indicates as clearly as anything can the rapidity with which developments appear to be occurring.

Let's look at the current "birth pangs."

1. WARS AND RUMORS OF WARS

Virtually everyone who listened regularly to radio or television or who read the newspapers throughout 1982, was made very much aware of three large scale wars which raged in that year—one of which is still ongoing at the time of this writing.

The Falklands, Lebanese and Afghanistan wars were truly major conflicts. The Afghanistan war, which began in December 1979, drags on with no sign of an end in sight.

And while people could scarcely escape the

fact of these major 1982 wars, what few realize is that, in the past few years, literally dozens of wars have been going on in scores of nations around the world.

Consider just a few of the headlines and items I've pulled from my files:

On January 11, 1980, the *Chicago Tribune* reported in a news map feature:

> At this moment, in nations scattered throughout the world, 23 major armed conflicts are taking place. More than 8 million soldiers and paramilitary personnel are directly or indirectly involved.... As many as 5 million have already been killed. The total number of wounded and maimed could be three times that.[139]

In March 1980, Major General Donald McNichol, Commander of Canada's Air Defence Group, said "War with USSR [is] 'inevitable.'"[140]

U.S. News and World Report carried a Special Report—Powder Keg entitled, "Central America: Why Such a Hotbed?"[141] And *Christian Life* carried this item in 1980:

> ...Harvard's 'Russian Research Center' has concluded that the Soviets believe they can fight, win and survive a nuclear war. The House Armed Services

Committee has reported that the U.S. strategic position has deteriorated so greatly that 'we are now unable to deter a first strike by the USSR....'The *Intelligence Digest* of England says that the most probable time for the Russians to be militarily aggressive is within the next three to five years....China's Vice-Premier has stated that World War III is "unavoidable." ' [142]

The Economist, in September 1981, published a newsmap of Africa which showed 39 African nations in which a total of 150,785 soldiers from Russia, Cuba, France, Morocco, South Africa, Britain, the U.S., East Germany, Israel, Egypt, Libya, Red China, Belgium, North Korea and several eastern European nations were active in nations other than their own. On that date, five "major conflicts" were in progress. [143]

"Can U.S. Stem Tide of Revolution At Its Doorstep?" a *U.S. News and World Report* article asked of the massive upheaval going on in Central America. [144]

A November 1980 *Moody Monthly* article entitled "Wars and Rumors of Wars" began with the statement: "Two dozen major and minor armed conflicts around the world are documented by the Center of Defense

Information in Washington, D.C." [145]

The sobering cover of *Maclean's* magazine, February 15, 1982, asked the question: "Is World War III Inevitable?" The feature story inside concluded that it is. [146]

United Press International reported on March 7, 1982, that "Europeans Prefer War to Russians." A Gallup poll throughout Europe revealed that a majority of those polled felt it would be better to go to war than accept Russian domination. [147]

The June 28, 1982, *Newsweek* cover carried the bold yellow title "Wars Without End" on a bright red slash across two war scenes. [148]

The August 16, 1982, *U.S. News and World Report* article, "Where the Military is in Charge," cited 38 nations under such control, and reported that "military strong men have seized power on every continent except North America and Australia within the past year." [149]

"Almost Unnoticed, Central America's Civil War Has Begun"—declares a Vancouver, B.C., *Province* headline. "Grenada falls under Soviet spell" is another headline on the same page. It details how avowed Marxist-Leninists had replaced a pro-American government. Grenada's is the third Marxist government in the Western Hemisphere. A major naval base and airport, accessible to Soviet ships and planes, are under construction on the island.[150]

"UN Urged to Combat 'New Global Anarchy' " the Reuters news agency reported. UN Secretary General Javier Perez de Cuellar warned, "We are perilously near to a new international anarchy." He criticized "the current tendency to resort to confrontation, violence and even war" in pursuit of what are seen as vital interests, claims or aspirations. "Such a trend must be reversed before once again we bring upon ourselves a global catastrophe and find ourselves without institutions effective enough to prevent it." [151]

Whether or not the experts quoted above are accurate in their assessments of the future is not really the issue. The fact is that their speculations and pronouncements, right or wrong, certainly constitute "rumors of wars" to go alongside many actual wars.

Of course there have always been wars throughout human history—but now, tragically, the tempo and severity of war is rapidly accelerating. In the twentieth century alone we have had over 200 armed conflicts.

There have been the "minor" wars: the Russo-Japanese war (1904-05); the Balkan wars (1912-13); the Spanish Civil war

(1937-39); the Colombian Civil war (1948-53); the Korean war (1950-53); the Viet Nam war (1963-73); the Lebanese Civil war (1973-82); the Afghanistan "Civil" war (1979-), as well as the Falklands and Lebanese wars (1982). In these wars well over 2.5 million soldiers and another million or so civilians died.

There have also been the two major World Wars, in 1914-18 and 1939-45, in which 10 million and 51 million, respectively, perished.[152]

And the frightful arms race goes on. More and more nations are expected to join the nuclear arms club, with 35 projected to possess such arms by the end of the 1980s.

Awesome new weapons—superkiller subs, planes, chemical warfare, neutron bombs and fearful space laser weapons—are being steadily added to the major arsenals of the world. In an article entitled, "How Do You Measure a Trillion Dollars?",* Dennis Robertson says that a conservative estimate of the money spent by all nations on national defense since World War II is *$4 trillion!*[153]

And the fear grows when one remembers the chilling observation that "mankind has

---

*For a person to spend a trillion dollars, at the rate of $1 million per day, would require that person to live 2.75 centuries!--according to Robertson.

yet to invent a weapon it has not eventually used.''

An editorial in the January 18, 1983, issue of *The Vancouver Sun* seems to sum up how most informed people feel about the possibility—or probability—of all-out war. The editor says:

> If the 136-page secret document made available to United Press International by what the news agency describes as ''sources familiar with defence issues'' represents only a part of U.S. thinking and planning on nuclear arms control, the world is already under sentence of death.
>
> The document, accompanied by a covering memorandum dated March 22, 1982, signed by U.S. Defence Secretary Caspar Weinberger, ignores as a general guideline any possibility of accommodation or peaceful coexistence with the Soviet Union, concentrating instead on preparations for winning an extended nuclear war and for waging war ''effectively'' from outer space. [154]

Wars and rumors of wars indeed.

2. EARTHQUAKES

Again, earthquakes are not unique to our

age. But, as with wars, their frequency and severity is dramatically increasing.

A prominent historian of seismology, after nearly a lifetime of study, reckons that major earthquakes have increased in frequency from 137 in the fourteenth century to thousands in our time.[155]

The 1976 World Almanac reported that 38 of the 57 greatest earthquakes in history occurred in this century. Another six major quakes that year alone added to the percentage of recent quakes.

A *Gemini News Service* article, "The Age of Disaster," says "experts warn that we are in the 'age of earthquakes.' The period up to the middle 1980s will be one of exceptional activity." [156]

The 1981 *Readers' Digest article*, "Where Will the Next Earthquake Strike?", details the fears of seismologists over the "50 percent chance that a major quake [in southern California] will occur within a decade." [157]

Tragically, the reports of earthquakes, with their attendant human suffering and loss of life, are frequent news headlines. The following is a listing, with dates, of a few of the main captions from my files:

August 30, 1980 "Deadly Krakatoa Builds

Up for Another Big Explosion—due to shifting of earth's crust"

November 29, 1980 "Biting winds, mud piling new misery on quake survivors" (3,000 dead, 1,500 injured, 300,000 homeless in Naples, Italy)

February 5, 1981 "Strong Quake Kills 5 in Greece"

March 11, 1981 "Second Quake Hits Greece"

March 21, 1981 "The Quake Menace" (Feature story detailing the quake danger in Vancouver, B.C.)

March 30, 1981 "Washington State is Jittery over its Rash of Earthquakes"

April 17, 1981 "San Francisco Recalls its Shaky Past" (with a major earthquake drill)

February 7, 1982 "Plans Made to Find Killers after Possible L.A. Quake"

March 20, 1982 "Volcano Explodes Twice" (Quakes beneath Mt. St. Helens trigger eruptions)

June 20, 1982 "Salvador Death Toll Rises in Aftermath of Big Quake"

December 20, 1982 "Death Toll Hits 3,000 in Quake" (North Yemen devastated)

January 8, 1983 "Quakes Rattle California" [158]

The beginning of "sorrows"? It very much looks like it.

3. FAMINES

Somewhere around the year 2004, this already hungry planet of ours will have 55 percent more people on it than it has right now. [159]

Dr. Albert Sabin, developer of the polio vaccine which bears his name, made a statement in 1974 as reported in the *Toronto Star-News*: "If changes are not made now, by the year 2000 there is doubt as to whether we will survive. By that time, there will be six billion people in the world and four and a half billion of them will be *starving*, un-educated and totally desperate." [160]

George Borgstrom, former professor of food sciences at Michigan State University wrote in *The Hungry Planet*:

> The rising tide of people threatens to deprive the human race of its future....If the world population continues to expand at the present rate, within 120 years the present production of food stuffs will have to be increased *eightfold* if even present standards are maintained, and yet these are inadequate for more than half of the *present* number of people.[161]

Again, glance over my shoulder at some of the headlines from my files:

July 13, 1979 "Peasants' struggle to eat

'deserves more concern' '' (UN Food Conference)

August 15, 1979 ''More Go Hungry Than Ever Before''

August 30, 1979 ''Famine Plagues Brazil''

November 19, 1979 ''Unchecked Food Shortages Will Cause Disaster, UN Says''

January 21, 1980 ''Grain Becomes a Weapon''

March, 1980 ''Famine Stalks Northern India''

September 17, 1980 ''Food Crisis For UN''

December, 1980 ''No matter what we do now, millions will die!'' (World Food Council executive director Morris Williams)

October, 1981 ''Experts say: Heading toward Universal Famine'' [162]

The outlook on famine is not a hopeful one.

4. PESTILENCES

A short time ago it was being suggested that technological advances and scientific ''know-how'' were going to eliminate pestilence from the earth.

Not any more.

A *Parade* magazine article on September 30, 1979, entitled ''Superbugs: A New Biblical Plague?'' indicated that insect pestilence is a major problem.

Describing some of the 364 "superbugs" which have become resistant to the poisons developed to destroy or hold them in check, the article calls them "the shock troops of a global insect army locked in constant combat with man, challenging us for our food and fibre supplies and bringing death, disease and discomfort to millions, particularly in Asia, Africa and Latin America."

Viewed in terms of war, it is the insects that are on the offensive. "They are beginning to tip the scales in their favor," warns Dr. Paul Schwartz, a U.S. Department of Agriculture (USDA) entomologist. "The potential for disaster is always present—in agriculture or in disease."

The United Nations Environment Program, in its recent State of the World report, noted with alarm the rapid gains made by insects, mites, ticks, rodents, weeds and fungi in becoming increasingly resistant to pesticides. This poses a grave threat to world health and food production. [163]

Killer bees, fire ants, locust invasions and similar pestilential insects really do appear to be "on the march." In the late 1970s, according to a UPI release out of Rome, Italy, the threat of an astronomical "locust plague" is described by UN locust specialist Jean Roy as containing the potential for disaster for Africa and Asia. [164]

The pollution of earth's atmosphere and resources is a fearful, though largely unknown pestilence—unknown because it is apparent no one *really* knows the long-term effects of hazardous waste and chemical contamination (like Love Canal); the "garbaging" of earth's oceans; [165] the underground contamination of water supplies; the threat of earth's oxygen supply through industrial pollution and the savage destruction of earth's forests—like the Amazon rain forest which is said to supply *half* the world's oxygen; [166] the awesome acid rain* and "Arctic haze" threat—products of both North American and Soviet industry; [167] or the danger of unknown effects on the earth from the enormous amounts of dust blasted into the atmosphere by recent volcanic action in the U.S., Mexico and Indonesia. (The El Chichon volcano's cloud is said to block five to ten percent of the sun's light in a solid belt around the earth from the equator to Texas.)

Then there are the sexually transmissible diseases—nearly two dozen of them, divided into bacterial, viral, protozoan, fungal and ectoparasitic. According to documented information in "The New Silent Epidemic" by D.D. Schroeder, more than twenty of these sexually transmissible diseases are out of control. The best known sex disease is the viral herpes—for which there is no known cure. *Time* magazine calls it "the new sexual leprosy." [168] Though dating back to before the Roman Empire, its incidence has, in recent years, exploded as a result of the "sexual revolution." *U.S. News and World Report* calls it "a worldwide epidemic," and reports it is associated with human cancers. [169] A strain of gonorrhea which is "totally penicillin-resistant" has also emerged and become widespread since 1976. Many of the sexual diseases were unknown a decade ago.

Most fearful of all, in terms of sexually transmissible disease, is AIDS—acquired immune deficiency syndrome. This incurable fatal ailment was first detected in 1979. AIDS strikes primarily at homosexual men, drug addicts, Haitians and hemophiliacs, but (as outlined in a July 1983 *Discover* article entitled "AIDS: A Plague of Fear") may be spreading to the general public. In May of 1983 the U.S. Public Health Service designated AIDS its "number one priority." [170]

There is also the continuing, but relatively unnoticed, stream of newspaper and magazine headlines and stories that tell of other diseases, often virtually epidemic, affecting vast numbers of earth's people. "Malaria parasite grows immune to most drugs"...."Worldwide resurgence of malaria—the worst health problem in the world, killing an estimated three million people a year"...."Disease after disease grips Upper Volta"...."Each year 5 million children in the developing world are killed and another 5 million permanently harmed by just six diseases—including 1 million malaria victims in that total".... [171]

Leprosy, cancer, heart disease, and stress, as well as "exotic" diseases like bubonic plague (again getting a grip in areas of Asia) and cholera are major factors today.

The significant thing about all of these pestilences is that they are either new to this era, or have recently become epidemic *in spite of scientific and medical measures* which may have previously held them in check.

5. UNUSUAL OCCURRENCES IN THE HEAVENS

When the term "heavens" is used in

Scripture it can have one of three meanings: the *atmospheric heavens*; the *cosmical heavens*, home of the heavenly bodies we call planets and stars; or the *dwelling place of God* and the inhabitants of heaven.

The *atmospheric heavens* have unquestionably been the arena of unusual occurrences in recent years, with the media full of reports of most unusual weather patterns and other phenomena.

A January 16, 1983, report sums up the situation in these words, under the headline "WACKY WEATHER: Scientists Baffled": "Snow in the Middle East. No snow in Quebec. Daffodils in Sweden in winter. India freezes. Moscow warms up."

If you're baffled by the recent topsyturvy weather, you are not alone. Some of the world's top weather scientists freely admit they don't understand what's happening either. Or why. [172]

Record heat waves, droughts, rainfalls, floods, blizzards and cold spells, often in areas where such events have not occurred, are results of the "wacky weather." A *U.S. News and World Report* article asks, "Is Mother Nature Going Berserk?"[173] as it reviews the strange occurrences in weather around the world. The debate rages as to whether the world is heading into another "ice age" or into a wet and warm "greenhouse effect" period, or into a time of unprecedented drought.

The fact is that there definitely are tremendous changes taking place. Furthermore, manipulation by man, — such as the grandiose Soviet plan to reroute her Arctic ocean rivers, and the possibility of "environmental warfare," — could create even more massive and dangerous shifts in climate. And such problems could create an even more serious global food shortage—as shorter growing seasons, heat waves, widespread drought or repeated floodings in the food-producing areas of the world combine to take their toll.

A UPI release out of Geneva in March 1982 quotes the experts convened by the World Meteorological Organization, United Nations Environmental Program, and the International al Council of Scientific Unions as seeing weather changes "materially affecting food production and water supplies." [174]

Another phenomenon possibly classifiable as an unusual occurrence in the heavens is that of the UFOs. An enormous amount of interest in, and debate over, the existence of Unidentified Flying Objects continues year after year. Books, articles, movies, television shows, lectures and investigations have all focused on the elusive UFO. In late 1981 an intense legal battle began over the freeing of 131 secret documents about UFOs from the files of the U.S. National Security Agency. The attempt was spurred by the 1978 release of Air Force and CIA reports which revealed that reliable military personnel, in 1975, saw UFOs over a number of U.S. military sites and installations.[175]

One of the best books I've come across—and I've done a good deal of research on UFOs—is *Encounters with UFOs* by John Weldon. Weldon points out that, while accounts of UFOs are to be found even in ancient history, the number of recorded sightings for *all* time up to 1954 was around ten thousand. Since then there has been a dramatic increase of sightings into the *millions*!

Weldon makes an extremely well-documented, reasoned and sane case for the view that UFOs are demonic and, as such, are definite indicators of the impending return of Christ . The subject is too deep to attempt to get into here—except to point out that these objects in the sky, coming as they appear to do in waves of sightings, certainly qualify as "signs in the heavens."

Another level of "heavenly" sign may well be in the planets. The discovery by University of Arizona physicists of 50-mile high gas waves on the sun's surface adds credence to long-held theories that fire storms on the face of the sun also affect the earth.[176]

Marsha Adams, of the research firm SRI International, says it is believed that solar flare activity has an effect on weather, earthquakes, electrical malfunctions, human illness and fatigue, as well as riots, crime sprees and political instability. Increased sun storm activity in the next few months is predicted, according to the September 15, 1982, UPI release.[177]

Meanwhile, other scientists note with concern a dip in solar energy. Physicist Richard Willson of the Jet Propulsion Laboratory, Pasadena, California, is not sure whether the dip is a temporary one, or the beginning of a long-term trend.[178]

Whatever the implications of these and other events, the fact remains that—taking the various meanings of "the heavens" into account—there do appear most certainly to be "signs in the heavens" in our time.

6. JERUSALEM RESTORED TO THE JEWS

It is a fact of history that Jerusalem was totally lost to the Jews in A.D. 70, at which time the Jews were dispersed worldwide, and ceased to exist as a nation. We noted this in chapter eight.

Until June 1967, the city of Jerusalem was controlled either totally or in part by non-Jewish, that is, Gentile, peoples.

However, on June 6, 1967, during the Six-Day War, for the first time in over 1,900 years, the Holy City was returned to Jewish control. Shortly after the capture of Old Jerusalem, and while the war was still raging, the late General Moshe Dayan marched to the Wailing Wall—that last remnant of the Old Temple—and said, "We have returned to our holiest of Holy Places, *never to leave again*."[179]

Since then, in the face of a great deal of worldwide opposition, the city has been made the capital of the State of Israel—with the seat of government being moved from Tel Aviv, and the Hebrew spelling, "Jereshulayim," restored.

7. DISTRESS OF NATIONS

The various present-day conditions which have been discussed in this book—inflation, economic concerns, war, famine, pestilence, ecological problems, the rape of irreplaceable resources—these and many more are all *international* problems.

Their enormity is compounded by their almost universal presence. The result is a high degree of concern and distress among the leaders of nation after nation.

Disarmament, trade wars, economics, the "north-south" dialogue, and a myriad of similar matters are viewed internationally with a sense of gloom and foreboding.

The leaders of the U.S., Britain, France, Japan, Italy, Germany and Canada have been meeting periodically over the past several years in summit sessions in an effort to address earth's problems. Venice, Italy, in 1980; Montebello, Quebec, Canada, in 1981; and later that year, Cancun, Mexico, for the much publicized "North-South," rich-poor conference, have been the sites for hopeful gatherings—the 1981 session being called the "most important summit ever held."[180]

However, following the 1982 summit meeting in Versailles, France, the pronouncements were uniformly gloomy. Canadian Prime Minister Trudeau bitterly described the talks as totally non-productive—a waste of time. So the leaders of the seven most powerful western nations obviously do not have, and cannot discover, solutions to the distressing problems facing the world.

Nor are the token summit talks among Communist, Third World, or OPEC groupings any better.

There is genuine distress of nations today.

8. FEAR

International terrorism in recent years has seen thousands of individuals brutally murdered. It has created a climate of fear that seems to be a symptom of our times. Providing security for the leaders of nations, prominent businessmen, artists, or athletes has become a big business. The fear is not unfounded.

But it is not just the prominent who fear. In the U.S., violence was described by the Surgeon General, C. Everett Koop, as the number one health problem in his nation in late 1982. Murders, suicides, rapes, muggings and related violence has created unprecedented fear in major U.S. cities and suburbs, in particular.[181] Elsewhere, too. A *U.S. News & World Report* article on violence is headlined, "Abroad, Too, Fear Grips the Cities."[182]

The September 1981 issue of *Psychology Today* reported that a nation-wide survey in the U.S. revealed that the greatest fear Americans have is the fear of war—with 41 percent so responding. A U.S. poll by Associated Press/NBC in late 1981 found that 75 percent of Americans feared the U.S. would go to war in the next few years. [183]

In another area, a 1980 headline in *U.S. News & World Report* reports that "Americans are Haunted by a Fear of Technology"[184] while the May 1982 issue of *The Bible in the News* cites reports that "millions of Americans are victims of 'cyberphobia'—the name tagged on to anxiety attacks, triggered by unhappy experiences people have had with computers." " 'It's safe to predict that within the next 10 years an unbelievable 100 million people will be affected,' " says Professor S. Weinberg, director of the Cyberphobia Laboratory Project at St. Joseph's Hospital in Philadelphia, Pa."[185]

March 10, 1982, (dubbed "Doomsday" because of the predicted effects of a rare planetary alignment on that day) found people in many areas of earth, particularly in the Third World, being swept by an "epidemic of fear."[186]

In Canada, Toronto pollster Martin Goldfarb discovered that in mid-1982 Canadians, "almost with a single voice were expressing a litany of fear."[187]

The Canadian Press revealed that at Christmas time, 1982, letters to Santa reflected "the worry of the times," while a Gallop poll of people in 31 countries found Europeans more pessimistic than optimistic in the closing months of 1982.[188]

And in early 1983, a "War of Worlds" type of radio program, with a nuclear twist, sparked panic throughout Illinois, and was yanked off the air.[189]

Unquestionably, fear stalks the earth.

9. FALSE CHRISTS

The date was April 25, 1982. On that day, full-page paid advertisements proclaiming that "The Christ is Now Here" appeared in *The New York Times*, *The Los Angeles Times* and major newspapers in 30 other cities of the world. The ad said that "the World Teacher, Lord Maitreya, known by Christians as Christ, the Jews as the Messiah, Buddhists as the Fifth Buddha, Moslems as the Iman Mahdi and the Hindus as Krishna—all names for one individual—has been in the world literally since 1977." Acknowledgement of the Christ's identity would be made within two months of the publishing of the ad through a worldwide television and radio broadcast, and his message would be "heard inwardly, telepathically by all people in their own language."

No acknowledgment was ever made.[190]

Nevertheless, the financial resources and clout sufficient to place full-page ads in major world-class papers sets this particular claim apart. In other senses, however, this "Christ" is only one of a number of false Christs who have been legion in recent years.

Rev. Sun Myung Moon came upon the American scene from Korea in 1972, claiming to be the Messiah. He has attracted a large following for his controversial Unification Church, using extremely questionable methods, and in 1982 was convicted of tax, immigration and charity violations. He is another of the present-day "Christs."

Jim Jones, the fanatical false Savior who led or forced over 900 people to commit mass suicide at the People's Temple in Guyana in November 1978 was another.

And there are, or have been, others—like Father Divine, Charles Manson, Guru Ji—men who have claimed to be Christ.

Undoubtedly there will be still others, until the man of sin appears. After his defeat at the word of Jesus Christ, the true Son of God will reign.

10. WORLDWIDE
PROCLAMATION OF THE GOSPEL

The Matthew account of Christ's answer to His disciples' questions about the timing of His return contains what many believe to be a most significant sign.

In Matthew 24:14, Jesus said, "And this gospel of the kingdom shall be preached in all the world for a witness unto all nations; and then shall the end come."

There are several views held by prophetic students concerning this sign. One view suggests that before Christ will return for His church the gospel must be proclaimed to all nations. This view has proven to be a great impetus to the foreign missionary effort.

Another view holds that this global preaching will be done by a group of 144,000 Jewish "evangelists" sealed against harm by God to proclaim the gospel during the tribulation period—after the church has been snatched away.

Regardless of the view held, however (and proponents of each view can make a good case for their position), it is most significant that some *unusual* and *very major developments* are taking place right now in terms of global missionary effort.

In recent years, major groups like

Operation Mobilization, Youth With a Mission, and World Literature Crusade—with its Every Home Crusades—have stimulated a renewed thrust in missions. Campus Crusade for Christ, with some 14,000 on staff, is seeking to give the gospel to the world through "Here's Life" campaigns in scores of nations. Scripture translation and distribution is at a record level, with organizations like Living Bibles International having an impact.

Many missionary groups and denominations have set goals for vastly expanded outreach. And in 1978, the U.S. Center for World Mission was created. This interdenominational effort, which envisions the establishment of sister centers of world mission around the world, has as its stated goal the preaching of the gospel in the world's 16,500 cultures in which no Christian church currently exists. The Center, in its brief lifespan, has identified these groups and begun to enunciate studies and strategies to reach them.

Consultations on World Evangelization, beginning with the one called by Billy Graham in the early 1970s, have continued and certainly have stimulated interest in unreached frontiers and the accomplishment of the global task of telling the world of Christ.

The possibility of the Word of God being preached in all the world even prior to the efforts of the 144,000 "sealed ones" is a very real one—especially when radio, gospel recordings, films and satellite TV to even remote villages and areas with "gospel" dish receivers are taken into consideration. To many observers it's an exciting potential sign.

So—whether fulfilled before or after the rapture—the signs of gospel proclamation in all the world are building up.

DANIEL'S UNIQUE WORD

In Daniel 12:4, an intriguing prophecy is recorded, in the context of end-time events:

> But thou, O Daniel, shut up the words, and seal the book, even to the time of the end: many shall run to and fro, and knowledge shall be increased.

Bible scholars generally agree that this prophecy is a clear statement about the "time of the end" in which the events predicted throughout Daniel's writings would occur. According to the prophecy, the "time of the end" will be characterized by *extensive travel* and by an explosive *expansion of knowledge*. Without going into great detail, it should be obvious to even the most casual observer that these two are uniquely characteristic of our era.

This generation has seen mankind move from the early days of the automobile to space travel, with the development of a whole new travel "industry" to care for the needs of earth's busy travellers.

So far as the increase of knowledge is concerned, an incredible "knowledge explosion" is underway, geometrically increased by the advent of the computer and the microcomputer. Seventy-five percent of all scientists who have ever lived throughout human history are alive and active today. [191]

Futurist author Alvin Toffler in his newest book, *The Third Wave*, divides history into three "waves": the agricultural, the industrial and a rising "Third Wave," which is driven by computer technology that threatens to transform the way most of the world lives and thinks into a world of "info-spheres," "techno-spheres," "bio-spheres" and "psycho-spheres." [192]

Without doubt, this age is witnessing a tremendous increase in travel and knowledge. The fulfillment of these prophecies of Daniel just by themselves would not be too conclusive—but when they combine with the many other signs of fulfillment which we've been considering, they become yet another important piece of the prophetic puzzle falling into place.

IN SUMMARY

Taken all together, the affairs of this period in human history have to be viewed as being, at the very least, *the beginning* of the "birth pangs" of earth's climactic final events!

The climax of the ages most certainly must be near!

For Further Reading:

Chant, C., R. Holmes and W. Koenig. *Two Centuries of Warfare*, (Hong Kong: Octopus Books, 1978).

Larson, Bob. *Larson's Encyclopedia of Cults*, (Wheaton, Ill.: Tyndale House Publishers, 1982).

PART FIVE

The Climax of the Ages

THE SIGN OF SAFETY

Safety!

It's one of mankind's most basic needs and desires.

But only those who have lived through a grave threat to life can fully appreciate the wonder of receiving a sign, or indication, that a place of safety is at hand.

Amidst the dreadful signs of this dark period in human history—signs which point to an awesome climax of earth's ages—is another sign.

It's the "sign of safety."

It points to a safety that is for real.

Bona fide.

Believable.

And available.

> *"And a man shall be as an hiding place,*
> *and as a covert from the tempest."*
> —The prophet Isaiah.

CHAPTER FOURTEEN

The Only Sure Shelter

As a child, I was very keenly interested in the work of E.J. Pace, a gospel cartoonist, whose excellent pen-and-ink drawings were extremely popular at the time. The artist's skill in illustration was matched by his ability to "cartoon" biblical truths in an understandable and graphic fashion.

One of those early cartoons which made a vivid impression upon my childish mind, and which I can still visualize clearly some decades later, had to do with a place of safety in storm.

In this cartoon, Pace depicted in the

distance a fearful, tornado-like storm sweeping across the land. In the foreground were people—men, women, children and youth—running as fast as they could toward a huge outcropping of rock. Under the overhang, and in the crevices of the rock were people who had already reached a place of security.

The rock that provided shelter from the impending storm, upon examination, was seen to resemble the huge head of a Man—Jesus Christ, as artists tend to depict Him.

The cartoon contained the text from Isaiah, "And a man shall be as an hiding place, and as a covert from the tempest" (Isaiah 32:2). It was captioned, "The Only Place of Safety."

The truth of that old cartoon is more valid than ever today.

An awesome storm of end-time events is brooding over the world at this very moment. Contained in those dark, lowering, ominous clouds are the events—predicted by the prophets—which we have been considering in the foregoing chapters of this book.

These include the horrendous scenario of the diabolical Antichrist's demonic reign; the horror of a world from which the Church has been removed—a world gone mad with sin and hatred, violence and lust; and the terror of a planet literally reeling under the righteous judgments of a holy, but justly wrathful, God.

To fully appreciate how indescribably terrible this impending "storm" will be, read carefully the book of the Apocalypse—The Revelation, last book of the New Testament. Chapters six through twenty detail the awesome judgments and describe the three distinct series of divine retributions which are visited upon earth.

There has never been, in all of human history, a "storm" to remotely rival this coming holocaust!

There is only one sure place of safety from that storm. That hiding place is a Person, the Lord Jesus Christ.

No other refuge or option is adequate. For a person to wish for or invite death to try to escape the climax of earth's ages is utterly foolish. To die without being in a right and real relationship to God, through Jesus Christ, is to go "from the frying pan into the fire." It is *not* a solution.

To look to any savior or hope other than Christ is ultimately to face disillusionment and eternal loss. Jesus said, "I am the Way, the Truth, and the Life. *No man comes to the Father but by Me*" (John 14:6, emphasis mine).

Perhaps you have experienced, at one time or another and in one degree or another, what it is to place your confidence in a thing or person and to be disillusioned. Many have lost everything, including their lives, through such misplaced confidence. Not *every* refuge is a secure place of safety in our world of nature!

Or in the far more important spiritual realm.

But Jesus Christ *can be trusted*. His claims to Deity are fully documented, and can be depended upon—completely.

It was the famed British theologian and writer C.S. Lewis who suggested the following argument in support of the claims of Christ:

There are only four possible conclusions a thinking person can come to concerning Jesus Christ. He's either a *liar*, a *lunatic*, a *legend* or He is *Lord*! In the light of the claims He made about Himself and the things the prophets said of Him, He has to be one of these four.

Consider: if He knew the claims He made were not true, but He made them anyway—then, of course, He was a *liar*.

If He believed His claims, but they weren't true, then He was deluded. And in view of the nature of these claims, nothing short of a *lunatic.*

If He didn't make the claims attributed to Him—but they were simply the work of an enthusiastic but misguided band of followers—then He is merely a *legend.*

The truth is that history gives the lie to each of these "options" about Jesus Christ. The only logical conclusion a thinking person can come to is that He is who He claimed to be.

He, and He alone, is worthy to be *Lord!*

And history does support Christ's claims. Dr. Peter Stoner, in his fascinating book, *Science Speaks,* applies the test of the science of probability to the prophecies concerning Jesus Christ. His conclusion is that fulfilled prophecy—as it relates to Jesus Christ and as it is documented in history—is an absolutely conclusive demonstration of His authenticity and Deity.

He is who He claimed to be—the Divine Son of God, and only Savior.

As such He, and He alone, can be a place of safety.

A PERSON A HIDING PLACE?

But, you may ask, how can a *Person* be a hiding place? How does one go about hiding in Christ?

Good questions.

The answer to the first is that safety comes when a man or woman places complete hope for salvation in Christ, is forgiven, cleansed and born again. Then, as a child of God, he is in God's family, under Christ's care, and will be kept or removed (in the rapture) as earth's cataclysmic climax comes.

The Bible says that "He [Jesus Christ] is able to keep that which is committed unto Him, until the final day" (2 Timothy 1:12). And "[God] who has begun a good work in you will perform it until the day of Jesus Christ" (Philippians 1:6).

God is well able to look after those who are His own. So safety comes through a Person, because when a man or woman has come to know the Person of Christ, then he or she belongs to God, and is *His* responsibility.

To answer the second question, "*How* does one go about hiding in Christ?" it is necessary to take what I call "the ABC steps." These stand for:

1. Agree
2. Believe, and
3. Call

First, *agree* with God in all that He says in His Word, the Bible, about the fact that you

314

are separated from God by your sin. Admit that you are a sinner who has broken God's righteous laws.

Agree with God that sin deserves His punishment, because He is a just, holy, *righteous* God. Admit that *you* are properly under that sentence and that you fully deserve it in all its awesomeness.

The Bible makes these facts very clear:

"For all have sinned, and come short of the glory [the standard] of God" (Romans 3:23).

"Thou [Lord] art of purer eyes than to behold evil, and canst not look on iniquity" (Habakkuk 1:13).

"There shall in no wise enter into [heaven] anything that defileth" (Revelation 21:27).

"All unrighteousness is sin" (I John 5:17).

"The wages of sin is death" (Romans 6:23).

The Bible describes three kinds of death: *physical* death (the state experienced when life leaves our bodies); *spiritual* death (spiritual separation from a holy God caused by our sin—a person can be alive physically but dead spiritually, Ephesians 2:1); and *eternal* death (the fixed state entered by the individual who dies physically while he is still dead spiritually).

It is eternal death in particular which is the horrible result or "wages" of sin. The Lord Jesus Christ frequently described such a death as being eternal (without end) in a destiny which He called hell. He described hell as a place of judgment (Matthew 13:41); a place of everlasting fire (Matthew 18:8); a place of torment (Luke 16:24,28); a place of wailing and gnashing of teeth (Matthew 13:50); a place of remorse (Mark 9:44); of bitter memory (Luke 16:25); and a place originally prepared for the Devil and his angels (Matthew 24:41). In fact, Jesus more often warned about hell than He spoke about heaven. It is not God's will or desire that *any* person should be consigned to perish in hell (II Peter 3:9), but rather that all should come to repentance.

But, as God's justice requires, "The soul that sinneth, it shall surely die" (Ezekiel 18:4).

So—agree with God, admitting that you are a sinner under God's just condemnation for that sin and that you are in need of His salvation.

SECOND: BELIEVE

Then—*believe* that God does not want you to perish eternally in the torment of hell because of your sin. Believe that God loves you—so much that He provided a way whereby He could still be a just, holy and righteous God, and yet pardon you—a sinner.

Believe that God did not just overlook sin, but that He sent His only begotten Son—the Lord Jesus Christ—to provide salvation by personally paying the penalty for sin.

Believe that Jesus Christ (whose life, death, burial and resurrection is the best-attested fact of antiquity*) did come to earth to live, die, rise again and ascend to heaven in order to provide justification and salvation for all who trust Him.

Believe that He, and He alone, *can* save you because He has fully satisfied the just demands of God. Believe that you can't become righteous in God's sight on your own.

Believe that He *wants* to save you and that He *will* save you.

The Bible provides a solid basis for such belief:

----

*See **Evidence that Demands a Verdict, More Evidence that Demands a Verdict, More than a Carpenter** and **The Resurrection Factor** - all by Josh McDowell.

"The Lord...is longsuffering to us-ward...not willing that any should perish but that all should come to repentance" (II Peter 3:9).

"For God so loved the world that He gave His only begotten son—that whosoever believeth in Him should not perish but have everlasting life" (John 3:16).

"But God commendeth His love toward us, in that while we were yet sinners, Christ died for us" (Romans 5:8).

"God hath set forth [Jesus Christ] to be a 'payment for sin' through faith in His blood...that He might be just and the justifier of Him which believeth in Jesus" (Romans 3:25,26).

"I declare unto you the gospel [the good news]...how that Christ died for our sins according to the scriptures; and that He was buried, and that He rose again the third day..." (I Corinthians 15:1-4).

"Neither is there salvation in any other [than Jesus], for there is none other name under heaven given among men whereby we must be saved" (Acts 4:12).

Jesus said, "I am the way, the truth, and the life. No man cometh unto the

Father, but by me" (John 14:6).

Jesus said, "Come unto me all ye that labor and are heavy laden and I will give you rest" (Matthew 11:28).

Jesus said, "Him that cometh to me I will in no wise cast out" (John 6:37).

Jesus said, "Behold I stand at the door [of the heart] and knock. If any man hear my voice and open the door, I will come in to him..." (Revelation 3:20).

THIRD: CALL

But, *it is not enough* to agree with God, admit your need, and believe that Christ can and will save you.

You must act upon those facts.

You must repent of sin. That is, you must be sorry for your sin—sorry enough to completely turn from it and from your own efforts, or any other hope. You must come to Christ, *calling* upon *Him* for salvation, and then counting on the fact that He will do what He has promised. This means simply taking the gift of pardon and eternal life which He offers.

Merely believing *about* Jesus Christ without coming to Him makes as much sense, and is as effective, as believing that a medication can successfully treat a fatal disease, but failing to take it.

Again the Bible provides the basis for such statements:

"He that believeth on the Son is not condemned: but he that believeth not is condemned already because he hath not believed in the name of the only begotten Son of God" (John 3:18). (The word translated "believe" here means to "rest one's entire weight and trust on the object or person in which the belief is placed." It requires *action* in keeping with the intellectual assent of that "belief.")

"Whosoever shall call upon the name of the Lord shall be saved" (Romans 10:13).

"...the gift of God is eternal life through Jesus Christ our Lord" (Romans 6:23).

The logical question at this point is:
How do you come to Christ and call upon Him?

"Calling upon the Lord" is just another term for "praying," or talking to God. To talk to God is not a complicated process, dependent upon some special rituals. God invites people to approach Him, through His

Son, in simple, straightforward terms. In fact, Jesus spoke with commendation of the dishonest, despised tax collector who simply prayed, "God be merciful to me—a sinner."

While the *exact* words of your prayer to God are not of vital importance (since God sees and knows the attitude of your heart), the following is the kind of prayer that you could pray in calling upon God for salvation:

Dear Lord Jesus: I realize that I need You. I admit that I have sinned and that I deserve Your just, eternal punishment for that sin. But I am sorry for my sin and sincerely willing to turn from it. I believe that You died and rose again to pay sin's penalty, on my behalf. I come to You now, and open my heart to You. I ask You to come into my life, forgive me for all my sin, cleanse me from it, and make me Your child. I invite You to take control of my life and to cause me to be the kind of person that You want me to be. And I thank You for doing this—because You have promised that whoever calls upon You, as I have done now, shall be saved.

If this prayer expresses the desire of your heart, I urge you to sincerely and genuinely express it to God as YOUR prayer, in the name of His Son, Jesus Christ.

Then, once you have, verbally share the fact of what you have done with someone. The Bible says that when we believe on the Lord Jesus Christ in our heart, God forgives our sins and counts us righteous, and that when we openly confess with our mouths what we have done in our hearts, God gives us *assurance* of that salvation! (Romans 10:9,10).

Follow up your decision by taking time, on a daily basis, to read and memorize God's Word (I Peter 2:2). Talk to the Lord in prayer regularly. Share with Him your desires, needs, burdens and blessings. Thank Him and praise Him—in everything (I Thessalonians 5:18).

Find a local church where the pastor and people really believe and teach the Bible—and where they are committed to obeying God in the power which He gives by His Holy Spirit.

Make a practice of regular attendance at such a church (Hebrews 10:24,25) and talk to the pastor about what the Bible teaches concerning obedience to Christ in baptism, and how to grow as a Christian. Daily invite God to control and direct your life (Ephesians 5:18).

Share your faith in Christ as often as you have opportunity—and daily anticipate the return of your Lord. Surely He must be coming soon!

And if you are someone who has come to the place of trusting Christ for salvation at some time prior to reading this book, be reminded that, as His children, God wants us to be eagerly anticipating the return of our Lord.

Jesus told His disciples, and His word comes down to us, that they were to watch for His return (Matthew 24:42). In addition, our Lord directed us to be busy serving Him until He comes (Luke 19:13).

The Apostle John adds that "every man that has this hope [the hope of Christ's return] in him, purifies himself even as He is pure" (I John 3:2). This obviously means that believers who really are anticipating the Rapture will commit themselves to a life of separation from all that defiles and a life of obedience to God, in the power which He supplies through His Holy Spirit.

And when we realize the horrific events which are to come upon this earth after the Rapture—as well as the desperate need for salvation by all who have not yet been born again—there will be strong motivation for us to share the Gospel with others as often as possible.

The Apostle Paul, near the end of his amazing life of service to the Lord—a life characterized by anticipation, even then, of Christ's return—wrote:

For I am now ready to be offered, and the time of my departure is at hand.

I have fought a good fight, I have finished my course. I have kept the faith:

Henceforth there is laid up for me a crown of righteousness, which the Lord, the righteous judge, shall give me at that day: and not to me only, but unto all them also that love his appearing.
—II Timothy 4:6-8

Obviously then, there is a special reward prepared for all those who love our Lord's appearing. May all of us who know Him live in such a way—watching, waiting, working and witnessing for Christ—until He comes, that it may be our great joy to receive such a crown.

Maranatha! The Lord is coming!

If you have prayed to receive the Lord Jesus Christ as Savior during the reading of *The Economy To Come*, I would be grateful to know of your decision and will be happy to respond with suggestions for growth in your new Christian life.

Kindly address me at:

Pastor Bill
2575 Gladwin Road,
Abbotsford, British Columbia,
Canada, V2T 3N8

Run For Your Life!

One of the ancient provisions in the nation of Israel was the concept of "cities of refuge."

Under this divinely instituted plan, several cities throughout the nation were designated as places of refuge to which a man who had taken a life without intent could flee and be guaranteed protection from avengers until justice could be assured. Such an endangered person, *if wise, lost no time in running to the place of refuge.*

It always makes sense to run for safety. Only the foolhardy fail to do so in the face of danger.

And our world is facing the ominous storms of the climax of the ages. The evidence has been presented in the pages of this book. The wise will flee the tempest.

However, quite apart from the impending judgments predicted for this world is the fact that *every individual upon earth* is under condemnation for his or her sin, and needs to run for his or her life. The only place of safety is a Person—Jesus Christ.

While you have opportunity, *run for your life*...your eternal life!

Run for safety to Christ—*today*!

Appendices

APPENDIX A
PROPHETS
Source: Apocalypse Next by W. R. Goetz, pp. 43 to 51.

Those ancient Hebrew prophets, who have given us the detailed prophecies which we will now consider, were men men who had to be willing to stake their very lives on the absolute truth of their prophetic messages.

Here's how.

THE ACID TEST

Israel's great deliverer and leader, Moses, writing in the Pentateuch, said that through the course of the nation's history many prophets would come to declare God's Word to the Jewish people. Moses was asked at that point how the nation could "know the word which God has not spoken." His answer, recorded in Deuteronomy 18:22, was simple, and is the acid test of a true prophet: "When a prophet speaks in the name of the Lord, if the word does not come to pass, that is a word which the Lord has not spoken."

And the penalty, under Jewish law, for **falsely** claiming to be a prophet was **death**. Capital punishment by stoning.

Even under such harsh conditions, however, many of the prophets made **short-term prophecies**, which could be, and were, fulfilled in **their** lifetimes. Obviously, they were for real.

Others gave long-range prophecies, or prophecies which undoubtedly had a double reference, that is, both a short- **and** a long-term meaning. Many of such prophecies, especially prophecies about the Messiah, have **short-term references**—to Christ's first appearance on earth (already fulfilled and documented by history)—as well as **long-term references**—to His second coming.

Frequently, the prophets did not themselves understand

the significance of their own utterances, as the Apostle Peter points out in his New Testament book II Peter.

Of course, to be valid, a prophecy must be of such a nature that the one who utters it cannot influence its fulfillment—prevented either by time or circumstances from interfering in its outcome.

It must also be in sufficient detail that it can't have numerous possible meanings, so that the prophet cannot cop out.

THOSE ANCIENTS MEASURE UP

The Hebrew prophets, whose utterances (given as long as 3-4,000 years ago) have been preserved for us in the Bible, clearly meet all of these criteria.

In fact, **all** of the short- and many of the long-term prophecies (all those due for fulfillment) have actually come to pass.

ISAIAH IS RIGHT ON

For example, Isaiah prophesied over a span of about 60 years during the reign of four successive kings of Judah. His authenticity as a bona fide spokesman for God, when submitted to Moses' acid test, was demonstrated time and again.

During the reign of Hezekiah about 710 B.C., the mighty Assyrian army led by the cruel King Sennacherib invaded and beseiged Jerusalem. As recorded in Isaiah 37:36-38, the prophet made a **short term** prophecy that, contrary to Sennacherib's plans and threats, he would not attack Jerusalem. Instead, he would return to his own land.

History records that's how it happened. When a rumor of internal problems at home reached Sennacherib, he abandoned the siege, returned home and was assassinated—with his own sons doing the dastardly deed!

Isaiah also made long-range predictions.

In chapter 39:5-7, he predicted that Babylon would destroy Judah and carry away all the treasures of Israel...with the surviving sons of royalty becoming eunuchs at Babylon. **Just over 100 years later**, in 586 B.C., this prediction came to pass.

Then, as recorded in Isaiah 13:17-22, the prophet foretold that the invincible Babylonian Empire would be conquered and the city of Babylon so completely destroyed that it would be uninhabitable. That prophecy meant really going out on a limb, for at the time it was uttered Babylon was considered to be an impregnable city with walls 150 feet high and so thick that five chariots abreast could drive on top of them. The city, one of the seven wonders of the ancient world, was also so self-sustaining that it was thought to be impervious to siege.

But approximately **150 years** after Isaiah prophesied, on October 16, 539 B.C., Babylon fell to the Medes and Persians. Ultimately, the city sank into ruin from which it has never recovered...though Iraq is currently attempting to reconstruct that ancient city.

Again Isaiah prophesied that a king whom he actually named—Cyrus—would make possible the rebuilding of the Temple and Jerusalem by allowing any Jewish captives who wished to do so to return to Palestine for this work. The prophecy is recorded in Isaiah 44:28 to 45:4. **Two hundred years** later the Persian King Cyrus granted Jewish exiles, remaining from the Babylonian captivity, to return to Jerusalem for the work of reconstruction, even providing requisitions for materials!

It's quite an impressive record for Isaiah—**if** he was just guessing. A most unlikely short-term prophecy...right on; then three completely accurate long-term forecasts of 100, 150 and 200 years. And these are only four of numerous prophetic utterances by the major Old Testament prophets. Only divine revelation can explain such feats of foresight.

Some scholars who would like to explain away the miracle of prophecy have charged that Isaiah lived later in history than claimed. Their "late dating" of Isaiah implies that he wrote his so-called prophecies after they actually happened, making him a fraud.

But such a charge makes more than Isaiah a fraud. It also makes the Jewish people, who have retained for posterity Isaiah's writings and whose Museum of the Scroll in Jerusalem houses the Isaiah manuscripts found in the 1940s, deceivers and charlatans, to say nothing of its violation of the consistent witness of history.

Obviously Isaiah was for real.

SO WAS EZEKIEL

Consider one other example.

Both Isaiah and the prophet Ezekiel prophesied the destruction of the powerful commercial center of Tyre. Ezekiel added the intriguing details that the walls and towers of Tyre would be broken, the very dust scraped from her site and that site made like the top of a rock—a place for the spreading of nets (Ezekiel 26:4-5).

At the time of the prediction (588 B.C.) it must have seemed absurd, for Tyre was then indeed a strong city-state. In fact, so well-fortified was the city that for thirteen years (from 585-573 B.C.) it withstood Nebuchadnezzar's attempts to overthrow it. Nebuchadnezzar succeeded only in destroying the mainland fortress, but the island city of Tyre—just a short distance off-shore—remained free and the excellent Phoenician sailors inhabiting it continued their commerce.

But in 332 B.C., Alexander the Great, determined to take Tyre, constructed a causeway out to it, in the process literally scraping the soil from the site of the city down to the bare rock. Thus mainland Tyre was so devastated that the ancient site can scarcely be identified. Fishermen now spread their nets on the rock where once it stood!

Daniel, Jeremiah, Ezekiel, Micaiah, David, Micah...on and on the list could go...prophets who passed the test. Their prophetic utterances came to pass. To be fair, we must acknowledge that there are those who dispute the claim of inerrancy for the prophets. But such positions are invariably taken when the "law of double reference" is ignored.

Concerning the birth, life, death and resurrection of Jesus Christ, over 60 prophetic utterances by more than a dozen different prophets were literally fulfilled—though given, in some cases, as much as 1,000 years previous to His birth.

Josh McDowell, in **Evidence That Demands a Verdict**, points out that Peter Stoner (**Science Speaks**, Moody Press, 1963) demonstrates that the possibility of **coincidence** in the fulfillment of the 60 specific prophecies through Christ's birth, life, death and resurrection is **ruled out** by the science of probability. Stoner says that by using the modern science of probability in reference to **just eight** of these,

> we find that the chance that any man might have lived down to the present time and fulfilled all eight prophecies is 1 in 10^{17} That would be 1 in 100,000,000,000,000,000. In order to help us comprehend this staggering probability, Stoner illustrates it by supposing that we take 10^{17} silver dollars and lay them on the face of Texas. They will cover all of the state to a depth of two feet. Now mark one of these silver dollars and stir the whole mass thoroughly, all over the state. Blindfold a man and tell him that he can travel as far as he wishes, but he must pick up one silver dollar and say that

this is the right one. What chance would he have of getting the right one? Just the same chance that the prophets would have had of writing these eight prophecies and having them all come true in any one man, from their day to the present time, providing they wrote them in their own wisdom....Now these prophecies were either given by inspiration of God or the prophets just wrote them as they thought they should be. In such a case the prophets had just one chance in 10^{17} of having them come true in any man, but they all came true in Christ.

This means that the fulfillment of these eight prophecies alone proves that God inspired the writing of those prophecies to a definiteness which lacks only one chance in 10^{17} of being absolute.

Stoner considers 48 prophecies and says, "We find the chance that any one man fulfilled all 48 prophecies to be 1 in 10^{157}."

To visualize a number so large is a virtual impossibility. And remember, it was not just 8, or 48, but 60 prophecies which Jesus completely and totally fulfilled, demonstrating that prophecy completed in Jesus Christ is a powerful testimony to both **His** and the **prophets'** authenticity.

These are historical facts that cannot be successfully disputed. Sir Robert Anderson of Scotland Yard spent many years of his life verifying and validating the details of Daniel's prophecy. Anderson's book, **The Coming Prince**, published in 1890, clearly underscores the fact that Daniel gave not only specific years but a sequence for future major events, the accuracy of which cannot be denied.

Obviously, these men were not mere **seers** or **psychics**—with a record of partial accuracy. They were **prophets**, whose utterances have been vindicated as being from God because all their prophecies whose time for fulfillment has already come **have been literally fulfilled** with 100 percent accuracy.

Their noble ranks include even Jesus Christ—the greatest of all Prophets, for He uttered many specific prophecies—and the apostles, like Peter, Paul and John of Patmos, whose Revelation is the final book of the sacred canon.

And so the word of these men, in terms of prophecies still to be fulfilled, may be **completely depended upon.** Their utterances have the stamp of divine authenticity upon them. While much of what they said is still future, it is apparent that we are beginning to see fulfillment of many of their predictions...in our time.

NOTE ON APPENDICES B - E

The author does not endorse the following quotes in their entirety. They are being included, however, for the *reader* to consider in deciding whether or not there is, indeed, a conspiracy to create a "New (One) World Order." Sources, in most cases primary, are indicated.

I want to reiterate what I said in chapter one: I do not believe that those who are part of the international organizations described in this book *necessarily* have evil motives. I feel sure that many really are convinced that their approach is for the ultimate good of mankind. They undoubtedly believe that the power and wealth which will be theirs as a result are just rewards for their efforts to save our world.

What I am certain of is that they do not know the extent to which they have been influenced in their thought by the direct involvement of the enemy, Satan, through the philosophy of humanism—which totally rules out God and deifies man.

I must agree whole-heartedly with a paragraph by editor Ron Marr, writing in the June 1980 *Christian Inquirer* Special Report:

> While far from providing an entirely satisfactory explanation of the massive effort to transform society and produce a new world order, Malcolm Muggeridge had something when he observed in a trans-Atlantic telephone conversation with me back in 1976 that, if there is a conspiracy, it is from hell itself. And on this, perhaps, most true Christians can agree.

APPENDIX B

TRILATERALISM
[Boston: South End Press, 1980, pp 1-8]

INTRODUCTION

When Jimmy Carter became president of the United States in January 1977, he made an under-"Statement to the World" which began: "I have chosen the occasion of my inauguration as president to speak not only to my countrymen—which is traditional—but also to you, citizens of the world who did not participate in our election but who will nevertheless be affected by my decisions." With equal candor members of the Trilateral Commission—an organization in which Jimmy Carter was an active participant—might have added: "We have chosen the occasion of President Carter's inauguration to speak not only to our membership, the Business Roundtable, the Council on Foreign Relations, and other such elite planning organizations—which is traditional—but also to you, citizens of the world who are not familiar with our organizations and did not participate in our appointment but who will nevertheless be affected by our decisions."

In 1973 the Trilateral Commission was founded by David Rockefeller, Chase Manhattan Bank chairman, Zbigniew Brzezinski, Carter's national security advisor, and other like-minded "eminent private citizens." Some 300 members (up from about 200 members in 1973) are drawn from international business and banking government, academia, media, and conservative labor.

The Commission's purpose is to engineer an enduring partnership among the ruling classes of North America, Western Europe, and Japan—hence the term "trilateral" —in order to safeguard the interests of Western capitalism in an explosive world. The private Trilateral Commission is attempting to mold public policy and construct a framework for international stability in the coming decades. Throughout this book, "trilateralism" refers to the doctrine of world order advanced by the Commission.

Shortly before Jimmy Carter's election in 1976, Richard

Ullman wrote from inside the foreign policy establishment: "In the U.S.—among elites, at any rate—trilateralism has become almost the consensus position on foreign policy." But it was only at the time of Carter's election that the Trilateral Commission was given much media attention. "Sound the Alarm: the Trilateralists are Coming!" teased William Greider in a postinaugural article on the Carter Administration and the Trilateral Commission. Jimmy Carter has picked no less than twenty-five trilateralists to serve in the highest posts of his administration. Besides Brzezinski, founding director of the Trilateral Commission, we find: Vice-President Walter Mondale, (former) Secretary of State Cyrus Vance, (former) Ambassador to the United Nations Andrew Young, Secretary of Defense Harold Brown, and Chairman of the Federal Reserve Board Paul Volcker.

Trilateralists don't make a habit of speaking directly and openly to us, the mass of world citizens (whether they are in government or out of government). But from their publications and other statements as well as by their actions, we can glean a clear sense of their ideology, goals, and strategy. Key themes of trilateralism are captured in the following statements:

The public and leaders of most countries continue to live in a **mental universe which no longer exists—a world of separate nations**—and have great difficulties thinking in terms of global perspectives and interdependence.

The liberal premise of a separation between the political and economic realm is obsolete: **issues related to economics are at the heart of modern politics.**

—**Toward a Renovated International System**
(Trilateral Task Force Report: 1977)

340

The vulnerability of democratic government in the United States (thus) comes not primarily from external threats, though such threats are real, nor from internal subversion from the left or the right, although both possibilities could exist, but rather **from the internal dynamics of democracy itself in a highly educated, mobilized, and participant society**. [Italics ed.]

> **The Crisis of Democracy: Report on the Governability of Democracies to the Trilateral Commission**
> (New York University Press, 1975)

To put it simply, trilateralists are saying: (1) the people, governments, and economies of all nations must serve the needs of multinational banks and corporations; (2) control over economic resources spells power in modern politics (of course, good citizens are supposed to believe as they are taught; namely, that political equality exists in Western democracies whatever the degree of economic inequality); and (3) the leaders of capitalist democracies— systems where economic control and profit, and thus political power, rest with the few—must resist movement toward a truly popular democracy. In short, trilateralism is the current attempt by ruling elites to manage both dependence and democracy—at home and abroad.

TRILATERAL ORIGINS

Trilateralism is rooted in a long tradition of elite ideology and corporate planning. For example, a private U.S. organization called the Council on Foreign Relations (CFR), founded in 1918, remains a powerful force in shaping public policy and perception.

> It is a board of initiation—a Board of Invention. It plans to cooperate with the government and all existing international agencies and to bring them all into constructive accord.

341

The CFR had its special chance to be a "Board of Invention" during and after World War II when it played a pivotal role in formulating U.S. war aims, constructing the post-World War II international economic and political order, and guiding U.S. policy over the last quarter century. (See Shoup and Minter.) In the postwar period, it was relatively easy to bring all parties into "constructive accord." Western Europe and Japan were in ruins; the U.S. emerged from the war as the unrivaled economic, military, and political power. Through massive economic and military assistance programs like the Marshall Plan and the North Atlantic Treaty Organization (NATO) Western Europe and Japan were reconstructed, following U.S. specifications, into stable trading partners and bulwarks against the "communist threat." The World Bank, the International Monetary Fund (see article by James Phillips), and other international organizations were founded during that early period. They became pillars of the postwar international trade and monetary system known as the Bretton Woods System (because it was established at Bretton Woods, New Hampshire in 1944); the Soviet Union and other "Socialist bloc" countries dropped out in the early stages when it became clear the system was to be designed mainly by and for the United States.

A lesser-known companion institution to the CFR is the Bilderberg Group. Bilderberg, founded in 1954, is a European-led organization which is well attended by heads of state and other "influentials" from Western Europe, the U.S., and Canada. The catch-word for the times was "Atlanticism" not "trilateralism"; Japan had not yet earned its place in the so-called "club of advanced nations" which formed the Atlantic Alliance.

Domestic stability and international stability were closely linked under the umbrella of the welfare/warfare state. (Alan Wolfe discusses this in Part VIII.) Policy makers and presidents like John F. Kennedy and Lyndon Johnson stepped up efforts to fight the world-wide "war on communism" (read "war for capitalism") alongside the domestic "war on poverty"—with the support of liberals, big labor, and big business. ("Cold War liberalism" is the name given to the dominant ideology of the postwar period.) Corporations reaped lush profits from domestic military production and rapidly expanded out into the empire which U.S. foreign aid remodelled and U.S. **guns** protected. Stability at home was maintained with varying doses of **butter** (expanding social welfare programs in the context of a prosperous economy) and political repression (McCarthy era of the 1950s; FBI and CIA counter-intelligence programs to disrupt and destroy progressive movements in the 1960s and 70s; systematic police brutality against Chicano/as, Blacks, Native Americans, and Puerto Ricans.)

With the sixties and early seventies came the collapse of the postwar international economic system and crisis in the welfare/warfare state. In advertising a 1979 feature story, "The Decline of U.S. Power: the New Debate Over Guns and Butter," **Business Week** exclaims:

READ IT AND WEEP....Between the fall of Vietnam and the fall of the Shah of Iran the United States has suffered a series of shocks signaling a steady erosion of U.S. power throughout the world....The entire U.S.-created post-World War II global economic system is in danger of destruction.

What are some of these shocks? Broad and militant protest and sustained political mobilization shook the stability of trilateral governments. The struggle for workers', students', and peasants' power brought France near revolution in May 1968—a climactic year throughout Western Europe, the U.S., and Japan. Watergate was a public display of government deceit and immorality. As trilateralists see it, a "crisis of democracy" plagued the West. (Carter sermonized about the continuing crisis in July 1979, calling it a "crisis of confidence"—in government, national purpose, the future.)

The rout of the U.S. military from Vietnam—formalized by the Paris treaty of 1973 and finalized with the fall of the Thieu regime in April 1975—undermined severely the U.S. role as global police for international capitalism. Domestic constraints were placed on direct and covert U.S. military action as the public said no to massive intervention abroad and Congress took steps to curb the imperial presidency and its zealous scouts, the CIA.

The "oil shock" came with the October 1973 Arab oil embargo (against the U.S. and the Netherlands because of their support for Israel during the October War) and OPEC price hikes of 1973-74. OPEC's success awakened Third World and Western leaders alike to the potential of "commodity power" on the side of raw material producers (and not just the "middlemen" corporations and consumer nations, as before). Oil gave OPEC the clout to force the rising Third World call for a New International Economic Order (NIEO) onto the Western agenda.

> 1973 [observes Brzezinski] was the year in which for the first time the new nations—the Afro-Asian nations, so to speak, inflicted a political reversal on the advanced world...In some respects, if 1945 was the beginning of the existing international system, 1973 marked the beginning of its end and hopefully the beginning of its renovation and readjustment.

But the post-World War II economic order began to disintegrate even before OPEC and Vietnam cracked the

344

armor of Western imperialism. The new menace of "stagflation"—stagnant economic growth with associated widespread unemployment **plus** rampant inflation—proved immune to modern economic medicine, highlighting the deepening economic crisis of world capitalism. Trade rivalry was mounting among the U.S., Japan, and Western Europe. West Germany and Japan were fast becoming economic Frankensteins, challenging U.S. hegemony over the international capitalist system. By the mid-sixties the traditionally large U.S. trade surplus had begun to erode; by 1971 the U.S. was running trade deficits, importing more than it exported. A huge buildup of dollars outside the U.S.—a result of hegemonic military and foreign aid activities—became disruptive of international monetary relations. Through inflation and speculation the dollar weakened against the Japanese yen and West German mark. International economic reform was needed. But before mutually agreeable reforms could be initiated President Nixon and Treasury Scretary John Connally unilaterally demolished the tottering Bretton Woods System on 15 August 1971 (an important date on the international business timeline), and attempted to reassert U.S. supremacy with a strongly protectionist "New Economic Policy."

The "Nixon shocks" violated the rules of "free trade"—the unobstructed flow of money, goods, and services between countries—enshrined in Bretton Woods. Indeed, such a harsh display of economic nationalism raised the specter of trade wars between the so-called free world powers, and horrified corporate captains such as David Rockefeller for whom international free enterprise is gospel.

On the political front, Nixon and Kissinger attended to the emerging U.S.-China-USSR triangle to the neglect of the Cold War alliance. Western Europe welcomed detente with the Soviet Union, but not at the expense of its special relationship with the U.S. The overtures to Peking marked by Kissinger's secret trip in July 1971 and Nixon's pageant in February 1972 came as a special shock to an uninformed Japan.

The Trilateral Commission was launched before all the tremors described above had yet registered on the economic/political seismograph. The Commission's aim is to "nuture habits and practices of working together" among the trilateral regions in order to: promote a healthy (i.e., mutually beneficial and not mutually suicidal) level of competition between the capitalist powers; forge a common front against the Third World and Soviet Union; "renovate" the international political economy in the interest of global business and finance; make trilateral democracy more "governable."

The trilateral regions, Commissioners point out, "have the largest shares of world trade and finance and produce two-thirds of the world's output." The Commission's overriding concern is that trilateral nations "remain the vital center" of management, finance, and technology (i.e. power and control) for the world economy—a world economy which (in Brzezinki's words) would "embrace" and "co-opt" the Third World and gradually reintegrate the Soviet Union, Eastern Europe, and China (known as the "dropouts" in trilateral lingo).

Trilateral Commissioners assert: **"history shows that every effective international system requires a custodian."** Today, the supereconomies—West Germany and Japan—must share the custodial role with the United States. Trilateralism, a form of "collective management" under U.S. tutelage, is the necessary response if corporate capitalism is to endure and prosper.

APPENDIX C

NEW WORLD ORDER

Source: **Thoughts on International Development, No. 9, 1975 and Christian Inquirer Special Report, June 1980.**

Paul Gerin-Lajoie, at that time President of the Canadian International Development Agency (CIDA), in booklet #9 in the Thoughts on International Development [series], published in 1975, reviewed the international development over the preceding two years leading to the call for a New World Economic Order and looked forward to the year 1980 in explaining his government's position on the subject....

...The process of profound change is irreversible, although it will be progressive. New sets of rules, national and international, will govern the international monetary system and will deal with larger transfer of resources....

I believe we must now go beyond the concept of a new economic order and design instead a new global order.

The transition towards a new project of universal civilization is not only possible; it is necessary. That is the direction which international cooperation should take.

...The Sixth Special Session of the U.N. General Assembly in April, 1974—with its milestone Declaration and Action Program for the Establishment of a New International Economic Order—reflected a dramatic change of mood....

Between the Sixth and Seventh Special Sessions, other conferences have echoed the themes of the New International Economic Order.

347

...After these and many other conferences and meetings, we arrived finally in September 1975 at the Seventh Special Session of the General Assembly—a major event in the history of international relations....

...The Special Session produced a resolution that does not make value judgments on national motives, but offers specific proposals and undertakings to help shift the world's trade and payments system so it will yield more benefits to those who need them most.

...It is encouraging to note in passing that even before this breakthrough in the General Assembly, a poll of college students in the United States showed the United Nations to be the most trusted of political and economic organizations.

...The Strategy for International Development Cooperation 1975-1980, recently adopted by the government of Canada, is a response to the moral and political demands for a new world order.

...This stocktaking, the first in 25 years of Canadian development cooperation, is centred upon five major themes:

—the sharing of wealth, a concept which permits a distribution of material and human wealth to the poorest members of the human family;...

—new types of relationships among nations, characterized by accord between equal partners engaged in the search for a better world order, in essence a global, organic and multidimensional approach to the problems of world development....

...The advent of a new world order consists primarily in the formation of new relationships among nations.

...Clearly, appeals on moral or sentimental

grounds will not suffice in the future to win the public's sympathy in the rich countries, much less draw tax dollars of voluntary contributions in favor of the sustained program of development cooperation. What is needed is a deeper understanding of the interdependence of nations....

Hinting at a government propaganda machine, Gerin-Lajoie said:

...To ensure public support for international development, governments of industrial countries must, therefore, re-examine their public information policies, redefine their target publics and direct their information increasingly to specific groups, using arguments which relate to their own search for social improvement.

One of the most urgent needs is to increase the dialogue with those sectors who fear their particular interest may be adversely affected by development cooperation, especially in the new, wider approach involving new trade and financial arrangements.

...The demands of the developing world must be explained and justified, and the consequences of ignoring the new interdependence must be fully explored.

In reference to education for a New World Order, he said: ...Any national public education and information strategy must not only cover all levels of society and all age groups, particularly the youngest, but also provide a stimulus for public participation. No amount of education or information can instill the commitment created by personal involvement.

APPENDIX D

WORLD GOVERNMENT THREAT GROWS

Source: Christian Inquirer, April 1981.

A largely unknown Private Member's Motion by Canada's present External Affairs Minister moved that the new constitution "should specifically commit Canada to the goals of...(3) transferring agreed national powers to world authorities where this would facilitate world peace...."

"The ultimate goal is, of course, world government in the sense of a federal world government," stated Mark MacGuigan, Nov. 9th, 1979, in making that motion while he was a member of the Opposition during then Prime Minister Clark's brief stay in power.

Quoting from a World Federalist brief to the Joint Committee on the Constitution of Canada, MacGuigan said: "We recommend that in recognition of the interdependence of all nations and people, Canada declare its willingness to transfer by legislation certain sovereign powers to a world authority such as the United Nations or a federal world government...."

"WE WILL SEE WORLD GOVERNMENT"

Another MP speaking on this motion was Douglas Roches, at that time Parliamentary Secretary to the Secretary of State for External Affairs, who wholeheartedly endorsed MacGuigan's motion. Also warmly supporting the motion was Ian Waddell, the Vancouver NDP member, who added:

"I believe that we will see a world government one day...(and) when it arrives, I think that it will come...**through the back door in a functional way, with the** social agencies having gradually intertwined themselves through the nations of the world." (emphasis added)

Parent activists have for many years been accusing government of employing change agents in the educational system and the social welfare structure.

They have pointed out its emphasis on, among other things, interdependence, opposition to patriotism, breaking down of traditional values and parental authority.

They have exposed the preparation of our youth to docilely accept the replacing of national loyalties by an internationalist world view essential to the acceptance of world government.

It is reported that on January 15, 1980, Ottawa signed an agreement in regard to certain products, including petroleum and agriculture, the effect of which is to transfer Canadian sovereignty in certain respects to a world authority.

CONTROL OF WORLD ECONOMY SOUGHT

Trudeau and his External Affairs Minister MacGuigan are pushing Canada into increased foreign aid. Presiding over an effectively bankrupt economy, the federal government wants Canada to sink another $500 million into oil and gas exploration in developing countries.

The reason, MacGuigan says, is a "humanitarian one." Some world observers see a far different motivation.

The International Monetary Fund is dovetailing activities with the World Bank's projected $25 billion plan to promote energy exploration in developing countries.

They are geared up for massive new petro dollar flows: the fund has augmented borrowing quotas by 58% to $75 billion; the bank has more than doubled its capital base to $85 billion, says Next magazine.

Canada has allocated some $250 million toward

petroleum development in Latin America and the Caribbean.

Control of energy is the name of the game.

Homes aren't heated, factories don't run, agriculture doesn't produce, economies grind to a halt, governments fail wherever and whenever there is a lack of energy, the ability to transport it or the funds to buy it.

It is interesting to note that internally, the Trudeau government has been busily pressing to nationalize energy production and distribution in Canada.

ECONOMIC COLLAPSE IN THE MAKING

Meanwhile, the stage is being set for a massive economic upheavel worldwide.

For several years, America's big banks have been lending billions to developing nations—by the late 1970s, they had extended some $57 billion.

Now it looks like some of these loans may never be repaid, according to the article in Next magazine, Jan.-Feb., 1981.

And the banks believe that "a single default could rumble through the world's economic structures and perhaps topple other banks in a domino effect," reports Next. "And if enough defaults occur, the banks will become insolvent."

There has been speculation that Moscow could provoke a Polish default as a way of collapsing Western economies. By 1979, Western banks had extended $20 billion in credit to Poland.

In desperation, the banks have appealed to the world's most powerful monetary institution—the International Monetary Fund.

The IMF is currently building up its resources to some $75 billion in currencies and $60 billion in gold.

The fund has "enormous power," says **Next**—"no other world organization has enjoyed even remotely comparable authority to meddle in national affairs."

The scenario emerges apparently something like this: the World Bank and the IMF are accumulating massive control over both the world economy and energy, the chief economic factor, to such a degree that the independence of nations is on the verge of becoming a myth.

It is no longer necessary that there be significant political preparation for world government. It appears that it could virtually be imposed by those who hold the real power through the control of energy and the world economy.

NEW ECONOMIC
ORDER TO PRODUCE CONTROLS

The steady propaganda over the last few years concerning the Third World and the New International Economic Order has been intense. Much of the material on this issue, aimed at church groups and student bodies, carried the imprimatur of the major church bodies.

The American federal debt is just tipping $1,000 billion—well over twice the total of the unpayable Third World debt. And this is not the limit of its debt.

Over the last few years, federal agencies have "borrowed" from the U.S. Treasury as much as $22 billion which doesn't appear on the books.

The Canadian federal debt has long ago topped $70 billion—$3,000 for every man, woman and child in Canada.

COMMUNIST LEADERS PLAY KEY ROLE

The World Bank is reportedly seeking to establish a new monetary system under the name, Bancor. It is seeking the control of credit.

The Institute of Economic Democracy said in a March bulletin: "Anticipating the coming crash, the emerging coalition between world financiers,...liberals in Western governments and churches, and Communist bloc leaders, have all agreed on the formula for a new international economic order, with its global control of banking, international reserves, and world production of foodstuffs, fibres and minerals.

The endless procession of conferences, reports, meetings and summits, feverishly putting this structure together and stretching from UNCTAD and UNIDO gatherings to the report of the ubiquitous Brandt Commission is generally known as the 'North-South Dialogue.'"

COMMUNISTS DEMAND NEW ORDER

"Not long before his death, President Tito of Yugoslavia addressed the Sixth Conference of non-aligned countries in Havana, Cuba. So non-aligned, in fact, that Fidel Castro was elected the group's spokesman!

"Tito, the Communist, put it this way: '...We have initiated long-term actions for the establishment of the new international economic order. We have contributed to the realization of the universality of the United Nations, and to the strengthening of its role and importance...

The establishment of the new international economic order is the only way to cope with the pressing problems of development and the profound crisis into which the world economy has fallen...'"

THEY SEE IT AS A
TRANSITION PHASE TO COMMUNISM

"Immediately following this Havana conference,

354

Fidel Castro spoke to the United Nations General Assembly on the imperative need for a new international economic order...

In the same month, the World Bank and the International Monetary Fund held their annual general meeting in Belgrade, Yugoslavia. Again, Tito opened the conference, and again demanded the introduction of the new international economic order.

Twelve months earlier, the Soviet Union had published its official view of the new international economic order in Moscow. Its publication, written by Soviet Professor Ernest Obminsky, one of almost 400 Soviet Communists on the United Nations payroll...said:

'The question of restructuring international economic relations on a just and equitable basis was originally put on the agenda of international affairs by the first socialist state in the world...' (**Cooperation**, Ernest Obminsky, Novosti Press Agency Publishing House, Moscow, 1979).

The booklet went on: '...The new international economic order cannot be anything but a mechanism possessing the ways and means of curbing the negative consequences of the capitalist method of production which is still continuing to function on a part of our planet. Equally obvious is the transitional nature of such a mechanism which can, nonetheless, in Lenin's words, make up an "entire epoch" in the period of transition from capitalism to socialism...'

No wonder the Tito's and the Castro's were so enthusiastic!

INTERNATIONAL TAX PROPOSED

"In February 1980, a special European Commission, under the chairmanship of ex-German Chancellor Willy Brandt—who had been forced from office by the disclosure of his sanctioning a top Soviet agent amongst his Cabinet—produced the Brandt Report, which advocated large-scale transfer of resources to developing countries, an international energy agency, a global food program and a start on major reforms in the international economic system. Included was the suggestion that the international income tax be introduced.''

APPENDIX E
EXPERT SEES WORLD GOVERNMENT BY A.D. 2000—"LIKELY HIGHLY REPRESSIVE"

Source: **On the Creation of a Just World Order by Mendlovitz, 1975 and the Christian Inquirer Special Report, June 1980.**

Dr. Saul H. Mendolovitz, director of the World Order Models Project, contends that there "is no longer a question of whether or not there will be world government by the year 2000.

The questions are how it will come into being (cataclysm, drift, more or less rational design), and whether it will be totalitarian, benign or participatory (the possibilities being in that order).

Mendlovitz is a professor law at Rutgers University and a member of the Council on Foreign Relations. He has taken great pains "to thank the Carnegie Endowment for International Peace and the Rockefeller Foundation for the support which they gave to specific research within the World Order Models Project."

"I believe," says Mendlovitz, "that the most likely governance by the end of the century—compelled by the arms races and outbreaks of violence, the food, population and environmental imbalances as well as large-scale, serious injustice—will be oligarchic and highly repressive."

To forestall that, he contends, we will need

356

"disarmament," a world police force and other machinery.

Princeton Professor Richard A. Falk is another member of the Council on Foreign Relations.

In the 1975 volume, **On the Creation of a Just World Order** (edited by Mendlovitz, New York, Free Press), Falk lays out a map.

The seventies, he reveals, were to be the decade of "consciousness raising," the eighties of "mobilization," and the nineties the decade of "transformation."

This approach was to involve early the transformation of the European Economic Community into a regional government.

The first direct elections to a European Parliament were held in 1979.

Regionalism is also going forward at other levels. The Trilateral Commission is developing the "partnership" of Western Europe, North America and Japan.

David Rockefeller's college roommate, and longtime director of the Council on Foreign Relations, George S. Franklin, was chosen as the Commission's first North American Secretary; meanwhile, Zbigniew Brzezinski, another CFR member, became the first director of the Trilateral Commission. At least 13 Trilateral Commission members have held top positions in the Carter Administration.

They include President Jimmy Carter, Vice President Walter Mondale, National Security Advisor Brzezinski, former Secretary of State Cyrus Vance, Secretary of Defense Harold Brown, former United Nations Ambassador Andrew Young, and former Secretary of the Treasury Michael Blumenthal.

Professor Richard Ullman commented concerning the Trilateral Commission in **Foreign Affairs** for October, 1976, that the desired "result—to quote Zbigniew

357

Brzezinski, the former Director of the Trilateral Commission—would be 'a community of the developed nations.' "

During his address to the Chicago Council on Foreign Relations, as recorded in the Congressional Record of May 11, 1976, candidate Carter said: "...Our policies should be aimed at building a just and peaceful world order, in which every nation can have a constructive role.

President Carter declared in his inaugural "Statement to the World" of Jan. 20, 1977: "The United States will meet its obligation to help create a stable, just and peaceful world order."

Of Europe, North America and Japan, he said: "We can make our societies the strong and stable inner core around which world cooperation, prosperity and peace can develop.

"...If our aim is to construct an international order, we must also work through the international bodies that now exist."

Professor Richard A. Falk, a Senior Fellow at the Institute for World Order, Inc., in a booklet entitled "Future Worlds," published as part of the Foreign Policy Association's Headline Series in 1976 (No. 229) said:

> ...The sheer complexity of a world system in which more than 150 sovereign states interact on a wide variety of issues creates a powerful urge toward some form of centralized political management.
>
> International pressures upon advanced industrial countries like the United States will heighten

national receptivity to global reform to the point where candidates for elective office might seriously begin to stress world order issues as early as 1980.

...One can conclude that a new system of world order is necessary, but that governments and national leaders are not likely under present circumstances to take sufficient initiatives toward its attainment.

...The first step toward a new world order is to build a consensus in this country and elsewhere in support of the idea. Such a consensus-building process will vary according to the domestic system of public order; the degree and quality of democratic accountability will determine the degree to which a new concensus depends on convincing national leadership groups or the citizenry as a whole.

...The broad movement for global reform presently taking shape in various parts of the world remains largely in the prepolitical stage in which the prime task is to form a more alert public opinion.

Hence some good old-fashioned education...propaganda...brainwashing seems in order—at least in the free world. Such wasteful efforts are, fortunately, unnecessary in other parts of the world—or isn't that what the professor is saying?

To achieve this, central institutions would have to be equipped with police capabilities while national institutions would be substantially deprived of military capabilities.

If the following statement taken from the Foreign Policy Association's Headline Series No. 228 can be considered accurate, the World Order propaganda and training is having its calculated effect on the government of the United States. In it, Lincoln and Irirangi Bloomfield say:

...A recent survey of 126 state department officials not noted for sentimental or woolly thinking on international relations showed 73% favoring turning over at least some elements of national sovereignty to an internationally elected body. A majority of U.S. military officers polled gave the same answers.

But promoters of the New World Order are becoming more cautious.

Professor Richard N. Gardner, a top Carter advisor who was Ambassador to Italy, explained the strategy in the Council on Foreign Relations journal, Foreign Affairs for April of 1974.

The hope, announced Gardner, lies "not in building up a few ambitious central institutions of universal membership and general jurisdiction as was envisaged at the end of the last war, but rather in the much more decentralized, disorderly and pragmatic process of inventing or adapting institutions of limited jurisdiction and selected membership to deal with specific problems on a case-by-case basis, as the necessity for cooperation is perceived by the relevant nations."

In short, said the Columbia professor, the " 'house of world order' will have to be built from the bottom up rather than from the top down....An end run around national sovereignty eroding it piece by piece will accomplish much more than the old-fashioned frontal assault."

He continues, "The hopeful aspect of the present situation is that even as nations resist appeals for 'world government' and 'the surrender of sovereignty,' technological, economic and political interests are forcing them to establish more and more far-ranging institutions to manage their mutual interdependence."

The Aspen Institute (for Humanistic Studies) spells it out in a brochure: "The most important changes will be modifications in attitudes which, in the nature of our pluralism, must first take place in the reasoning consciences of millions of individuals. The most important adjustment of all will be to blur, then erase, the psychic frontier between 'domestic affairs' and 'international affairs.' "

We are to be conditioned to forget that we are Americans or Canadians or whatever and become citizens of the New World.

Way back in April, 1966, the **Daughters of the American Republic** Magazine contained these words:

> Only an awakening of the American people to the realization that they are exchanging their once free Republic for a materialistic, atheistic, centralized government, and their heritage for a mess of pottage, can save them from the fate of earlier civilizations.
>
> Americans must refuse to surrender their liberties! A heavy hand is already knocking on their door!
>
> Only through a reversal of policies and the restoration of government by the people, for the people and of the people, can we reach onward and upward to greater heights of achievement and abundance....
>
> A grave responsibility rests with the American people at this time in our history. For if the lights of freedom are snuffed out within our country, they will be extinguished for all the world.

APPENDIX F

PART ONE

1. (Dan. 8:23). In this verse the Antichrist is called a "king of fierce countenance." However, before the significance of this name is examined, we must consider a prior question. Is the reference here to the Antichrist, or is the subject Antiochus IV, who is clearly in view as the little horn of verse 9? In Daniel 8 there seems to be a movement in verses 9 through 27 in which Daniel at first sees Antiochus IV as a type of Antichrist and then moves on to a vision of the prototype - the Antichrist himself. Perhaps the transition occurs at 8:23 where Antiochus IV, the Greek little horn, becomes the king of fierce countenance, the Antichrist. [193]

Moreover, there is another evidence that a transition from Antiochus to Antichrist occurs in this vision, for the vision which Daniel had of the little horn in verses 9-14 is a clear reference to the reign of Antiochus IV. But the interpretation which Gabriel gives to this vision carries the subject far beyond Antiochus IV and the second century B.C., to the end-time reign of the Antichrist. In fact, in these verses which follow the vision of Daniel in verses 9-14, the "time of the end," or its equivalent, is mentioned three times, verses 17, 19, and 26. So it is not a question of who is in view in Daniel 8, **either** Antiochus IV **or** the Antichrist. **Both** are in view. Daniel first sees Antiochus IV (vv. 9-14) and then moves in vision to the time of the end (vv. 23-27) and describes the reign of the Antichrist, whom he calls the king of fierce countenance.

PART TWO

2. Antiochus IV: A Type of the Antichrist

During the first year of the reign of Belshazzar, king of

Babylon, Daniel the prophet had a dream, the substance of which is recorded in Daniel 7:1-28. He sees four beasts emerging from the great sea. These beasts represent the four great world empires whose succession **constitutes the times of the gentiles**. They are Babylon, 7:4; Medo-Persia, 7:5; Greece, 7:6; and Rome, 7:7.

THE TWO HORNS OF DANIEL SEVEN AND EIGHT

As Daniel contemplates the fourth beast which represents ancient Rome, he describes it as "terrible and powerful, and strong exceedingly; and it had great iron teeth; it devoured and brake in pieces, and stamped the residue with its feet; and it was diverse from all the beasts that were before it." He **also notes that the beast has ten horns**. Out of these ten horns "there came up among them another horn, a little one, before which three of the first horns were plucked up by the roots; and, behold, in this horn were eyes like the eyes of a man, and a mouth speaking great things" (Dan. 7:8). Without taking note of the age of the church which separates the ancient Roman empire from the revived Roman empire of the last days, Daniel views the Antichrist arising out of the ten-nation confederation that constitutes this revived form of the Roman empire during the tribulation period. This little horn which has the eyes of a man and which speaks great things is the Antichrist. This is clear from the fact that he will make war with the saints and "prevailed against them; **until** the ancient of days came (that is, until the second coming of Christ), and judgment was given to the saints of the Most High, and the time came that the saints possessed the kingdom" (Dan. 21-11)

Daniel sees a different little horn in chapter 8. "And out of one of them came forth a little horn, which waxed exceedingly great, toward the south, and toward the east and toward the glorious land" (Dan. 8:9)

If the little horn of Daniel 7 & 8 is the Antichrist, then what is the identity of the little horn of Daniel 8:9? Does this little horn also represent the Antichrist? An answer of yes or no must be qualified. Only typically can the little horn of Daniel 8:9 be construed as the Antichrist. Actually, the little horn of Daniel 8:9 represents a person whose coming was yet future in Daniel's day, but who has already crossed the stage of history as far as we are concerned. The little horn of Daniel 8 is the sinister ruler of the house of Seleucus, Antiochus IV Epiphanes, who reigned in Syria between 175 and 163 B.C. This identity is made clear in Daniel 8:19 and following. The identification of this little horn with Antiochus IV is also clarified by comparing the text of Daniel with the history of the Greek world in the second, third, and fourth centuries B.C. In addition, note that the little horn arose out of **one** of the four notable horns (8:8-9). The **one** of the four notable horns was the horn that represented Alexander's General Seleucus. For he, along with Ptolemy, Cassander, and Lysimachus, inherited Alexander's empire when he died. Antiochus IV arose several generations later out of the horn which represents the Seleucid dynasty. [194]

PART THREE

3. Twice Daniel describes the reign of Antiochus IV: Daniel 8:9-14, and again in 11:21-45. But each time he moves beyond the reign of Antiochus IV and pictures the coming reign of the Antichrist. Just as Isaiah begins with a description of the King of Babylon and lapses into a description of Satan (Is. 14:1-20), and just as Ezekiel begins with a description of the king of Tyre from which he moves on into a description of Satan (Eze. 28:1-19), so

Daniel employs the same literary method to present the Antichrist. In each case he begins with Antiochus IV, but his vision soon moves to the end of the age where his picture of Antiochus IV merges with a picture of the Antichrist. This is consistent with the method of the Hebrew prophets, however, for they often move into the prophetic future by describing some contemporary event. This is not to say that Daniel is conscious of the fact that he is seeing two different persons who are separated from each other by many hundreds of years--already more than two millennia. Daniel is only recording his vision and the interpretation of this vision which was given to him (Dan. 8:15-17). However, in the light of the fuller revelation of God in the prophetic word, we now recognize that Daniel is actually presenting the person of the Antichrist by first presenting the person of Antiochus IV. 195

PART FOUR

4. John uses it in a unique way, for he has in view the contemporary spirit of the Antichrist, more than the person of the Antichrist who will appear in the last days.

It is the contemporary dimension of the Antichrist that is set forth in John's writings. Daniel hints at this idea when he uses Antiochus IV as an historical example, indicating in this that the spirit of Antichrist was already present in Antiochus IV. It is for this reason also that Daniel could move in his discussion of Antiochus IV to the Antichrist without even indicating transition. Paul also hints at this same idea when he says that "the mystery of lawlessness doth already work" (2 Thess. 2:7), even before the revelation of the lawless one. But it is John who most clearly enunciates this contemporary theme in his theology of the Antichrist.   196

5. When the Antichrist emerges as a new caesar at the head of the revived Roman empire, he will face the same problem that Antiochus IV faced. Daniel says that the empire which the Antichrist will head will be like a mixture of iron and clay. It will be an empire as strong as iron, but with the constant potential of falling apart. The Antichrist will have to spend the first part of his reign in welding together his empire--just as Antiochus IV did. And just as Antiochus used the force of ideas embodied in Hellenism to accomplish this unity, the Antichrist will also use the force of ideas to accomplish the unification of the people in his domain. The Hellenistic ideas that Antiochus used had a strong religious element in them. The Antichrist will also use religion to weld together his empire. During the first three and one-half years, the forces of cohesive religion will center in Judaism and in the apostate church. But during the great tribulation period, the religious maelstrom will have the Antichrist himself at its center.

At first the Antichrist will permit the Jews to practice their ancient religion. This seems to be his policy until mid-tribulation period (cf. Dan. 9:27). He will also permit the apostate world church to continue its worship. But this too he will terminate at mid-tribulation (cf. Rev. 17:1ff). When he stops the worship of both Jews and gentiles at mid-tribulation, he will then divert the religious inclinations of these two groups to himself, just as Antiochus IV tried to stamp out Judaism and divert the worship of the Jews to himself.

The Crash of '87:

How Does it Fit into the Prophetic Scenario?

Black Monday. October 19, 1987!

TIME magazine's November 2, 1987 cover succinctly told the story in bold black headlines: "THE CRASH: After a wild week on Wall Street, the world is different."

On Black Monday, the Dow Jones industrial average dived by 22.6%, far more than on the worst day of the ill-famed 1929 crash, which plunged the world into an incredible recession and turmoil. And, as TIME pointed out, the Crash of '87 sent stock markets around the world plummeting to record losses.

All around the globe people wondered--was this the beginning of the end? Was Black Monday the first indication that the many predictions, made for years by scores of economists and authors, of an unprecedented global economic collapse were coming to pass?

In the days immediately after October, 19, I (probably because of having written this book) was approached for an opinion by numerous individuals, several reporters and by the editor of a regional newspaper. I was invariably asked whether I saw Black Monday to be a key factor which would speed the onset of the Biblically-predicted Antichrist, who, as has been shown throughout this book, will be earth's final dictator, and certainly an economist.

My response was to, first of all, make it very clear

that I am neither an economist nor a prophet. Consequently, I am unable to speak with any authority on the economy in the immediate future.

Having established that fact, however, I indicated that I did not believe Black Monday was the end in terms of a global financial collapse. Rather, I said I believed it to be just a factor (a very important one, to be sure) in the continuing "setting of the stage" for the appearance of the Antichrist.

I hold that opinion even more firmly, eight months later, as this update is being prepared. Certainly, as Larry Burkett said in his *Christian Economic Newsletter* of December, 1987: "I think it's safe to say (after Black Monday) that we dodged the bullet that could have plunged us into the next great depression." Burkett went on to say:

> We dodged this bullet because of three basic factors: one, the rest of the economy was basically sound; two, we had a stable, authoritarian president; and, three, we had no other major crisis at hand. But under different circumstances we might be reading headlines about companies collapsing, banks closing, food rationing and riots in the cities.
>
> We have weathered a genuine crisis in the stock market. The rapidity of this crisis and the realization of how close we came to a full-blown collapse should capture everyone's attention. This economy is so vulnerable to any emotional reaction that anything can happen. Once it starts, it's too late to do anything about it. But memories are short and this too will pass and things will get VERY tough for a long

time. We have been, and are, living beyond our means.

Many other voices are warning that, though the world has apparently survived the Crash of '87, the global economic outlook is not encouraging. Glance over my shoulder as I flip through my files on this subject:

THE MCALVANY INTELLIGENCE ADVISOR, January 1988, P. 2: "The Roaring 20's and the Soaring 80's are looking more alike all the time." Further, it quotes billionaire Ross Perot speaking in the *Wall Street Journal*:

The crash was like a giant tapping us on the shoulder. But what have we done about the deficit? Nothing. What have we done about the Third World loans? Nothing. What have we done about our savings and loan system? Nothing. We had this big shock-- everybody was frightened--but now we're just bumbling along.

And as Julian Snyder recently wrote in *International Moneyline*: 'As the country moves into recession, the dollar will collapse as foreign investors lose all confidence in the U.S. The Fed will be forced to respond by raising interest rates, which will catapult the economy into depression...the government will impose drastic controls on foreign exchange; America will be financially quarantined, and Americans won't be allowed to take any money out of the country.

TIME, December 28, 1987, p. 54:
Rain or Shine? Black Monday has had surprisingly little economic impact, but dangers still loom.... Pes-

simists see parallels between the stock market today
and just after the 1929 Crash. At that time, stocks
rallied for several months and did not collapse again
until September 1930. In retrospect this interlude
was seen as the 'sucker's rally' that preceded the
Great Depression. If nothing is done to curb borrowing and reduce deficits, history may yet repeat
itself.

MACLEAN'S, April 11, 1988, p. 5:
The depressing truth is that the Third World cannot
pay its way--and yet must borrow to develop.... That
aside, Canada is doing what is right by becoming
one of the few countries to realize that we are at the
brink and that the Third World may have no choice
but to eventually balk at paying for part of its loans.

HOW TO MANAGE YOUR MONEY, April 15,
1988, p. 6:
We are in a HIGHLY unstable economic cycle where
anything could happen. A crash could occur over a
minor economic incident, but so could a rally. When
weighed in the balance, I would say the chances of
an economic downturn outweigh the chances of an
upturn by at least three-to-one.

MACLEAN'S, April 25, 1988, pp. 36, 37: "Many
stock market analysts...predict that a severe recession will occur in late 1989 or early 1990 and that
when it comes it will be aggravated by high consumer, corporate and government debt."

FORTUNE, April 25, 1988, p. 121: "Conducting
the monetary affairs of a debtor nation means less
manoeuvering room for the Federal Reserve. Yes-

terday's pat answers don't work anymore."

TIME, April 25, 1988, p. 38:
The bad news hit the financial markets last week like a right cross from Heavyweight Champ Mike Tyson. An unexpected rise in the U.S. trade deficit knocked down the dollar against foreign currencies and sent the U.S. stock and bond markets reeling...the threat of a downturn--and another stock-market crisis--loomed once again.

FORTUNE, April 25, pp. 87: *"Has the Debt Binge Gone Too Far?* Not yet, says the latest assessment. But with recession possible and debt disasters popping up, it's time for most companies to reign in the impulse to borrow."

THE PROVINCE (Vancouver), Sunday, May 8, 1988, p. 43: "Share prices in New York and Toronto slipped Friday for the third consecutive day as investors continued to worry about higher inflation and interest rates."

FORTUNE, May 23, 1988, pp. 77-79: *"To the U.S. From the IMF: Shape Up!* As America's foreign debt swells, the scourge of prodigal nations prescribes cutting the federal budget deficit and consuming less...more and more economists argue for tough action."

TIME, May 23, 1988, pp. 34-36:
Blowing Off Some Steam. With the economy threatening to overheat, Greenspan (Federal Reserve Chairman) fights to avert an inflationary explosion. What is going on here? By all accounts, the 5 1/2-year-old economic expansion should be fizzling out.

Already ancient by historical standards, the upswing appeared to have suffered a devastating blow when the stock market crashed last October. But, defying expectation, the economy is still running and even blowing off enough steam to inspire fears that it may actually be overheating. Forget about a recession, many economists counsel, and start worrying about inflation. Once a faint and far-off danger, rising prices may now pose the gravest threat to economic stability.

"Controlling inflation long-term is hopeless," says internationally noted economist Jerome Smith, author of *The Coming Currency Collapse*. "Around the corner is what appears to be the final blow-off in the great inflationary cycle of the last 50 years."

So the economic world is very jittery as the end of the 80's comes upon us. And apparently with good cause.

But, someone asks, how does all this fit into the preparation for the unveiling of the Antichrist? To answer that question it's important to understand what has been called the "Blueprint for Building the New World Order."

An excellent analysis of this "blueprint" has been developed by Peter Lalonde, researcher and co-editor of the monthly *Omega-Letter*. (See note 1 end of chapter.)

The extensive article, quoted here by permission of Mr. Lalonde, points out that

the New World Order consists of three central parts--a World Government, a World Economy and a single, united One-World Religion--all of which we believe to be a clear fulfillment of the prophetic Word.

World Government: '...and power was given over all kindreds, and tongues, and nations' (Rev. 13:7). 'The fourth beast shall be the fourth kingdom upon earth, which shall be diverse from all kingdoms, and shall devour the whole earth, and shall tread it down, and break it in pieces' (Daniel 7:23).

World Economy: 'And he causeth all, both small and great, rich and poor, freed and bond, to receive a mark in their right hand, or in their foreheads: And that no man might buy or sell, save he that had the mark, or the name of the beast, or the number of his name' (Rev. 13:16-17).

World Religion: 'And they worshipped the dragon which gave power unto the beast: and they worshipped the beast, saying, who is like unto the beast? who is able to make war with him? (Rev. 13:4). 'And all that dwell upon the earth shall worship him, whose names are not written in the book of life of the Lamb slain from the foundation of the world' (Rev. 13:8).

In our analysis of these trends, we look at many seemingly diverse and unrelated issues-- from constitutional issues to monetary issues to New Age mega-events to the technological developments in electronic banking. However, it is of utmost importance that we understand how these apparently diverse issues are related. And, as we shall see, their relationship is not restricted to their fulfillment of Bible prophecy, they are also integral parts of the Blueprint that most globalists and New Agers are following in their attempt to bring forth their envisioned New Age of Peace and Prosperity.

The Blueprint. At one time, not too many years go, students of Bible prophecy, who were watching the trends leading toward the envisioned New World Order, had a relatively easy time. All they had to do was watch a few key organizations such as the United Nations or the Council on Foreign Relations and see exactly what these powerful globalist institutions were espousing in terms of their desire to build a World Community. Today, however, with the proliferation of the New Age Movement and thousands of different groups working toward this New World Order, the task has become far more difficult.

This increasing difficulty not only has to do with the vastly increasing number of groups working in this direction but also has to do with the fact that many of the groups working toward this New World Order do not appear on the surface to be doing so at all.

Lalonde goes on in his very penetrating, perceptive and well-researched article to detail the various aspects of "The Blueprint." He lists these aspects as: world government, piece-by-piece; global management by crisis; critical instability as a factor, with the present economic system being shown to be at a point of critical instability; and transformation to world government through (1) social movements; (2) new science (which accepts the psychic human potential); the new image of man ("man is more than the sum of his mundane experiences: he is a spiritual entity, the *ultimate reality* is to be found in the realm of the spiritual and mystical, rather than the material and empirical"); and (3) a new central project for mankind (guided as Willis Herman suggests, by the new image of man ie. a spiritual being with psychic potential).

At the conclusion of the blueprint is a world leader. Lalonde writes:

> Ervin Laszlo, of The United Nations Institute for Training and Research (UNITAR), in speaking of how all of the various crises--environmental, overpopulation, economic and political-- combined with the new image of man, could bring about a moment of critical instability and thus a transformation to a New World Order, also noted another occurrence that will accompany the coming moment of critical instability:
>
> He said, 'How does all this apply to the contemporary condition of humankind? The answer is, I believe, obvious. We are now about to enter an epoch of critical instability. Unlike past such epochs, it will not be locally confined. Our world is so strongly interdependent that an instability in any sector or any part can and will spread with great rapidity and destabilize all societies.'

Such new realities as high speed communication, instant worldwide media coverage and the political-economic interdependency of the world, according to Laszlo, means that any major crisis will be worldwide in scope and any solution will also have to be global. And likewise with regard to the leader who will be thrust forward at this moment of critical instability, Laszlo concludes that he 'will not be locally confined. He will become a worldwide leader.'

Historian Arnold Toynbee claims that 'we are ripe for the deifying of any new Caesar who might succeed in giving the world unity and peace.'

And as Henry Spaak, the former Secretary General of NATO, claimed as early as 1957: 'We do not want another committee; we have too many already. What we want is a man of sufficient stature to hold the allegiance of all people and to lift us out of the economic morass into which we are sinking. Send us such a man and be he god or devil, we will receive him.'

And much like the globalist leaders believe that the moment of critical instability will greatly amplify the call for a New World Order, they also believe that this 'crisis of leadership' will be greatly magnified when a crisis or series of crises of unbelievable proportion hits the earth. It is in such a moment of crises that it seems that the Antichrist will emerge to fill this great leadership vacuum. And the Bible is very clear that the Antichrist will have great leadership capabilities... (Dan. 7:20; Dan. 7:8,11; Rev.

13:5; Dan. 7:25; Rev. 13:8;).

Lalonde notes that it is not only the globalists who are looking for their 'savior,' but so are the Buddhists, the Moslems, the Hindus, the Jews and the New Agers. All expect their 'savior' to come and set up the kingdom of God here on earth. All are wide open to the deception of the miracle-working Antichrist (*Omega-Letter*, July-August 1987, pp. 15-17).

I am convinced that events like Black Monday and similar future upheavals are an important part of the development of the "critical instability" which will create the one world scenario in which the Antichrist will star.

Peter Lalonde says it well:

The secret to a managed crisis is to have people accept something as a resolution to the crisis that they would never have accepted if that 'crisis' had not been brought to their attention. And when one begins to watch the highly publicized crises in the world today and the solutions being proposed to solve them, he begins to notice that in each instance the proposed solution is always a World Government, a World Court, World Law or a New International Economic Order--all parts of a New World Order (*Omega-Letter*, July-August 1987, p. 7).

Donald McAlvany, in his March 1988 *McAlvany Intelligence Advisor*, p. 6, comments that globalists such as the Rockefellers, Hammers, and others dream of a new "partnership" and "convergence" between America and the Soviet Union and that a one world monetary system, with a new world currency called the Phoenix, will give the needed impetus to international cooperation on such a level. The system would be controlled by automatic sanctions which would be beyond the control of the governments, forcing a relinquishment of national egotism. So says Edouard Balladur, the French Minister of Finance. Balladur continues:

'That is why I propose that the international community *entrust a small group of distinguished people of unquestionable moral authority...with the task of lighting our way.... Economic freedom will have little hope for the future unless it is based on a world order accepted by all and binding on all!*'

...One other interesting aspect of the *Wall Street Journal* article... were the illustrations. Note the eye in the triangle in each picture. Ever see it before? It's on the U.S. dollar bill.

It is also the symbol of the Illuminati, a group founded amongst the wealthy banking families of Western Europe in 1776 and dedicated to establishing a one-world global government. The Illuminati (the illumined ones) could be the dynamic behind... the current drive toward a global currency, monetary system and world order. The dynamic behind the Illuminati is that they are Satan worshippers--they worship Lucifer.... (Note the interesting language in the Balladur article: *'Entrust a small group of distinguished people of unquestionable moral authority with the task of lighting our way'* -- the illumined ones.) (*The McAlvany Intelligence Advisor*, March 1988, pp. 6-7.) (See note 2 end of chapter.)

When these disturbing economic developments occur against the backdrop of an incredible worldwide surge of interest and involvement in what is called "The New Age" movement, certainly we must conclude that *the hour is late*.

When European 'unification' (as predicted in FORTUNE magazine, Feb. 1, 1988) is anticipated for 1992, we sense that *the hour is late*.

When technological advances which boggle the mind continue to tie our world together, we must conclude that *the hour is late*. (Such advances are affecting even Third World countries. A missionary from Gabon, Africa, showed me her newly introduced Gabonese ID card which is compatible to the computerized lazer-scanned system so common to the Western world.)

So--stay tuned for future developments.

But above all else keep your ear cocked for the "sound of the trumpet."

And do be *sure* you're qualified to hear that sound--for if you're not (and it occurs) *you've lost everything*!

While you can (if you've not already done so), *run* to The Rock for safety.

Note 1: *Omega-Letter*, P.O. Box 744, North Bay, Ontario, Canada, P1B 8J8. Published monthly eleven times a year. Annual subscription $25.00 (Canadian currency).

Note 2: *The McAlvany Intelligence Advisor* is an explicitly Christian monthly analysis of global economic, monetary and geo-political trends as these impact the precious metals market. Subscription Office: P.O. Box 84904, Phoenix, AZ 85071.

For Further Reading:

Groothuis, Douglas R., *Unmasking the New Age*, (Downers Grove, IL, InterVarsity Press, 1986).

Hoyt, Karen, *The New Age Rage*, (Old Tappan, NJ, Fleming H. Revell Company, 1987).

Hunt, Dave, *Beyond Seduction*, (Eugene, OR, Harvest House Publishers, 1987).

Martin, Walter, *The Kingdom of the Cults*, (Minneapolis, MN, Bethany House Publishers, revised 1985).

Notes

Prologue

1. *Time*, September 7, 1981, p. 23.

Chapter One

2. Factual material for scenario excerpted from *The Coming Currency Collapse, Crisis Investing, After the Crash* and *The EcoSpasm Report* (see bibliography).

3. Jerome Smith, *The Coming Currency Collapse*, (Toronto, Bantam Books, 1981), p. 125.

4. Ibid., p. 126.

5. Ibid., p. 178.

6. Ibid., pp. 173-175.

7. Ibid., p. 179.

8. Ibid., pp. 185-187.

9. Douglas Casey, *Crisis Investing*, (New York: Pocket Books, 1981), pp. 235, 236.

Chapter Two

10. G. Abert, *After the Crash*, (Scarborough: New American Library, 1979), inside front cover.

11. *Canadian Business Magazine*, December 1979, p. 43.

12. *USNWR*, May 19, 1980.

13. *World Market Perspective*, November, 1980, p. 1.

14. *The Vancouver Sun*, February 2, 1982, p. D2.

15. *Business Week*, January 18, 1982, p. 28.

16. *The Economist*, January 18, 1982, p. 64.

17. *The Economist*, September 11, 1982, p. 56.

18. *The Vancouver Sun*, September 11, 1982, p. A2.

19. Edward Schumacher, *New York Times*, (reported in *The Province*, Vancouver, B.C., January 14, 1983, p. B2.

20. *The Province*, Vancouver, B.C. January 16, 1983, p. A3.

21. *The Province*, Vancouver, B.C., February 3, 1983, p. B12.

22. *Time*, January 10, 1983, pp. 34-41.

23. *The Vancouver Sun*, Vancouver, B.C. September 17, 1982, p. A1.

Chapter Three

24. *The Christian Inquirer: New World Order--Special Report*, June, 1980, p. 2.

25. Ibid., p. 2.

26. Material drawn from H. Lindsey, *The 1980's: Countdown to Armageddon*, (New York, Bantam Books, 1981; D. Stanton, *Mystery 666* (India, privately published, 1980, and various issues of *American Opinion*.

27. *The Christian Science Monitor*, February 7, 1977, p. 16.

28. One such step was the creation in March 1969 of a new medium of exchange--Special Drawing Rights (SDR). Don E. Stanton, in *Mystery 666*, explains:

The world was given a little insight into the future monetary system, on March 31, 1969, when the IMF (International Monetary Fund) announced that the nations were ready to start business, using a new type of exchange which would eventually replace all other currencies and even gold. This new medium was referred to as "Paper Gold," but it is neither paper nor gold. It is a number/credit system of Special Drawing Rights (SDR).

This was a big step forward, and on that same day, Pierre Schweitzer declared, "Gentlemen, we are right on schedule." In 1976 the IMF declared that gold would be replaced by SDR as the reserve of the Fund. Since then the Fund has been auctioning off its gold holdings.

SDR are simply numbers in the international "books" which represent the credit of the member nations. SDR are now being used for international trade. No currency is used, but the account of the nation is debited or credited for purchases or sales. SDR presents a unified unit for international trade. Existing currencies have a value in relationship to

SDR--for instance, one SDR may be worth $1.20 on the IMF books.

Eventually, however, all currencies will become obsolete and cancelled. SDR will then be the means for transactions for all individuals as well as nations. Naturally if the leading nations adopt the system (and they are doing that step by step) then all nations must follow. The only alternative would be complete isolation from world trade.

The changeover can be seen in many areas already. From 1977 on, airlines have been quoting passenger fares and cargo rates in SDR. The OPEC oil countries are considering an SDR pricing system.

The need is, however, not merely for a unified currency but for an instantaneous means of payment (other than handing over cash on the spot). SDR, of course, can't be "handed over," for they are numbers. They can only be debited or credited in the "books." And the "books" are not ordinary books, but computers.

SDR, though not the solution sought, are nevertheless an integral part of the "New Order."

D. Stanton, *Mystery 666*, (India, privately published, 1980), p. 53.

29. *Newsweek*, June 16, 1975, p. 45.

30. As quoted by H. Lindsey in *The 1980's: Countdown to Armageddon*, p. 122.

31. Ibid., p. 122.

32. *Foreign Affairs*, July 1975, p. 31.

33. As quoted by H. Lindsey, op. cit., p. 123.

34. *Atlantic Monthly*, September 1975, p. 28, 30.

35. *The 1980's: Countdown to Armageddon*, p. 124.

36. *U.S. News & World Report*, February 21, 1977, p. 34.

37. *U.S. News & World Report*, February 21, 1977, p. 33.

38. *The 1980's: Countdown to Armageddon*, p. 125.

39. Ibid., p. 125.

40. *"W" Magazine*, (Fairchild Publications, 7 East 12th, New York, N.Y., 10002), August 4-11, 1978, p. 21.

41. *The 1980's: Countdown to Armageddon*, p. 127.

42. Ibid., p. 128.

43. W.C. Skousen, *The Nake Capitalist*, (Salt Lake City; published privately, 1970), pp. 4,5.

44. C. Quigley, *Tragedy and Hope*, (New York: The MacMillan Company, 1966, pp. 136-144.

45. *American Opinion*, October, 1982, p. 84.

46. *American Opinion*, October 1982, pp. 26, 81, 83.

47. *American Opinion*, October, 1982, p. 84.

48. *CRF Special Study, No. 7*; November 25, 1959.

49. *American Opinion*, November, 1982, p. 94.

50. W. Wood, Jr., *New Money for a New World*, September, 1981, p. 3.

51. As quoted in *The Coming Currency Collapse*, p. 21.

52. H. Lindsey, op. cit., p. 128.

Chapter Four

53. *Houston Chronicle*, January 10, 1975, p. A2.

54. R. Hendrickson, *The Cashless Society*, (New York: Dodd, Mead & Company, 1972), pp. 283-285.

55. *Maclean's*, November 16, 1981, p. 42.

56. *San Bernardino News*, August 22, 1981, p. 22.

57. Quotation from sound track of the film, "The Future is in Your Hand."

58. *The Globe and Mail*, Toronto, May 11, 1980, p. B4.

59. *Burroughs Clearing House*, January, 1975, p. 12.

60. *Maclean's*, November 16, 1981, p. 42.

61. *Toronto Star*, November 10, 1981, p. 2.

62. *The Houston Post*, Houston, Texas, October 12, 1981, p. 15A.

63. *The Vancouver Sun*, Vancouver, B.C., September 8, 1981, p. A1.

64. *The Province*, Vancouver, B.C., October 26, 1981, p. B2.

65. *Smith Line Forum, Vol. IV, No. 1*, February, 1982, p. 2.

Chapter Five

66. As quoted in *The Coming World Dictator*, J.W. White (Minneapolis: Bethany Fellowship, 1981), p. 26.

Chapter Six

67. L. Dekostar, "Whither Bound, America?", as condensed in *The Christian Reader*, June 1981, pp. 6-9.

68. Ibid., p. 9.

69. J.C. Bennett, *Foreign Policy in Christian Perspective*, (New York: 1966), p. 63.

70. *The Pittsburg Catholic*, October 6, 1966, p. 3.

71. Z. Brzeninski, *Between Two Ages*, (New York: Penguin Books, 1973), p. 134.

72. *The Vancouver Sun*, December 27, 1981, p. A1.

73. *The Vancouver Sun*, April 3, 1980, p. A5.

74. *U.S. News & World Report*, March 16, 1980, p. 28.

75. *New York Times*, September 9, 1982, p. A3.

76. R. Steele, *The Mark Is Ready, Are You?* (College Place, Wash.: Project Research, 1978), pp. 34-65.

77. *Tacoma News Tribune*, Tacoma, Wash., December 14, 1980, p. B1.

78. W. Wood, *Cashless Society: World Without Money*, (Oklahoma City: Southwest Radio Church, 1977), p. 12.

79. *Houston Chronicle*, August 19, 1975, p. 1.

80. *Worldgram*, July, 1981, p. 3.

81. Michael Baigent, Richard Leigh and Henry Lincoln, *The Holy Blood and the Holy Grail*, 1982.

82. M. Abley, *Maclean's*, February 21, 1982, pp. 54, 55.

Chapter Seven

83. Quoted in H. Lindsey, *The Late Great Planet Earth*,

(Grand Rapids, Mich., Zondervan, 1970), p. 85.

84. *The Vancouver Sun*, January 10, 1982, p. A7.

85. *The Vancouver Sun*, November 16, 1980, p. A6.

86. *The Vancouver Sun*, September 16, 1981, p. A6.

87. Ibid., p. A6.

Chapter Eight

88. Micha Livnek and Ze'ev Mischel, *Masada*, a publication of the National Parks Authority of Israel, November, 1965, pp. 16, 17.

89. L. Lathan, *Israel: A Secret Documentary*, (Wheaton Ill.: Tyndale House Publishers, 1975).

90. C. Taylor, *Today in Bible Prophecy*, November, 1973, p. 8.

Chapter Nine

91. D.W. Gesenius, as quoted in *The Beginning of the End*, pp. 63, 64.

92. Statistics taken from an address, September 18, 1980, by Dr. L.L. King, New York, N.Y., President of The Christian and Missionary Alliance.

93. *Baltimore Evening Sun*, March 11, 1982, p. A2.

94. *The Houston Post*, November 20, 1981, p. 1.

95. *Time*, January 18, 1982, p. 38.

96. *Midnight Call*, February 1982, p. 4.

97. *Time*, March 1, 1982, p. 67.

98. *Pittsburg Press*, March 16, 1982, p. A1.

99. *Business Week*, March 22, 1982, p. 42.

100. C. Pack, Ed. *Dry Bones: Two Sticks and Falling Dominoes*, (Oklahoma City: Southwest Radio Church, 1974), p. 43.

101. *James Sinclair Report*, February, 1980, p. 3.

102. *Today*, (Gannet Westchester newspapers), March 27, 1979, pp. 1, 14.

103. *Aviation Week and Space Technology*, February 22, 1982, p.21.

104. *Bible in the News*, June 1982, p. 8.

105. Dr. L. L. King, address.

106. *The Vancouver Sun*, November 14, 1982, p. D12.

107. *The White House Years*.

108. *The Province*, August 31, 1982.

109. *The Vancouver Sun*, September 11, 1982, p. A2.

110. *Los Angeles Times*, October 6, 1977, p. B1.

111. *Los Angeles Times*, August 31, 1977, p. A7.

112. "The Terror Network," *The Readers' Digest*, July 1981, pp. 79-84.

113. *The Economist*, London, June 19, 1982, p. 23.

114. *The Jerusalem Post*, July 11, 1982, p. 11.

115. *The Jerusalem Post*, November 9, 1982, p. 2.

Chapter Ten

116. *The Vancouver Sun*, September 16, 1981, p. A6.

117. *The End Times Digest*, March, 1980, p. 7.

118. S. Kirban, *The Salem Kirban Reference Bible*, (Huntingdon Valley, Pa.: Salem Kirban, Inc. 1979), pp. 213-215.

119., J. Walvord, *Armageddon, Oil and the Middle East*, (Grand Rapids: Zondervan Publishing House, 1975), p. 46.

Chapter Eleven

120. H. Halley, ed., *Halley's Bible Handbook*, (Chicago: H.H. Halley, 1951), pp. 82, 83.

121. H. Lindsey, *There's A New World Coming*, (Santa Ana, Ca.: Vision House Publishers, 1973), p. 236.

122. As quoted in *Five Minutes to Midnight*, (London: Victory Press, 1971), pp. 49-52.

123. *The Christian Beacon*, June 11, 1970, p. 1.

124. *The Christian Inquirer*, March, 1981, p. 7.

125. "$125,000 to Guerillas," *Globe and Mail*, Toronto, September 22, 1981, p. A3.

126. *Signs of the Times*, January 1981, pp. 10, 11.

127. *Canadian Ecumenical News*, November/December, 1982, pp. 4, 5.

128. Ibid., p. 1.

129. A 1973 Canadian Crusade Evangelism *Special Newsletter*.

130. B. Alexander, "The Coming World Religion," *The Christian Reader*, July/August, 1981, p. 5.

Chapter Twelve

131. B. Bright, "Humanism--The Grand Delusion," *Worldwide Challenge, Vol. 8, No. 3*, March 1981, pp. 6-9.

132. C. Lamont, *The Philosophy of Humanism* (New York: Frederich Unger Publishing Co., 1967), p. 83.

133. *Torcaso v. Watkins*, 367 U.S. 488, 1961.

134. Adapted from pp. 47-83 of T. LaHaye's *Battle For The Mind*, (Old Tappen, N.J.: Fleming H. Revell Company, 1980).

135. F. Schaeffer and C.E. Koop, *Whatever Happened to the Human Race?* (Old Tappan N.J.: Fleming H. Revell Company, 1979), p. 21.

136. As quoted in "Humanism--The Grand Delusion."

137. P. Blanschard, "Three Cheers for Our Secular State," *The Humanist*, March/April, 1976, p. 17.

138. *Dittman, et al v. Western Washington University*, Cause No.1 C-79-1189-V. In United States District Court, Western District of Washington at Seattle, Washington (1979). Amicus brief filed by Center for Law and Religious Freedom.

Chapter Thirteen

139. *Chicago Tribune*, January 11, 1980, p. A3.

140. *The Christian Inquirer*, April 1980, p. 7.

141. *U.S. News & World Report*, May 19, 1980, pp. 23-26.

142. *Christian Life*, July 1980, pp. 26-29.

143. *The Globe and Mail*, September 26, 1981, p. 9.

144. *U.S. News & World Report*, November 3, 1980, pp. 57-60.

145. *Moody Monthly*, November, 1980, pp. 32-41.

146. *Maclean's*, February 15, 1982, cover.

147. *The Vancouver Sun*, March 8, 1982, p. A2.

148. *Newsweek*, June 28, 1982, cover.

149. *U.S. News & World Report*, August 16, 1982, pp. 58, 59.

150. *The Province*, August 27, 1982, p. B2.

151. *The Vancouver Sun*, September 8, 1982, p. C8.

152. C. Chant, R. Holmes, W. Koening, eds., *Two Centuries of Warfare*, (Hong Kong: Octopus Books, 1978).

153. *The Plain Truth*, October 1982, p. 7.

154. *The Vancouver Sun*, January 18, 1983, p. A4.

155. Quoted from Dr. John W. White in *World War III*, (Grand Rapids: Zondervan Publishing House, 1977), pp. 46-50.

156. *The Vancouver Sun*, April 8, 1979, p. A5.

157. *The Readers' Digest*, June 1981, pp. 159-166.

158. *The Vancouver Sun*, August 30, 1980, p. C16; November 29, 1980, p.A1. *The Seattle Post-Intelligencer*, February 25, 1981, p. A10; *The Province*, March 11, 1981, p. A6; *The Vancouver Sun*, March 21, 1981, p. A1, 8; March 30, 1981, p. A10. *The Province*, April 14, 1981, p. E1; February 7, 1982, p. F10. *The Vancouver Sun*, March 20, 1982, p. A1; *The Province*, January 20, 1982, p. D2; December 20, 1982, p. A3; January 8, 1983, p. A1.

159. *U.S. News & World Report*, August 2, 1982, p. 56.

160. As quoted by L. Ward in *And There Will be FAMINES*, (Glendale: Regal books, 1974), p. 24.

161. G. Borgstom, in *The Hungry Planet*, quoted in *And There Will be FAMINES*, p. 84.

162. *The Vancouver Sun*, July 13, 1979, p. A12; August 15, 1979, p. A5; **August 30**, 1979, p. A19; November 11, 1979, p. A10. *Time*, January 21, 1980, pp. 8-15; *The Plain Truth*, March 1980, pp. 24, 30 *U.S. News & World Report*, August 18, 1980, pp. 54, 55; *The Vancouver Sun*, September 17, 1980, p. B11; *Prophetic News Letter*, December 1980, p. 2; *The Globe and Mail*, March 12, 1981, p. 7; *The Leader Post*, Regina, May 25, 1981, p. C11; *U.S. News & World Report*, July 27, 1981, pp. 54, 55; *The Province*, October 7, 1981, p. A3; *Prophetic News Letter*, October, 1981, p. 4; *The Globe and Mail*, October, 28, 1981, p. 7; *The Province*, March 28, 1982, p. A3; August, 2, 1982, p. B2.

163. *The Sunday Oregonian Parade Magazine*, September 30, 1979.

164. *United Press International*, Rome, Italy, February 8, 1981.

165. *Newsweek*, August 31, 1981, pp. 68-71.

166. *The Province*, January 14, 1983, p. B2.

167. "The Invisible Enemy: Acid Rain could eventually destroy all life in the world," *The Province*, September 15, 1982, p. B2, December 6, 1982, p. A1.

168. *Time*, July 29, 1980, p. 58.

169. *U.S. News & World Report*, August 2, 1980, p. 61.

170. "AIDS: A Plague of Fear," *Discover*, July 1983, pp. 28, 29.

171. *The Province*, August 17, 1981, p. C8; *Sudan Interior Mission News Service*, June 1980, p. 10; *Globe & Mail*, November 12, 1981, p. 10; *The Vancouver Sun*, June 9, 1982, p. C7.

172. G. Utting, "Wacky Weather," *The Province*, January 16, 1983, p. B3.

173. *U.S. News & World Report*, February 22, 1982, pp. 66-69.

174. *The Province*, March 10, 1982, p. A2.

175. *The Vancouver Sun*, November 5, 1981, p. C3.

176. *The Province*, January 25, 1982, p. B8.

177. *The Province*, September 15, 1982, p. A1.

178. *The Province*, April 21, 1982, p. A3.

179. As Quoted in *The Beginning of the End*, p. 54.

180. *The Province*, June 28, 1981, p. B1.

181. *The Province*, October 27, 1982, p. A10.

182. *U.S. News & World Report*, February 23, 1981, p. 65.

183. *Psychology Today*, September 1981, pp. 27-29.

184. *U.S. News & World Report*, July 21, 1980, p. 70.

185. *The Bible in the News*, May 1982, p. 19.

186. *The Province*, March 9, 1982, p. A3.

187. *Maclean's*, July 26, 1982, p. 3.

188. *The Province*, December 17, 1982, p. A2.

189. *The Province*, January 14, 1983, p. A3.

190. *The Vancouver Sun*, April 25, 1982, p. A12.

191. J.W. White, *World War III*, pp. 31-38.

192. A. Toffler, *The Third Wave*, (New York: Morrow, 1980), cover.

Appendix F

193. Walter K. Price, *The Coming Anti-Christ*, pp. 45, 46.

194. Ibid., pp. 77, 78.

195. Ibid., p. 87.

196. Ibid., p. 150.

197. Ibid, pp. 122-124.

Bibliography

Abert, Geoffrey. *After the Crash*, Scarborough, Ont.: New American Library, 1979.

Allen, Gary. "Troubled Bankers." *American Opinion*, October 1982, pp. 1-6, 97-110.

_____ "Our Economy Trembles Atop the Banking Pyramid." *American Opinion*, January 1983, pp. 31-90, 77-82.

_____ *None Dare Call It Conspiracy*. Rossmoor, Ca.: Concord Press, 1971.

_____ "Insiders of the Great Conspiracy." *American Opinion*, September 1982, pp. 41-54, 73-78.

Balizet, C. *The Seven Last Years*. New York, N.Y.: Bantam Books, 1980.

Bloomfield, A.E. *How to Recognize the Antichrist*. Minneapolis, Minn.: Bethany Fellowship, Inc. 1975.

Campbell, D. *Daniel, Decoder of Dreams*. Wheaton, Ill.: Victor Books, 1972.

Cantelon, Willard. *Money Master of the World*. Plainfield, N.J.: Logos International, 1976.

Casey Douglas. *Crisis Investing*. New York, N.Y.: Pocket Books, 1980.

Clark, Doug. *The Greatest Banking Scandal in History*. Eugene, Ore.: Harvest House Publishers, 1981.

Collins, L. and D. Lapierre. *O Jerusalem!* New York, N.Y.: Pocket Books, 1973.

Goetz, W.R. *Apocalypse Next*. Beaverlodge, Alta.: Horizon House, 1981, Chaps. 2,6,8.

Gothard, W. *Be Alert to Spiritual Danger*. Wheaton, Ill.: IBYC, 1979.

Hendrickson, Robert. *The Cashless Society*. New York,

N.Y.: Dodd, Mead & Company, 1972.

Humanist Manifestos, I and II, 1933, 1973. Buffalo, N.Y.: Prometheus Books, 1973.

Kirban, S. *Satan's Angels Exposed*. Huntingdon Valley, Pa.: Salem Kirban, Inc., 1980.

_____ *The Rise of Antichrist*. Huntingdon Valley, Pa. Salem Kirban, Inc., 1978.

_____ *Satan's Mark Exposed: 666*. Huntingdon Valley, Pa.: Salem Kirban, Inc. 1981.

La Haye, T. *The Battle for the Mind*. Old Tappan, N.J.: Fleming H. Revell, 1980.

Larson, Bob. *Larson's Encyclopedia of Cults*. Wheaton, Ill.: Tyndale House Publishers, 1982.

Latham, L. *Israel: A Secret Documentary*. Wheaton, Ill.: Tyndale House Publishers, 1975.

Lewis, David A. *Magog 1982 Cancelled*. Harrison, Ark.: New Leaf Press, 1982.

Lindsell, H. *The Gathering Storm*. Wheaton, Ill.: Tyndale House Publishers, 1980.

Lindsey, Hal. *The 1980's: Countdown to Armageddon*. New York, N.Y.: Bantam Books, 1981.

_____ *The Late Great Planet Earth*. Grand Rapids, Mich.: Zondervan Publishing House, 1970.

_____ *There's a New World Coming*. Santa Ana, Ca.: Vision House Publishers, 1973.

McCall, T. and Z. Levitt. *Satan in the Sanctuary*. Irvine, CA.: Harvest House Publishers, 1973.

McDowell, Josh. *Daniel in the Critics' Den*. San Bernardino, CA.: Campus Crusade for Christ, 1979.

_____ *Evidence That Demands a Verdict*. Arrowhead Springs, Ca.: Campus Crusade for Christ, 1972.

Novak, N.D. "The Changing Scene in World Economics." *Canadian Banker and ICB Review*, August 1981.

Phillips, M. *The Spirit World*. (An abridgement of *The Bible, the Supernatural, and the Jews*.) Wheaton, Ill.: Victor Books, 1972.

Price, Walker K. *The Coming Antichrist*. Chicago, Ill.: Moody Press, 1974.

Relfe, Mary Stewart. *The New Money System*. Montgomery, Al.: Ministries, Inc., 1982.

Skousen, W.C. *The Naked Capitalist*. Salt Lake City, Utah: by the author, 1970.

Smith, Jerome. *The Coming Currency Collapse*. Toronto, Ont.: Bantam Books, 1981.

Stang, Alan. "New Book by Quigley adds more PROOFS OF A CONSPIRACY." *American Opinion*, October 1982, pp. 19-26, 81-84.

Stantin, Don. *Mystery 666*. Secunderabad, India: Maranatha Revival Crusade, 1978.

Steele, R. *The Mark is Ready, Are You?* College Place, Wash.: Project Research, 1978.

Stoner, P.W. and R.C. Newman. *Science Speaks*. Chicago, Ill.: Moody Press, 1976.

Toffler, Alvin. *The Eco-Spasm Report*. New York N.Y.: Bantam Books, 1975.

Van Impe, J. *Israel's Final Holocaust*. Nashville, Tenn.: Thomas Nelson Publisher, 1979.

Ward, Larry. *And There Will Be Famines*. Glendale, Ca.: Regal Books, 1974.

Weldon, J. and Z. Levitt. *Encounters with UFOs*. Irvine, Ca: Harvest House Publisher's, 1975.

Weldon, J. and C. Wilson. *1980s Decade of Shock*. San Diego, Ca.: Master Books, 1978.

White, John Wesley. *The Coming World Dictator*. Minneapolis, Minn.: Bethany Fellowship, 1981.

Williams, L. *The Energy Non Crisis*. Wheatridge, Co.: Worth Publishing Co., 1980.

About the Author

William R. Goetz, or "Pastor Bill" as he is better known, is Senior Pastor of the Sevenoaks Alliance Church in Abbotsford, B.C., a congregation which has grown during the 15 years of his leadership there from about 500 to a constituency now approaching 3,600 with nearly 2,500 in regular attendance.

A graduate of Canadian Bible College in Regina, Saskatchewan, "Pastor Bill" has been a long-time student of the prophetic Scriptures and current events as they relate to prophecy.

A former National Youth Director in New York for his church, and editor of COMPASS magazine, he has had a number of articles and pamphlets published. *The Economy to Come* is his second book. His first, *Apocalypse Next*, became an international bestseller, with over 300,000 copies in eight languages, in print.

Apocalypse Next, the author's first book, published in 1981, is available from the publisher.

Those who wish to circulate a number of copies of this book, or *Apocalypse Next*, are invited to address the publisher. Quantity discounts are available. Please call (619) 325-1770.